ROUTLEDGE LIBRARY EDITIONS:
TRADE UNIONS

I0131031

Volume 4

TRADE UNIONS AND THE STATE

TRADE UNIONS AND THE STATE

W. MILNE-BAILEY

R Routledge
Taylor & Francis Group
LONDON AND NEW YORK

First published in 1934 by George Allen & Unwin Ltd.

This edition first published in 2023
by Routledge
4 Park Square, Milton Park, Abingdon, Oxon OX14 4RN

and by Routledge
605 Third Avenue, New York, NY 10158

Routledge is an imprint of the Taylor & Francis Group, an informa business

© 1934 George Allen & Unwin Ltd

British Library Cataloguing in Publication Data
A catalogue record for this book is available from the British Library

ISBN: 978-1-032-37553-3 (Set)
ISBN: 978-1-032-39000-0 (Volume 4) (hbk)
ISBN: 978-1-032-39053-6 (Volume 4) (pbk)
ISBN: 978-1-003-34791-0 (Volume 4) (ebk)

DOI: 10.4324/9781003347910

Publisher's Note
The publisher has gone to great lengths to ensure the quality of this reprint but points out that some imperfections in the original copies may be apparent.

Disclaimer
The publisher has made every effort to trace copyright holders and would welcome correspondence from those they have been unable to trace.

TRADE UNIONS AND THE STATE

by

W. MILNE-BAILEY

LONDON
GEORGE ALLEN & UNWIN LTD
MUSEUM STREET

FIRST PUBLISHED IN 1934

TO MY MOTHER AND FATHER

Every study of freedom is a plea for toleration; and every plea for toleration is a vindication of the rights of reason.

Liberty in the Modern State

PREFACE

As the title indicates, this volume is written as a contribution to the study of political institutions. It makes no attempt to discuss the problems of economic theory associated with the aims and activities of Trade Unions: these problems must be left to be dealt with later.

It should be clearly understood that the opinions expressed are no more than personal views, and no organization whatever has any responsibility for them.

Even the casual reader will perceive something of the great debt I owe to Harold Laski's brilliant and suggestive work in the field of political thought, though he would not endorse some of the conclusions I have reached. For his generous counsel throughout the writing of this book I cannot adequately express my thanks.

To my wife I owe more than I can say for her constant help and encouragement; without it this volume would never have been completed.

W. M.-B.

CONTENTS

I

ORGANIZED LABOUR'S CHALLENGE TO THE STATE

II

THE TRADE UNION GROUP

III

TRADE UNIONS, THE STATE, AND THE LAW

IV

THE THEORY OF GROUPS IN RELATION
TO THE STATE

V

THE FUTURE OF TRADE UNIONS
AND THE STATE

I

ORGANIZED LABOUR'S CHALLENGE TO THE STATE

CHAPTER I

THE SETTING OF THE TRADE UNION CHALLENGE

IF only those institutions are happy that have no history, neither Trade Unions nor the State can claim to occupy a position of pleasant security. For more than two thousand years men have debated and wrangled and fought in endless controversy over the nature of the State, and have killed and been killed in the practical application of their theories.

The history of Trade Unions, though shorter, has been no less chequered and no less shot through with violence and bloodshed.

For men tend to make gods of their institutions, and religions of their institutional theories, and religions demand their martyrs and their human sacrifices. Renan has profoundly observed that "one is only a martyr for the sake of things about which one is not really sure," and despite the torrents of learning and eloquence that have gone to the elucidation of the problems of politics, despite the efforts and sacrifices of the protagonists, no one is really sure to-day where the Great Society stands and whither the growing complexities and subtleties of social and industrial organization are driving us.

If it be true that most of the political and social problems of the modern world are essentially economic problems, the radical difference between the politics of to-day and the politics of the societies of the past becomes apparent. It is no longer a question of a society in which the chief dynamic element is the conscious will to civic perfection in a given environment. Economic organization and economic forces are more than ever dependent on technology; the advance of science creates a constantly changing environment with which mankind is for ever trying to catch up.

B

Thus, the problem is not one of adjusting institutions to the nice differences of social policy in a comparatively static society, and still less is it one of adjusting human beings to pre-existing institutions. As well might one seek to imprison a stormy sea within a pasteboard harbour as to bring the changing forms of the modern industrial world under rigid categories that belong essentially to the past. Yet it is not the existence of categories, but their rigidity, that is the danger. For that "social heredity" which is the basis of civilization (and which is a modern rendering of the doctrine of natural rights) is to some extent embodied in and transmitted through institutions, and the perception of this fact leads most people to incline strongly towards continuity of organization. The problem, then, is to adapt and modify institutions rapidly enough to accord, roughly at any rate, with the kaleidoscopic changes in our economic and social life, and therefore to afford satisfaction to the individual human beings who are subject to the effects of these changes.

In the remote past the institution called the State evolved and served certain ends. Like other institutions that in name survive through the centuries, the State has undergone many changes. Such primacy among institutions as it has usually enjoyed is not to be ascribed to any real permanence in form, but rather to the emphasis that the circumstances of the time have placed on the specific functions of the State, concerned with the guarantee of security against aggression from without or revolt from within. In consequence, the State has in actual fact been the sovereign power, but only intermittently so, not continuously. What is this State? It is not society, it is not the community of individual men and women who make up a nation. It is an institution, as a joint stock company, a church, a municipal corporation, are institutions. Like them, it can only function through agents (called, briefly, the Government), and the policy and acts of the institution are the policy and acts of those agents.

The Trade Union is also an institution, created in the comparatively recent past, created by human beings for specific purposes and functions connected with their vocational life. It likewise functions through agents, and the sphere of action of those agents frequently intersects that of the Government. This is inevitable because the sphere of the State, politics, becomes, as has been pointed out, more and more dependent upon the economic forces and factors that are the peculiar province of vocational institutions like Trade Unions. Where spheres of action and policy intersect there are obvious possibilities of conflict, and these are frequently realized in modern times, often with grave results to human liberty and happiness, and even to human life itself.

If this were a temporary phenomenon, there would be little necessity for detailed examination and discussion of its causes, consequences, and cure. But it is very clear that economic considerations will, as time goes on, play a more and more important part in the entire politics of modern industrial States, and the already pressing problem of the relations between the State and Trade Unions will therefore become more urgent and its solution more necessary. It is with this problem that the present work is concerned.

The analysis that follows leads to the conclusion that the nineteenth-century State, and the conception of sovereignty it embodied, are quite inadequate to the needs of the present day since they fail to accord with the growing complexity of our economic life and institutions. Political democracy of the type that developed last century leads to irreconcilable conflict, not because of its element of democracy but because, being unitary in character, it cannot fit in with the tendency towards functional decentralization which arises inevitably out of the facts of economic growth. If the institutional pattern of society has to be modified on functional lines, a rigidly unitary conception of the State must be abandoned. An important place must be found for organizations like Trade Unions, which must play a large part in the orderly development and smooth working of the economic system. Politically and legally the State has cramped the growth of voluntary associations and, more recently, attempts to restore State absolutism have involved the suppression of free institutions such as Trade Unions.

To Trade Unionists "Life, Liberty, and the pursuit of Happiness" (to use the words of the American Constitution) mean the guarantee of economic sufficiency and security and a freedom and status corresponding to the vital functions they perform in society: these can only be achieved and social harmony secured if the workers' organizations take their proper place in a planned, democratic, and functionally decentralized State.

The conflict between the State and Trade Unionism during the past century and a half has taken many forms, of which the so-called "general strike" is the most spectacular. Apart from this very direct challenge to the sovereignty of the State, organized Labour in various parts of the world has frequently, in recent years, come into conflict with governmental authority. This is not an isolated phenomenon, of course, for other groups besides Trade Unions have taken up a similar attitude of opposition to the State on matters in which they were especially concerned, or on which they felt sufficiently strongly.[1] Some of these will be referred to incidentally, since they throw light on the actions and motives of Trade Unions.

The State has for many centuries claimed the allegiance of all its citizens. Multiple allegiance has been recognized only in so far as allegiance to the State, in those matters which it chose to regard as vital, remained unquestioned. If a citizen's allegiance to some other institution, whether Church or family,

---

[1] That Churches are still ready to take up this attitude is shown by the Covenant signed by two thousand pastors of the Evangelical Church in Germany, refusing to subordinate the Church to the Nazi State.—*Manchester Guardian*, October 24, 1933.

or to his individual "conscience" (i.e. his interpretation of the social heritage of morality and manners) came into conflict with the State's fiat, the latter must be obeyed. It has already been pointed out that obedience to the State has in actual fact been intermittent. Most of the matters in respect of which obedience is demanded do not seem sufficiently important to the average citizen to induce him to defy authority, even if he does not wish to obey. Since the agents of the State normally control the machinery of law and police, to say nothing of the armed forces, active disobedience is fraught with considerable peril. Nevertheless, there are at almost all times individuals who, in response to the order of some other institution or to their own private beliefs, do in fact defy the State. Whether it be the payment of certain taxes, willingness to undertake military service, or any of a hundred and one other obligations imposed by the State, there have been citizens who refused, whatever the result, to render obedience. And such action has not been confined to individuals, for organized groups, too, have deliberately called upon their members to rate their allegiance to such groups above allegiance to the State. It is to be noted that this attitude on the part of organized groups such as the Church and Trade Unions has not been one of revolt in the ordinary sense of the term. It has not been a challenge to the existing Government by a group aiming at the overthrow of that Government and the assumption of the sovereign power by itself. Rather has it been the assertion of a counter claim to the allegiance of groups of citizens in certain matters only. Thus, Trade Unions have never come into conflict with the State on claims to provide an alternative Government to the one in power, but only on claims that in respect of certain questions in dispute their members must obey their Unions and not the State.

Such disputes as these have become increasingly frequent with the growing industrialization of modern nations. There are two main classes of cases in which conflicts of this kind have occurred. Any ordinary industrial dispute is a dispute between employers (or employers' organizations) and workers (or workers' organizations). The State is not directly concerned, and the conflict is one between opposing groups of private citizens. Owing to the unequal strength and different economic functions of the parties the same tactics of struggle have not been available to both sides. Employers are normally more wealthy and the workers more numerous. In many cases the tactics of the workers have involved some breach of the ordinary laws relating to public order and the maintenance of the peace. This has brought in the State, nominally an impartial outsider engaged in "keeping the ring," in defence of the law which it is its business to uphold against violation by any party. In some cases special laws have been passed which handicap the workers in such struggles by prohibiting certain forms of activity that the Unions but not the employers wish to adopt. In either event, but especially in the latter, the workers are easily convinced that the State is in fact an agent of the employing class, and not an impartial institution acting for the whole of society. Taking a "behaviourist" view of the situation, indeed, it is difficult to come to any other conclusion!

The other class of case is steadily becoming more important, however, in which the State is from the outset a direct party to the dispute. This happens either because the Government is carrying on some industry or service in which the dispute occurs, and the State is therefore the employer; or because at an early stage the Government assumes responsibility for the continued operation of an industry or service which it considers essential to the national safety or well-being, and therefore, for the purpose of the dispute, takes the place of the employer. As more and more industries enter the category of public utilities—and this is the tendency—and as more and more services become nationally owned or controlled, we may confidently anticipate that the State will play a larger and larger part in the industrial sphere. Thus, the Postal Service,

Telephones and Telegraphs, Radio Broadcasting, Coal, Railways, the supply of Electricity, Gas, and Water, Public Health and Sanitation services, Sea transport, and other industries and services, are in one country or another publicly owned or controlled, and everywhere they are regarded as so essential to the welfare of the community that the Government must always use the whole of its power to ensure their uninterrupted operation. In Germany, where the State has in recent years greatly extended its participation in industrial enterprises, the situation becomes more complicated still. The diverse forms of "mixed undertakings" in which the State is a large shareholder all present similar opportunities for the assertion of State supremacy and the counter-assertion of the rights of organized Labour.

Such opportunities for conflict are multiplied indefinitely in Russia and Italy,[1] where very different conceptions of economic and political organization have led to the most extreme form of State domination over all other groups, including Trade Unions.

These cases will be considered in detail in later chapters, but it may be said here that, new as these experiments are, the practical difficulties arising from the peculiar relation of the State to industry have already become evident.

The bearing of M. Duguit's theory of the Public Service State on all these developments will also be discussed in a later chapter; at present we are concerned only with the outcome of these changed conceptions in the form of grave conflicts between the State and organized Labour.

So far the discussion has proceeded on the tacit assumption that strikes are the only form of such conflict that need be considered. It is true that in the last resort the withdrawal of labour, or the threat to withdraw it, is the Trade Unions' only reply to the employment of coercion by the State. There are,

[1] And of course in Germany and other countries ruled by dictatorships.

however, other and milder forms of action that may be adopted. In 1927, for example, the British Trade Union movement spent large sums of money in a great publicity campaign to try to rouse the country against the Trade Disputes and Trade Unions Bill that the Baldwin Government was forcing through Parliament. It may of course be said, and with truth, that this was not in any sense a challenge to the State, but merely the exercise of a right, common to all citizens and groups of citizens, to persuade the democracy that the Government of the day was pursuing a wrong policy. But striking is also the exercise of a right, and if the purpose of a strike is to bring pressure to bear, so, surely, is the purpose of such a campaign of publicity and propaganda. This was not merely an attempt to persuade the electorate to turn the Government out at the next General Election. It was an attempt, made very systematically, with the aid of special national, regional, and local machinery, with thousands of speeches, carefully prepared literature, and all the other aids to modern propaganda, to arouse the indignation of people to such a pitch that the Government would be deterred in its intention to place the Bill on the Statute Book. It did not succeed, but similar great campaigns have succeeded in the past in modifying the declared intentions of Governments. In 1869–71, for instance, the steady propaganda of the Trade Union movement, and especially the "lobbying" of Members of Parliament, forced the Government to introduce the Trade Union Bill of 1871, which was later hailed as the Charter of Trade Unionism.

That such tactics are very mild and gentle compared with the large-scale strike may be conceded, but if it is allowable to bring pressure to bear at all, to make things so uncomfortable by speeches, lobbying, etc., that the Government is constrained to act in a different way from what it had intended, can it be urged that a different kind of pressure (e.g. a strike), simply because it is likely to be more effective, is not allowable? This is an important issue in the discussion on the method of the general strike, and we shall not prejudge it at this point. The "man in the street," at any rate, draws a rough and ready distinction between the moral pressure exerted by public opinion and the physical restraint enforced by the cutting off of water and electricity supplies, for instance.

Another movement among Trade Unions that has sometimes been seen as a menace to the national State is the development of international Trade Union organizations. In so far as the affiliated bodies place a common international policy above national considerations they may easily come into conflict with their own Governments. For example, the French Confédération Générale du Travail was affiliated to the International Federation of Trade Unions in 1923 and joined in the opposition of the latter body to the Ruhr occupation then enforced by the French Government. Similarly, the British Trade Union movement challenged the Government's policy of non-recognition of Soviet Russia, when it formed the Anglo-Russian Committee in co-operation with the Russian Trade Unions in 1925.

International Trade Unionism has offered many challenges to national States by adopting programmes, and using all the means in its power to have effect given to them, in opposition to the policy of Governments, and this has occurred in cases where no organization affiliated to the I.F.T.U. has existed in the country in question. Thus a boycott against Hungary was declared by the I.F.T.U. at the request of the Hungarian workers in 1920 as a protest against the Horthy dictatorship. No Hungarian organization was a member of the I.F.T.U., so that this was not a case of a national body seeking the aid of an international organization of which it was a member. Rather was it an example of a State being criticized and its policies hampered by a purely external Trade Union body, though at the request of a number of its subjects. A more recent instance is the boycott of German goods declared by the I.F.T.U. in 1933 as a protest against the Hitler dictatorship.

International Trade Unionism, through the International Federation of Trade Unions, and also through national representatives at International Labour Conferences at Geneva, has also come into conflict with the Fascist Government of Italy and other Governments over their selection of Labour delegates to the Conferences, under the provisions of the Versailles Treaty.

CHAPTER II

STRIKES AGAINST THE GOVERNMENT

THE chief manifestation of collision between the State and Trade Unions is to be found in those strikes in which the Government combats the efforts of the Unions to secure their objectives by what is conveniently called "direct action."

Throughout the history of strikes Trade Unions have from time to time found their conduct of ordinary strike operations hampered and opposed by Governments. In most of the strikes of the nineteenth century where this occurred, the intervention of the State was regarded as an intervention by an outside party. Such action was resented as a combatant resents the action of an umpire who takes sides. By the parties the State was regarded as an outside authority whose function in industrial disputes was to see fair play. The State itself took the same view. It only intervened if one of the parties broke the law. In actual fact, so the Unions contended, the laws were so unfairly framed that it was always the Unions who broke them by the most innocent and necessary forms of strike activity such as picketing, boycotts, and other methods without which the effective conduct of strikes was impossible. In this way the State nearly always appeared to intervene on the employers' side, and thus it gained in the minds of the workers the reputation of being merely a tool of the employing class.

The Trade Union Act of 1871 which, as has been pointed out, was secured by persistent agitation on the part of the Unions, was accompanied by another measure, the Criminal Law Amendment Act, imposing very harsh penalties for picketing and other forms of strike activity. In effect it was lawful to strike, but unlawful to do anything to make a strike effective. In 1871, for instance, seven women were imprisoned in South Wales merely for saying "Bah" to a blackleg. On the other hand, employers were allowed to use the weapon of the black list and the boycott against workers. So in 1872 the imprisonment of a number of London gas stokers, with the approval of the Government, for "preparing for a simultaneous withdrawal of their labour," was naturally received by the Unions as a direct challenge to all they stood for, and the attitude of the Government was regarded as purely partisan. Hence the Unions conducted an energetic campaign against the Government, which was heavily defeated at the General Election in 1874, the offending legislation being repealed in 1875. This defeat of the Government has been attributed largely to the Trade Union agitation.[1]

Similar open hostility on the part of the Government had, of course, been shown on many occasions at a much earlier date. As early as 1831 Lord Melbourne, the Home Secretary, wrote as follows to Sir Herbert Taylor: "When we first came into office in November last the Unions of Trades in the North of England and in other parts of the country for the purpose of raising wages, etc., and the General Union for the same purpose, were pointed out to me by Sir Robert Peel in a conversation I had with him upon the then state of the country, as the most formidable difficulty and danger with which we had to contend; and it struck me as well as the rest of His Majesty's servants in the same light."[2] This sentiment was conscientiously acted upon by Lord Melbourne and his colleagues, for there were many prosecutions and harsh sentences for the most peaceful forms of strike action, all with the Government's warm approval.[3]

---

[1] Webb, S. and B., *History of Trade Unionism*, 286. (References are to the 1920 edition throughout.)

[2] *Ibid.*, 138.

[3] *Ibid.*, 143 ff. The transportation of the six Dorset labourers in 1834, merely for forming a Union (the technical offence being the "administration of an unlawful oath"), is the best known of these injustices.

All these conflicts, however, were not regarded as really menacing the State. Despite Lord Melbourne's alarmist words, the Government was far too strong and the Unions too small and puny to create any genuine fear in the minds of the governing class.

To be sure, when revolution was in the air, as during the last years of the eighteenth century, the Government took fright, fearing that the French virus might infect England. Again, at the time of the Chartist movement and the European Revolutions, in the middle of last century, the Government and its friends were impressed by these evidences of a new social force which had to be reckoned with. But although the first of these occasions saw the passing of the repressive Combination Acts, 1799–1800, and in the second period the growing power of the Unions led Bright to declare that they would become revolutionary if wage-earners were condemned to remain "a separate and suspected order in our social system,"[1] what was really feared was political revolution, the capture of the State machine by the common people. The winning of power by political means or even by violence was familiar enough, but the use of direct industrial action was scarcely thought of, because until then there had been no real power or solidarity in the Trade Union world; there were Trade Unions, but there was not yet a Trade Union movement to be feared as a separate industrial power, a threat to the political State. Even the general strike, a term first invented by William Benbow in 1831–32, when he published his proposal[2] for a Grand National Holiday (the very name is significant!), failed to arouse any great alarm. The possibilities of this weapon were not realized, and perhaps this is why Mr. Justice Erskine was able in 1843 to say that "honestly and peaceably to persuade

---

[1] Trevelyan, G. M., *The Life of John Bright* (1913), 280.
[2] See Plummer, A., "The General Strike during One Hundred Years," *Econ. J. Supp.*, May 1927, and Carpenter, N., "William Benbow and the Origin of the General Strike," 35 *Q. J. Econ.*, 491.

the working classes to cease their work for the purpose of obtaining the Charter is not in itself criminal."[1]

The really formidable challenge arising out of the growing Trade Union power did not come until the early years of the present century. Then, in many industrial countries simultaneously, arose the movement known as Syndicalism. To be more correct, the Syndicalist movement was merely that branch of a world-wide unrest that was equipped with a particular philosophy. Originating in France, the doctrine undoubtedly affected Labour thought and action in England, Italy, Spain, Scandinavia, and even the United States and Australia, but while it was only in the Latin countries that it took root, the actual unrest that was fundamental came at least as early and spread as vigorously in America and Britain. Sorel's philosophy was only the local dressing it received in certain countries, and not the cause, which lay deeper. The similarity between the wave of industrial unrest in Britain, with its Guild Socialism, the new I.W.W. Unionism in the United States with its militant Marxism, and the Syndicalist tactics of French and Italian Unionism, with their Sorelian theory, is very striking. These movements, coincident in point of time, were due neither to any one new doctrine nor to local and temporary economic conditions. The British unrest of 1909–14 is frequently attributed to a slackening in the rising curve of real wages. This doubtless helped, but the more important cause everywhere was that a stage in industrial evolution had now been reached at which the State became definitely the Industrial State, and, as an incident in this development, the workers became organized on a consciously anti-State basis. This change had been proceeding since about 1880 in Britain, and as the leading nations kept neck and neck in the industrial race, so did the workers' organizations in their reactions to it. The result was an unprecedented series of strikes, which for the first time appeared to have wider and

[1] *Rex* v. *Cooper* (1843), State Trials N.S. 1250.

more serious aims than immediate improvements in working conditions.

In Britain these strikes were viewed with vague alarm, but the Government at this time (1906–14) was somewhat nervous about the new political development of the Labour Party, first represented in the 1906 Parliament, and did its best to conciliate the Trade Unions rather than antagonize them further or attempt to meet the strike menace by repression.

In many Continental countries, however, the corresponding wave of unrest took the form of large-scale disputes and general strikes against governmental measures or for wider objectives than immediate economic aims. These European general strikes were perhaps the first sign, on a large scale, of the open challenge of organized Labour to the authority of the State. Thus there were general strikes in Belgium in 1902 and 1913 (it is worth noting here that Belgium had had a general strike as far back as 1893), in Holland in 1903, in Italy in 1904, in France in 1909, and in Sweden in 1902 and 1909. Some of these conflicts will be described, as it is important to examine the form they have taken in different countries.

The period of the World War was notable for two struggles especially that may be singled out, namely, the Norwegian general strike of 1916 and the South Wales Miners' strike of the same year. The period immediately following the war was marked by a series of grave conflicts in Europe, in many of which the Trade Union movement was the directing factor or was intimately concerned. Thus there were the German Revolution of 1919, the Italian workers' seizure of power in 1920, the French general strike of 1920, and the Danish general strike of 1920, as well as political revolutions, which do not so much concern us, in other countries. In Britain the Railway strike of 1919, along with the Police strike of 1918, may be singled out as significant of the new attitude of and towards Government. Finally, the so-called "general strike" in 1926 must be fully described. This list is not by any means complete.

The Australian strikes of dockers and seamen, the South African strike of 1922, the "general strike" in Winnipeg in 1919, and many others might be mentioned, but only the more significant will be described here. All of them, however, presented features quite outside the normal characteristics of a trade dispute, and in particular all involved a direct clash between the Trade Unions and the State. The post-war series differs from the pre-war series in being, generally speaking, more revolutionary in temper and more thorough-going in method.

CHAPTER III

PRE-WAR GENERAL STRIKES[1]

THE Belgian general strike of 1893[2] was political in aim, the objective being to compel the Government to introduce universal suffrage. It scored a half success owing to its novel character. The middle classes were seriously frightened by this new menace, and while the full demands of the strikers were not secured the result was a measure of universal suffrage combined, however, with plural voting. By 1902, when the second Belgian general strike was declared, the country had lost its earlier fear and the strike failed completely. The Swedish general strike in the same year also had universal suffrage as its aim. The question was postponed, so it cannot be said that the strike was either lost or won. In fact it was less a strike than a great demonstration. It was called at the request of the Socialist Party and its duration was fixed beforehand at three days—the same days on which the franchise question was being discussed by the Diet. As a collective effort it was a success, since about 120,000 workers, or nearly half the total number of trade unionists and three times the number in Unions affiliated to the national Trade Union Centre, took part.[3]

The next general strike was in Holland, in 1903.[4] This was aimed against projected legislation to prevent strikes in the public services, a very significant objective from the point of view of the present study. The strike was badly organized and it failed completely.

[1] See Georgi, E., *Theorie und Praxis des Generalstreiks* (1908). Crook, W. H., *The General Strike* (1931), and Plummer, A., *op. cit.*
[2] Georgi, *op. cit.*, 42.
[3] See Hansson, S., *The Trade Union Movement of Sweden* (1927), 37, and Georgi, *op. cit.*, 52.
[4] *Le Mouvement Socialiste*, April 15, 1903, 629.

The Italian strikes of 1904 were interesting because they were quite spontaneous.[1] A number of workers had been killed by troops called out by the Government to suppress disorder in connection with industrial disputes. All over Italy workers downed tools in protest, and this general stoppage lasted five days. The results were naturally negative, but the revolutionary organizations claimed a victory.

The Swedish general strike of 1909[2] was purely industrial, being the response of the Trade Union movement to the vigorous attempt of the employers to break the workers' campaign against wage reductions by means of a general lock-out. The employers were so well organized that they completely defeated the Unions. It is the attitude of the Government in this case that is the interesting feature. For the first time, probably, in the history of such strikes the Government organized essential services—a course of action that has more and more been followed in all countries. The supply and distribution of food were safeguarded, transport facilities were arranged, and public services generally maintained. In addition, military forces were assembled in case disorder should arise. Private "security associations" were also organized and corps of blacklegs created by the employers' federation. Notwithstanding all this provocation the strikers were perfectly orderly and law-abiding, strict instructions on this point being issued by the Trade Union headquarters. Indeed, the local organizations of strikers themselves organized "special constables" to prevent disorder and in most cases the strikers paid more regard to them than to the official police and military guards. Alcoholic drink was forbidden during the strike and this partly accounted, no doubt, for the small number of offences against the law committed during this period. Foreign aid was sought by the Unions, and not in vain. Norway, Denmark, and Ger-

---

[1] Georgi, *op. cit.*, 81 ff. *Nation* (New York), Oct. 20, 1904.

[2] *Les lock-out et la grève générale en Suède en 1909*. Swedish Dept. of Labour (1912).

many in particular sent donations, through their Trade Union Centres, while Swedish delegates went to England, the United States, and elsewhere to keep the workers' movement informed of all that was taking place. At one point the Press was completely stopped, but the strikers started their own newspaper. Later the other newspapers were able to get out limited editions. The similarity between the course of this conflict and the British National Strike of 1926 is remarkable, but one important difference is that in the former the railways continued in operation. Many of the Swedish railwaymen were employees of the State, however, and would have been dismissed if they had struck. Consequently all efforts to bring them out failed.

On attempts being made by the Liberal Party to induce the authorities to initiate conciliation proceedings the Government declined on the grounds that "When the struggle between Capital and Labour was extended by the general strike to industries in which the stoppage of work was fraught with great danger to the life and security of the community; when the strike was proclaimed in spite of binding agreements between masters and men, thereby violating the principle of good faith on which all social order must be based; when the strike leaders openly endeavoured to induce State employees to neglect their duties; then the strike was no longer a trial of strength between employers and workers, but a direct attack on the community at large. Under such circumstances it was not possible for the Government either to make, or to assist others to make, concessions to those who started the struggle. The latter must learn that above every class stood Society, and that the power and interest of Society were above those of the different classes composing it."[1]

It will be seen that this was precisely the attitude adopted by the British Government in 1926. The loyalty of other

[1] Montgomery, B. G., *British and Continental Labour Policy* (1922), 104.

workers to their fellows rather than to the Government was shown in the action of the non-Socialist Swedish Workmen's Federation, which joined in the strike solely out of the determination not to act as blacklegs, though it did not believe in the strike itself. The loyalty of the same organization to the Government at a later period, rather than to their fellow workers, was shown equally well in their return to work before the main body of strikers, on the ground that the breach of agreements and the stoppage of agriculture were a blow at the interests of the nation.

Seeing their case was hopeless, the Unions decided to call off the strike as far as employers were concerned who were not affiliated to the employers' body that had threatened the general lock-out at the beginning of the dispute. This converted the general strike into an ordinary industrial dispute, and the Government thereupon, logically enough, agreed to appoint a Conciliation Board. However, it proved impossible to reach a settlement owing to the employers' determination to have compulsory arbitration for future disputes, with the prohibition of stoppages during the hearings. This the Trade Union side refused resolutely to accept, and eventually the dispute came to an end without this being conceded. A somewhat full account has been given of this conflict because it remains a classical instance of the general strike, showing all the features of group challenge, group loyalty, State protection of public services, and State claim to universality of power that have to be discussed in later chapters.

The French general strike of 1909[1] was also a complete failure, as there was division in the Trade Union ranks. The famous Postal strike in the previous year was largely successful, however, and is worth mention because the whole problem of stoppages in the public services was presented in an acute form, and indeed an extensive literature has grown up as a result of this particular struggle. A similar problem was

[1] Crook, *op. cit.*, 41.

presented by the Police strike at Lyons in 1905, and the entire history of Trade Union organization in the public services in France is full of conflicts that were fought out, if not on the picket line, then in Parliament and in the courts. The action of M. Briand in breaking the French Railway strike of 1910 by calling the strikers to the colours and then assigning them, as soldiers, to their former duties is frequently cited to this day as an example of the State's superior power over Trade Unions and of the effective exercise of sovereignty in a crisis.

But there is no space to dwell upon the details of these pre-war events in France and other countries. The entire series of struggles that have been briefly mentioned as belonging to the pre-war period presents several interesting features which it is desirable to emphasize. In the first place, it will have been observed that there was no large aim common to all the disputes. There was a world-wide wave of unrest, yet the objects of the major strikes ranged from purely economic gains in wages and hours to purely political reforms such as universal suffrage. Some of the strikes were concerned with the protection of Trade Union liberties, others were protests against legislation, against governmental acts, or against lock-outs, while the majority were for economic improvements of the familiar kind. Syndicalist propaganda was certainly the inspiration of much of the French activity, and perhaps of the Italian, while even British, American, and Scandinavian strikes were indirectly affected by it, but there was assuredly no one philosophy or theory responsible for all these manifestations of unrest. Rather did the theorists use the prevailing movements and tendencies as the peg for their doctrines.

The second point to notice is that the lead in most cases was taken by Socialist Trade Unions. To be sure, the French Syndicalists bitterly attacked the orthodox Socialists, but their own objectives were essentially what would have been called Socialistic. Perhaps the less ambiguous way of expressing it would be to say that all the strike movements were anti-

Capitalistic in leadership. The conversion of the various Trade Union movements to Socialism had taken place between about 1880 and 1900. The conscious anti-Capitalistic fervour thus created was an important factor in determining the form of working-class activity, but the intensified conflict of the early part of the century affected non-Socialist as well as Socialist groups. In England, for instance, the miners were among the most active strikers, and no stoppage was more determined or more fraught with grave possibilities than the Coal strike of 1912. Yet the miners were almost the last group in this country to adopt Socialist theories, for their conversion cannot be said to have taken place until just before the war. As we have already pointed out, the Socialist tendency of organized Labour was itself an accompaniment of the industrial changes that were taking place, and not an unrelated phenomenon due to the teachings of any particular person. Because the process of industrial concentration was proceeding rapidly, and because the pace of economic change became speeded up, the soil became more fertile for the spread of Socialist ideas, and at the same time the Trade Unions were compelled to organize more closely and efficiently to defend their industrial position. Thus the general economic situation led groups of workers to form large organizations and at the same time provided a stronger incentive to use them in actual conflict. Whether they felt only the normal economic urge to protect their own industrial interests in the face of an increasingly threatening industrial system, or whether, as happened in many cases, they were inspired by wider Socialist or Syndicalist aims, the Trade Unions found it necessary to challenge the existing order, and any excuse was good enough; the phrase is used in no disparaging sense, for any excuse *was* good enough, since at whatever point they contemplated the working of government and industry they found abundant reason to say they would endure existing conditions no longer. For the first time they saw themselves clearly as independent groups with claims and

powers as against those of Governments, and the precise form
those claims took at a given moment was really unimportant.
They struck, in a sense, for the sake of striking; not with a
mere desire for disorder and dislocation, but with the intention
of showing that they were no longer a collection of individual
citizens subject completely to a despotic State. That this feeling
was real and this interpretation sound the ensuing events of
the war period show quite clearly.

CHAPTER IV

WAR PERIOD

ONE of the first results of the outbreak of war in all the belligerent countries was that organized Labour declared a truce in industrial conflict. All other loyalties were subordinated to the supreme force of patriotic sentiment. The solidarity of the nation became far more important than the solidarity of any other group, internal or international. The reason was partly that actual physical safety was at stake, partly a sentiment and tradition far older than those attaching to the newer groupings that had sprung up within and without the national State. The State was enthroned again after the ominous divisions revealed in the industrial conflicts of the preceding years. But not for long. The overwhelming appeal of national safety and national supremacy in war failed to maintain unity for more than a few months, for the State was openly and deliberately challenged by a Trade Union in the South Wales Miners' strike of 1915.[1] Even before this occurred the Yorkshire miners voted by a large majority in favour of a stoppage, as a result of the failure to settle a dispute that had dragged on since just before the outbreak of war. In January 1915 the Miners' Federation as a whole gave the Yorkshire Association sanction to take a ballot, which meant that in the event of a strike the national body would support the district. The district vote in favour of a strike was 26,676, and 7,211 voted against; as a result of this decisive verdict the employers agreed to settle on the terms demanded by the men.

Following conferences with the leading Unions connected with the supply of munitions, the Government passed the Munitions of War Act in July 1915, which provided, among

---

[1] Cole, G. D. H., *Labour in the Coal Mining Industry (1914–1921)*, (1923), 27 ff.

other things, for the application, by Proclamation, of compulsory arbitration to any vital industry where a stoppage was threatened. Where a proclamation was issued, a strike became illegal and heavy penalties were provided.

The South Wales miners were in the meantime engaged in a dispute over a new agreement, the old one terminating by three months' notice in June. The employers refused to negotiate and urged the continuance of the old agreement for the duration of the war. Only a few days before the expiry of the notices the Government intervened, and a crisis was averted for a fortnight during which negotiations went on. These proved abortive, and on July 12th a delegate conference of the South Wales Miners' Federation voted by a large majority in favour of a strike, despite the fact that on the 8th the Government had warned them that a dispute would be "proclaimed" under the Munitions of War Act. The Executive of the Miners' Federation (the national body) then appealed to South Wales to remain at work, and on the same day, July 13th, the Government "proclaimed" the dispute under the Munitions of War Act, and thus made a strike illegal. Notwithstanding these events, the strike took place on July 15th as arranged. The South Wales miners were defying not only their own national federation but the State itself, in face of the threat of severe punishment for all who stopped work. The Government naturally found that it could not take proceedings against two hundred thousand men, and therefore it gave way. Negotiations were opened, and on July 20th a settlement was reached giving the miners nearly all they asked. No penalties were exacted against anyone, and thus at the very first attempt to put the Act into operation the Government was successfully defied and the Act rendered a dead letter. Only a month later, when differences arose over the interpretation of the agreement of July 20th, and a verdict against the miners was given by the President of the Board of Trade, a new strike was at once threatened and the award was hastily reversed.

There were other instances of defiance of the Munitions of War Acts. In August 1915 the Ministry of Munitions sent out a circular recommending an extension of the employment of women on machine work. When a Scottish firm notified their employees of their intention to make the change, the Amalgamated Society of Engineers offered such opposition, hinting at strike action, that the Government withdrew the circular.

The history of the Munitions Acts, and indeed of the war-time regulation of labour altogether,[1] was marked by strikes and threats of strikes, and in the nature of the case the Government, when it was not concerned as employer, was nearly always as closely involved as either of the immediate parties to the dispute. In a large number of cases, of course, the law was invoked, Trade Unionists were imprisoned, fined, "deported," or otherwise punished, and governmental authority was vindicated. The war years were full of conflicts between bodies of workers and the Government, in some cases the challenge to authority being successful, in others not. The workers were in a very strong position because of the shortage of labour, and if the official Trade Union movement had not been as anxious as any section of the community to further the successful prosecution of the war, every demand of organized Labour would have had to be conceded. Where strikes were declared or were likely to occur without the backing of the whole Trade Union movement the Government was in a different position. It could and did threaten to call up the insurgent workers for military service, and this action was usually sufficient, in the later stages of the war, to avert trouble. In this way was ended a strike called by a conference of shop stewards in the engineering trades in July 1918. On being warned that they would become liable for military service, the strikers returned to work after a stoppage of six days without obtaining their objective.

---

[1] See Wolfe, H., *Labour Supply and Regulation* (1923), and Cole, G. D. H., *Trade Unionism and Munitions* (1923).

One of the most remarkable of all the war-time disputes was the London Police strike of 1918. Ever since 1913 efforts had been made to form a Police Trade Union, but the Government always refused to allow this, as the police, like the army and navy, were regarded as so intimately connected with the whole mechanism of sovereignty that organization on Trade Union lines could not be permitted for a moment. A Union was formed, however, though it was not recognized. Conditions of pay, etc., became so bad that in August 1918, angered by cases of dismissal which the men looked upon as victimization, practically the whole of the London police went on strike. Confronted with a revolt in the very citadel of authority, the Government gave many concessions but still refused to recognize the Union. The strike ended for the time, but in July 1919 the Union again called a strike of police in all parts of the country. This was poorly responded to, and the result was a foregone conclusion. The strikers were dismissed, and while increases of pay, pensions, etc., were granted, all subsequent efforts to secure reinstatement of the dismissed men failed. Further, by the Police Act, 1919,[1] the police were forbidden to form a Trade Union. An elective organization under official rules and supervision was established by the same Act, as a means whereby representations could be made to the employing authorities on any grievance, but affiliation to outside Trade Union or political bodies was prohibited.

Of a different character was the refusal of the National Union of Sailors and Firemen in 1917 to allow two Labour leaders, Mr. Ramsay MacDonald and Mr. G. H. Roberts, the latter being at the time Parliamentary Secretary to the Board of Trade, to proceed at the Government's request to Petrograd to arrange for an international Labour conference.[2] The seamen

[1] 9 and 10 Geo. V. c. 46. See Milne-Bailey, W., *Trade Union Documents* (1929), 50.
[2] Webb, *History of Trade Unionism*, 666.

struck work on the instructions of their Union, and so prevented the journey being made.

Before leaving the war period the general strike of 1916 in Norway must be mentioned.[1] The Norwegian Labour movement had shared in the general wave of unrest in the pre-war years, but it was not until 1915, when the Government introduced a Trade Disputes Bill which included provisions for compulsory arbitration, that matters reached a crisis. The employers, like the Unions, were opposed to such provisions, but they naturally did not view with enthusiasm the proposal of the National Confederation of Trade Unions to call a general strike. Full notice of the stoppage was given, and the General Association of Employers thereupon washed its hands of the matter, deploring "the fact that the Confederation . . . contemplates bringing pressure to bear upon the Government by measures which in the first instance must be detrimental to the industry and trade of the country. The responsibility for this action," it went on, "must be borne entirely by the Confederation."[2] The workers were so hostile to the introduction of the hated compulsory arbitration provisions that they pressed forward with their plans for a general stoppage, and in face of this menace the Government decided to delete the offending clauses. "The Government has not taken this step," declared the Prime Minister, "because of the threat of a general strike. The conclusive reason is the present European situation. The World War is carried on outside our very doors . . . and under these circumstances I dare not take the responsibility for the situation which may arise out of a general strike." Even so, the Act as passed contained very far-reaching provisions for the settlement of disputes by conciliation and arbitration, and in the following year the Government succeeded, despite the opposition of the Unions, in passing a temporary Act providing for compulsory arbitration in disputes which might involve danger to the community. A decree issued

[1] Montgomery, *op. cit.*, 330.　　　　[2] *Ibid.*, 330 ff.

at the same time applied the Act to any dispute which might arise out of its being passed into law. A general strike was the answer to this challenge. The Government was firm, and after five days' stoppage the strike was terminated, as the Confederation of Trade Unions did not wish to risk any further conflict over a law that after all was temporary. After several renewals the Act expired in 1921, employers as well as workers being opposed to it.

CHAPTER V

POST-WAR CONFLICTS

IT will be clear that both in belligerent and neutral countries the ever-growing clash between organized Labour and the State persisted during the war period, though naturally the prevailing circumstances and mood produced a temporary diminution in the struggle. As soon as the war ended, however, there was an immediate and widespread outbreak all over Europe, and indeed in other parts of the world too. Old industrial programmes and theories were brought out in new dress, the very fact that the war was over induced a spirit of optimism and relief that sought satisfaction in action, and above all the Trade Unions had attained to a position of numerical strength and economic power never before known. A new world was confidently expected, and as it showed few signs of coming of its own volition, organized Labour quickly determined to speed up the change. The years 1919 and 1920 were marked by outbreaks of industrial conflict more severe than any that had preceded them. At this point it becomes very difficult to disentangle industrial from political events, strikes from revolutions.

With the attempts of political parties to seize power by overthrowing the Government, whether by peaceable or violent means, this work is not concerned, except for those cases where the Trade Union movement played an important part. Thus the Russian Revolution was an economic as well as a political revolution, but it was organized and carried through by a political party, intent on capturing the State, and not by the Trade Union movement. In Germany, on the other hand, the Trade Unions were vitally concerned in the so-called Revolution of 1918–19, not only by reason of their close association with the Social-Democratic Party, but also in their policy and activities in regard to the carrying on of industry, and in their part in the making of the new Constitution. The Trade Unions were in a position to influence the construction of the new State and to obtain what seemed to them, at the time, safeguards against industrial and political tyranny.

In Italy the position was different again, for the Trade Unions were for a time sufficiently strong to take matters into their own hands and to seize industry in certain districts. There was more than a clash; there was apparently a complete separation between political sovereignty and industrial sovereignty. It did not last long, for the Fascist revolution soon swept the industrial organizations away, and set up a dictatorship under cover of which an entirely new Constitution took shape. These developments will be described in greater detail in the chapter on Italy.[1]

Leaving out of account countries like Poland, Hungary, and Spain where, peaceably or violently, the government passed into the hands of dictators, a survey of the more stable communities shows a succession of grave conflicts between organized Labour and the State. The general strike in France in 1920 and in Denmark in the same year are worth notice, but in Australia, Canada, South Africa, and the United States, to take the other side of the world, there were very significant struggles that are worth brief mention. In Britain itself the Railway strike of 1919, the coal disputes of 1921 and 1926, and the so-called general strike of 1926 are worth studying in view of the light they throw on the general question of Trade Unionism in relation to the State.

Turning first to France, we find that the general strike of 1920[2] was both political and economic in character. It was called not by the Confédération Générale du Travail, the central organization of Trade Unions, but by the Railwaymen's Federation. The immediate issue was nationalization of the

---

[1] See Chapter xxvi.
[2] C.G.T., *L'Action Confédérale et la Grève des Cheminots* (Paris, 1920), and Montgomery, *op. cit.*, 56 ff.

railways, and the date fixed was Labour Day, May 1st. The C.G.T. had, as a matter of fact, intended to call a one day's strike in all industries for that day, as a demonstration only, but despite the conviction of the leaders that anything more would inevitably fail, if only because of the lack of preparation, the railwaymen succeeded in persuading them to come in. It was finally agreed that the railwaymen would cease work on May 1st, the dockers, seamen, and miners on May 2nd, and the remaining trades were to remain at work. The weakness of French Trade Unionism was at once shown. Local Unions of railwaymen and miners refused to obey the strike call, while, on the other hand, Unions not included in the strike plan took measures in opposition to the C.G.T. Road transport, organized by anti-strike Unions, functioned effectively, strike leaders were arrested, and after a week's stoppage the Government asked the courts to order the dissolution of the C.G.T. Some discussion of this last point is necessary. One of the main Acts which in France legalize Trade Unions is that of 1884, limiting the objects of such bodies to the defence of their economic interests and giving the courts power to dissolve them for breach of this law. Strikes having an industrial object are therefore quite legal, but those having a political aim are not, and the Government took the view that this general strike was entirely political in that it sought to coerce the community into nationalizing the railways.

"The C.G.T.," said the Premier, M. Millerand, "is a power which claims to set itself up against the public authorities in order to obtain the triumph of its pretensions by stopping the life of the country and profoundly upsetting the habits, needs and interests of the public. . . . The C.G.T. insists, against the will even of the great majority of its own members, in placing itself above the law. It has no more right to do this than has any other organization in the country."[1] The middle-class elements of the population took an active part in defeating

[1] *Morning Post*, May 12, 1920, cited by Montgomery, *op. cit.*

the strike by organizing alternative forms of transport, etc., where needed. Many shopkeepers refused to sell goods to strikers. Worse still, there was a gradual drift back to work, until on the twentieth day of the strike the C.G.T. decided to terminate it, but to continue the stoppage on the railways alone. This move also failed, however, and the net result of the entire affair was a complete victory for the Government. In the legal action which followed the dissolution of the C.G.T. was ordered on the grounds that it had admitted civil service organizations, contrary to law, and that it had sponsored political strikes, and also political campaigns against French military expeditions in Russia. The result was that the C.G.T. was reconstituted, and the extreme "Left" elements now excluded formed a new organization, the Confédération Générale du Travail Unitaire (C.G.T.U.), which has maintained a separate existence ever since.

The Danish general strike of 1920[1] was the outcome of a very confused political situation, and its aims were really political, although several economic demands were made at the same time, these including the establishment of industrial councils on which the workers would be represented. The strike originated in a constitutional quarrel between the Socialist and Radical parties and their opponents, the issue being complicated by the King's intervention in the dispute. The Trade Union Confederation called the general strike, really at the request of the Socialist Party, in order to force the existing Government to give way. Hospital employees, water and gas workers, police, workers employed by Labour organizations, and workers on newspapers that had opposed the Government's policy were alone excepted from the order to stop work.

The crisis became so acute that a revolution was quite possible, and in these circumstances the Copenhagen City Council sent a deputation to the King to ask him in the interests of public safety to dismiss the Government. The Cabinet

[1] Montgomery, *op. cit.*, 132 ff.

D

thereupon resigned, and the new Government conceded the main demands of the Trade Union Confederation, economic as well as political. The general strike thus ended in a victory for the workers' organization.

During the early post-war years there were numerous conflicts between the Unions and State Governments in the United States, though there was no general strike. Several States have laws either forbidding or limiting strikes of certain types. These laws have not prevented the workers from striking, however. Colorado was one of the States with an anti-strike law, passed in 1915 and modelled on the well-known Canadian Act forbidding a stoppage in certain industries until an investigation has been held. Yet in 1919 there were strikes of coal miners, steel workers, and tramwaymen, the required thirty days' notice of a stoppage being given in none of these cases. At the beginning of 1922 the packing plant workers went on strike, and they remained out even after the State Industrial Commission had secured an injunction ordering their return to work. As a result, twenty-seven officials of the Union were sentenced to periods of imprisonment varying from one to sixty days. The strike continued nevertheless.

In Canada, there was something like a "general strike" in Winnipeg in 1919.[1] An entire community of nearly a quarter of a million people was shaken to its foundations for six weeks. The whole life of the town was paralysed by the strike of thirty thousand workers. The police force took sides with the strikers, and practically all of them were dismissed for refusing to sign a "no strike" pledge, being replaced by a special force recruited from ex-service men. Postal services were stopped, firemen left their posts, tramcars, telephones, and telegraphs were paralysed, and the newspapers had to stop publication. In clashes with the North-Western Mounted Police several fatalities occurred, and a number of strike leaders were charged with conspiracy against the State. The strikers were not led by

[1] Crook, *op. cit.*, 543 ff, and *The Times*, various issues in May 1919.

people of foreign origin, but by men coming from England or Scotland, and the issue of "workers' control" was a dominant one.

In Australia again, there was a general strike in 1917, important strikes of seamen and marine engineers in 1919, and of gas workers in 1920, notwithstanding the provisions of the compulsory arbitration law in force.[1]

In South Africa there was a general strike in 1922, martial law being proclaimed. Over 250 persons were killed and 1,000 wounded in the suppression, by the military forces, of this strike. This conflict, in fact, developed into something like civil war. Aeroplanes dropped bombs on a Trade Union hall, towns supposed to be leading the strike were besieged, artillery, aeroplanes, and machine guns being used, and trials for treason were afterwards instituted.[2] An indirect result of this terrible struggle was the passing of the Industrial Conciliation Act in 1924, which forbids a stoppage until the dispute has been considered either by an Industrial Council or by a Conciliation Board, both types of machinery being provided for in the Act. Strikes and lock-outs are also illegal if the term of a collective agreement has not yet run its course. This was South Africa's attempt—very similar to that made in other countries—to resolve the growing menace of the conflict that is the subject of these pages.

Space does not permit of more detailed description of these events nor even of reference to the many similar disputes in various parts of the world.

[1] The Australian general strike of 1917 has not been described as it presented no special features of interest from the point of view of this work. See, however, Sutcliffe, J. T., *History of Trade Unionism in Australia* (1921).

[2] See Gitsham, E., and Trembath, J. F., *Labour Organisation in S. Africa* (Durban, 1926), and *The Round Table*, March and June 1922.

CHAPTER VI

POST-WAR BRITISH STRIKES

WE must return to a consideration of the important post-war conflicts in Britain. The first of these was the Railway strike of 1919. This was in origin a dispute of an ordinary type, the issue being one of wage rates. The interest arises from the fact that the Government was, at the time, in control of the railways and was therefore in the position of employer. As agreement could not be reached a strike was declared which lasted for nine days, practically the whole of the railway systems of the country being tied up. The strike took place at the end of September, and subsequently the Prime Minister, Mr. Lloyd George, stated that the Government had been making preparations for it since the previous February. What these preparations were will be seen. Half a million workers were involved in the stoppage, and the Associated Society of Locomotive Engineers and Firemen, which was not directly concerned and was in some measure a rival organization to the National Union of Railwaymen which declared the strike, loyally joined their fellow workers. The Railway Clerks Association directed its members to do no work normally done by the men on strike, and the Unions of Post Office workers sought and obtained a guarantee from the Government that they would not be called upon to do such work either, so far as mail traffic was concerned. The Government felt it wise to announce that troops would not be used to run trains, though military detachments were sent out to guard railway stations. In a previous national railway strike in 1912, it is worth recalling, the Government had announced its intention to use troops to keep the railway services in operation.[1] In the 1919 stoppage the change of attitude was clearly seen. There was no disorder and no violence.

[1] Webb, S. and B., *History of Trade Unionism*, 529.

The Government put into operation the plans it had been perfecting for seven months, and road transport services manned by volunteers were organized to supply London and other towns with foodstuffs. Skeleton passenger train services were also organized in the same way, but industrial transport by rail was stopped so completely that after a few days collieries, steel works, etc., had to close down. The Co-operative Wholesale Society, through its bank and printing works, issued special cheques for the Trade Unions, payable at the co-operative stores up and down the country, as shopkeepers in many cases refused to sell goods to strikers. One of the most remarkable features of the strike was the publicity campaign carried on by both sides. Never before had a Government undertaken a great publicity drive against a Trade Union organization on strike. Public opinion was appealed to by both parties—and one of the parties was the State itself. At first the public was against the strikers, as was natural in view of the inconvenience caused to everyone. The Unions, however, voted a large sum for publicity, issued the Labour newspaper, the *Daily Herald*, in many thousands all over England, and engaged an expert body of men and women to write articles, make speeches, design posters, draw cartoons, etc., in support of the railwaymen. Printing workers on other newspapers threatened to stop work unless space was accorded by their papers to explanations of the strikers' case, and the space was given. The cinema was utilized, the railwaymen's leader being shown delivering speeches, and full-page advertisements were paid for in *The Times* and other newspapers for the purpose of replying to the Government's statements. The Government, on its side, followed similar methods, using the Press, posters, cinemas, etc. This unique battle of publicity unquestionably changed public opinion in the course of a week, as was shown by the tone of editorial articles.[1]

The strike was finally settled by the mediation of a Trade

1 Webb, *op. cit.*, 543.

Union Committee specially appointed for the purpose, the settlement being a victory for the Unions. The comment of the historians of Trade Unionism is as follows: "The Government has learned that Trade Unionism is not easily beaten, even when all the resources of the State are put forth against it and when public opinion is incensed."[1]

There were several important results of this strike. First, the Government set to work to elaborate its scheme for alternative services (transport, etc.) for use in case of large-scale strikes. These arrangements will be described fully on a later page. Second, a National Wages Board was established for the railways by an Act of 1921, the Trades Union Congress and the Co-operative movement being represented on it, as well as the Railway Unions. Finally, the experience of the Mediating Committee led the Trade Union world to consider seriously the greater consolidation of its forces and the establishment of a central executive body for the whole of organized Labour. This latter project was realized in 1920–21 by the formation of a General Council for the Trades Union Congress, which has since been the body recognized as empowered to speak for the whole Trade Union movement. From that time, too, the process of amalgamation of separate Trade Unions has gone on at a more rapid rate, stimulated by the General Council of the Trades Union Congress. For these important developments the Railway strike of 1919 was largely responsible.

In the same year the miners were also drawn into what might have proved a grave challenge to the Government. A national coal strike was threatened unless the British military intervention in Russia came to an end and compulsory military service definitely ceased. The Government announced that in fact both of these measures that were so objectionable to the Trade Unions were to be brought to an end immediately.[2]

In the following year Russian affairs caused another crisis which might easily have led to the most serious conflict. The

[1] Webb, *op. cit.*, 545.   [2] *Ibid.*, 667.

impression gained currency that Britain was planning to help Poland in her war with Russia then in progress. Immediately the whole Labour movement, industrial and political, rose in protest. "Councils of Action" were set up in a number of centres, and a national Council of Action was formed to direct the campaign against the Government's policy. A national conference of the entire Labour movement endorsed these steps and authorized a general strike against the projected war, as well as a levy on the Unions to provide a campaign fund. Public opinion was hostile to the Government's supposed policy also, and in the event no step was taken to give military aid to Poland. It is very probable that a general strike would have taken place had Britain entered the war, and the threat of direct action undoubtedly made a great impression on the Government.

We must now return to the miners. In 1920 the Government controlled the coal industry as well as the railways, and the 1920 Coal strike, lasting from October 16th to November 3rd, was therefore a dispute between the miners and the State. The only special feature to be noted, however, is that there was for a time a distinct possibility that the railwaymen and transport workers would also declare a strike in support of their partners in the Triple Alliance. As far back as 1915 this Alliance had been formed by these three groups of Unions for the purpose of affording mutual assistance in case of attack on any matter of vital principle.[1] This formidable combination was not brought into action in 1920, but largely as a result of the apprehensions to which it gave rise the Government passed the Emergency Powers Act[2] in October of the same year. This Act gives the Government very large powers in case of an emergency in which the supply of the essentials of life to the community is threatened. It is, in fact, a remarkable expression

[1] For constitution of Triple Alliance see Milne-Bailey, W., *Trade Union Documents*, 148.

[2] 10 and 11 Geo. V. c. 55 (1920).

of the Government's claim to take any and every action to prevent interference with essential industries. Its terms are as follows:—

1.—(i) If at any time it appears to His Majesty that any action has been taken or is immediately threatened by any persons or body of persons of such a nature and on so extensive a scale as to be calculated, by interfering with the supply and distribution of food, water, fuel, or light, or with the means of locomotion, to deprive the community, or any substantial portion of the community, of the essentials of life, His Majesty may by proclamation (hereinafter referred to as a proclamation of emergency), declare that a state of emergency exists.

No such proclamation shall be in force for more than one month without prejudice to the issue of another proclamation at or before the end of that period.

(ii) Where a proclamation of emergency has been made, the occasion thereof shall forthwith be communicated to Parliament and, if Parliament is then separated by such adjournment or prorogation as will not expire within five days, a proclamation shall be issued for the meeting of Parliament within five days, and Parliament shall accordingly meet and sit upon the day appointed by that proclamation, and shall continue to sit and act in like manner as if it had stood adjourned or prorogued to the same day.

2.—(i) Where a proclamation of emergency has been made, and so long as the proclamation is in force, it shall be lawful for His Majesty in Council, by Order, to make regulations for securing the essentials of life to the community, and those regulations may confer or impose on a Secretary of State or other Government department, or any other persons in His Majesty's service or acting on His Majesty's behalf, such powers and duties as His Majesty may deem necessary for the preservation of the peace, for securing and regulating the supply and distribution of food, water, fuel, light, and other necessities, for maintaining the means of transit or locomotion, and for any other purposes essential to the public safety and the life of the community, and may make such provisions incidental to the powers aforesaid as may appear to His Majesty to be required for making the exercise of those powers effective:

Provided that nothing in this Act shall be construed to authorize the making of any regulations imposing any form of compulsory military service or industrial conscription:

Provided also that no such regulation shall make it an offence for any person or persons to take part in a strike, or peacefully to persuade any other person or persons to take part in a strike.

(ii) Any regulations so made shall be laid before Parliament as soon as may be after they are made, and shall not continue in force after the expiration of seven days from the time when they are so laid unless a resolution is passed by both Houses providing for the continuance thereof.

(iii) The regulations may provide for the trial, by courts of summary jurisdiction, of persons guilty of offences against the regulations; so, however, that the maximum penalty which may be inflicted for any offence against any such regulations shall be imprisonment with or without hard labour for a term of three months, or a fine of one hundred pounds, or both such imprisonment and fine, together with the forfeiture of any goods or money in respect of which the offence has been committed: Provided that no such regulations shall alter any existing procedure in criminal cases, or confer any right to punish by fine or imprisonment without trial.

(iv) The regulations so made shall have effect as if enacted in this Act, but may be added to, altered, or revoked by resolution of both Houses of Parliament or by regulations made in like manner and subject to the like provisions as the original regulations; and regulations made under this section shall not be deemed to be statutory rules within the meaning of section one of the Rules Publication Act, 1893.

(v) The expiry or revocation of any regulations so made shall not be deemed to have affected the previous operation thereof, or the validity of any action taken thereunder, or any penalty or punishment incurred in respect of any contravention or failure to comply therewith, or any proceeding or remedy in respect of any such punishment or penalty.

3.—(i) This Act may be cited as the Emergency Powers Act, 1920.

(ii) This Act shall not apply to Ireland.

Even without this Act the Government had been able to make arrangements for the supply of foodstuffs and for transport in case the stoppage proved a long one, but armed with the powers conferred by the new legislation it was possible to devise a most elaborate organization for use in future disputes. The new plans were put into operation for the first time in the following year, when a much longer coal stoppage was precipitated by the sudden decontrol of the industry. The dispute concerned the new agreement offered by the employers, when the industry was handed back to them, large reductions in wages being involved on account of the slump in trade that had just set in. Apart from its large scale—over a million mine workers being concerned—and its effects on other industries dependent on coal, the stoppage was therefore an "ordinary" industrial dispute, in which the Government was not involved. The lock-out, which lasted three months, started on March 31, 1921, and on the same date the Government issued a Proclamation under the Emergency Powers Act, regulations being quickly issued thereafter conferring large powers on the officials administering the scheme for the provision of transport, foodstuffs, etc. Reservists were called to the Colours, troops were moved into the mining areas, special constables were enrolled, and a new Defence Force created, numbering eighty thousand men fully armed and uniformed.

Large stocks of coal had previously been accumulated in anticipation of the stoppage, so there was no apprehension of an immediate shortage of coal. The Government's preparations were, in fact, due to the expectation that the Triple Alliance would be brought into the conflict, and this would have meant a railway and transport strike, which would have been much more serious than a stoppage confined to coal. A strike order was actually issued by the Railwaymen's and Transport Workers' Unions on April 8th to take effect at midnight on April 12th, but it was postponed on the latter date to April 15th, as negotiations were still proceeding for a settlement of the stoppage. Other large Unions now formally decided to back up the Triple Alliance, in some cases by strike action, while the Co-operative Wholesale Society and the Distributive Workers' Union offered their help in supplying and distributing foodstuffs through the co-operative societies. The Government denounced the action of the Unions as being "political," unconstitutional, and revolutionary. The Triple Alliance leaders replied with a manifesto containing the following significant words: "We resent the suggestion made in Government quarters that the miners' fight is a political one. We are not proclaiming a revolution, we are standing shoulder to shoulder for fundamental Trade Union rights." As matters turned out there was no strike by the other Unions, and the Triple Alliance itself perished on Black Friday, as April 15th, when the strike order was rescinded, came to be called.

The large-scale challenge to the Government was thus withdrawn, but only temporarily, for a similar situation arose again in 1925 with the very important difference that this time it was the Trades Union Congress itself, instead of the Triple Alliance, that took up the miners' cause and threatened direct action.

CHAPTER VII

THE "GENERAL STRIKE" OF 1926

WHEN the General Council of the Trades Union Congress was established in 1920–21, its powers were very circumscribed, as the Congress looked upon the project as an experiment and desired to move cautiously.[1] As the new development prospered, there arose a willingness to concede wider powers to the central body, and in 1924 the General Council had its scope and authority added to very considerably. An important part of the new powers was contained in Standing Order 11,[2] which reads as follows:—

Industrial Disputes.

(*a*) It shall be an obligation upon the affiliated Unions to keep the General Council informed with regard to matters arising as between the unions and employers, and/or between one union and another, in particular where such matters may involve directly or indirectly large bodies of workers. The General Council shall, if they deem necessary, disseminate the information as soon as possible to all unions in the industry concerned which are affiliated to the Trades Union Congress, and which may be either directly or indirectly affected.

(*b*) The General policy of the Council shall be that unless requested to do so by the affiliated union or unions concerned, the Council shall not intervene so long as there is a prospect of whatever difference may exist on the matters in question being amicably settled by means of the machinery of negotiations existing in the trades affected.

(*c*) In the event, however, of negotiations breaking down and the deadlock being of such a character as to involve directly or indirectly other bodies of workpeople affiliated to the Trades Union Congress in a stoppage of work and/or to imperil standard wages or hours and conditions of employment, the Council may take the initiative

---

[1] See Trades Union Congress, *The Story of the T.U.C.*, and *The General Council*.

[2] *T.U.C. Standing Orders.*

by calling representatives of the unions into consultation, and use its influence to effect a just settlement of the difference. In this connection the Council having ascertained all the facts relating to the difference, may tender its considered opinion and advice thereon to the union or unions concerned. Should the union or unions refuse the assistance or advice of the Council, the Council shall duly report to Congress.

(*d*) Where the Council intervenes, as herein provided, and the union or unions concerned accept the assistance and advice of the Council, and where despite the efforts of the Council, the policy of the employers enforces a stoppage of work by strike or lock-out, the Council shall forthwith take steps to organize on behalf of the union or unions concerned all such moral and material support as the circumstances of the dispute may appear to justify.

The 1925 coal crisis was the first dispute in which these new powers were invoked and the aid of the General Council was sought by a Union.

A new dispute had arisen in the coal industry owing to the employers' proposals to reduce wages, and lower conditions of work in other respects, as a result of the severe depression in the trade. The miners, determined to resist, asked the General Council to support them. The Council agreed and appointed a special committee which thereupon took over from the miners the conduct of their case, and entered into discussions with the Government to see whether a settlement acceptable to all parties could not be reached. At the same time plans were made for a stoppage of work should one ultimately prove unavoidable. The International Federation of Trade Unions sent one of its secretaries to England to keep in touch with events from the international point of view, and the International Transport Workers' Federation was asked to arrange for an embargo on foreign coal destined for England, should this step be necessary. It was decided that at first, at any rate, active measures should be confined to the task of stopping the production and movement of coal. To allow the large stocks of coal that existed at the collieries and elsewhere to be used would only prolong the dispute and make a victory for the miners far more difficult. The Unions that would be first involved would therefore be the Transport Workers, Railwaymen, and Seamen. The last-named group had been for some years out of sympathy with the remainder of the Trade Union world and hostile to a sympathetic strike. It therefore had no part in the subsequent proceedings. The other Unions engaged in rail and road transport, docks, etc., met and agreed to support the General Council and the miners with an embargo on coal. Instructions were drawn up for the complete stoppage of coal transport, but allowing "safety men" to continue to work for safety purposes only (pumping etc.).[1]

At the last moment before the stoppage was timed to begin the Government averted the threatened crisis by offering a nine months' subsidy to the coal industry to give time for a full inquiry by a Commission (the Samuel Commission). The embargo on coal movements was immediately cancelled and the miners continued at work while the inquiry proceeded. The Government's concession was widely regarded as a great victory for the Trade Union movement, one which would not have been won but for the determination shown to stop the entire production and transport of coal.

In actual fact, of course, the problem was not solved but only shelved—for nine months. The situation had to be faced at the close of the Commission's labours and the crisis flared up again when the subsidy came to an end in May 1926. Then occurred the most momentous clash between organized Labour and the State that this country has yet seen, and one of the most remarkable conflicts in the history of Trade Unionism the world over. With the story of the investigations and negotiations of the nine months and the various offers that were made to the miners this study is not concerned. It must suffice to say that the miners resolutely refused to consider any reduction in wages or lengthening of hours, and in this

[1] For text of instructions see *Trade Union Documents*, 320.

policy they carried the General Council of the Trades Union Congress with them in the early stages. When the Commission's Report was issued it was seen that immediate wage reductions were recommended for certain classes of mineworkers at least, though in other respects the conclusions were favourable to the miners. The Miners' Federation, however, maintained their earlier position and refused a settlement with the Report as its basis. The mineowners were hardly more anxious to endorse the Commission's recommendations, so a stoppage seemed inevitable. The General Council, through its Industrial Committee, and in constant touch with the miners, continued negotiations with the Government in the hope of reaching some kind of settlement that would be acceptable to all parties, but in the meantime a special Conference of the Executive Councils of all Trade Unions affiliated to the Trades Union Congress was called to decide on the course to be taken in the event of a breakdown. This conference was held on April 29th and following days, and after full discussion it adopted, on May 1st, proposals presented to it by the General Council. These had been drawn up by a Committee of the General Council on the assumption that if no settlement was reached the workers in the most important industries would be called out on strike as and when required but not necessarily all at once. The scheme thus recommended was adopted by the Conference by the overwhelming vote of 3,653,527 against 49,911. It was as follows:—

PROPOSALS FOR CO-ORDINATED ACTION OF TRADE UNIONS[1]

(It should be understood that memoranda giving detailed introductions will be issued as required.)

1. SCOPE.

The Trades Union Congress General Council and the Miners' Federation of Great Britain having been unable to obtain a satis-

[1] *Trade Union Documents,* 342.

factory settlement of the matters in dispute in the coalmining industry, and the Government and the mineowners having forced a lockout, the General Council, in view of the need for co-ordinated action on the part of affiliated unions in defence of the policy laid down by the General Council of the Trades Union Congress, directs as follows:

Trades and Undertakings to cease Work.

Except as hereinafter provided, the following trades and undertakings shall cease work as and when required by the General Council:—

Transport, including all affiliated unions connected with Transport, i.e., railways, sea transport, docks, wharves, harbours, canals, road transport, railway repair shops and contractors for railways, and all unions connected with the maintenance of, or equipment, manufacturing, repairs, and groundsmen employed in connection with air transport.

Printing Trades, including the Press.

Productive Industries.

(*a*) Iron and Steel.

(*b*) Metal and Heavy Chemicals Group—including all metal workers and other workers who are engaged, or may be engaged, in installing alternative plant to take the place of coal.

Building Trade.—All workers engaged on building, except such as are employed definitely on housing and hospital work, together with all workers engaged in the supply of equipment to the building industry, shall cease work.

Electricity and Gas.—The General Council recommend that the Trade Unions connected with the supply of electricity and gas shall co-operate with the object of ceasing to supply power. The Council request that the Executives of the Trade Unions concerned shall meet at once with a view to formulating common policy.

Sanitary Services.—The General Council direct that sanitary services be continued.

Health and Food Services.—The General Council recommend that there should be no interference in regard to these, and that the Trade Unions concerned should do everything in their power to organize the distribution of milk and food to the whole of the population.

With regard to hospitals, clinics, convalescent homes, sanatoria, infant welfare centres, maternity homes, nursing homes, schools, the General Council direct that affiliated unions take every opportunity to ensure that food, milk, medical and surgical supplies shall be efficiently provided.

2. TRADE UNION DISCIPLINE.

(a) The General Council direct that, in the event of Trade Unionists being called upon to cease work, the Trade Unions concerned shall take steps to keep a daily register to account for every one of their members. It should be made known that any workers called upon to cease work should not leave their own district, and by following another occupation, or the same occupation in another district, blackleg their fellow workers.

(b) The General Council recommend that the actual calling out of the workers should be left to the unions, and instructions should only be issued by the accredited representatives of the unions participating in the dispute.

3. TRADES COUNCILS.

The work of the Trades Councils, in conjunction with the local officers of the Trade Unions actually participating in the dispute, shall be to assist in carrying out the foregoing provisions, and they shall be charged with the responsibility of organizing the Trade Unionists in dispute in the most effective manner for the preservation of peace and order.

4. INCITEMENT TO DISORDER AND SPIES.

A strong warning must be issued to all localities that any person found inciting the workers to attack property, or inciting the workers to riot, must be dealt with immediately. It should be pointed out that the opponents will in all probability employ persons to act as spies and others to use violent language in order to incite the workers to disorder.

5. TRADE UNION AGREEMENTS.

The General Council further direct that the Executives of the Unions concerned shall definitely declare that in the event of any action being taken and Trade Union agreements being placed in jeopardy, it be definitely agreed that there will be no general resumption of work until those agreements are fully recognized.

6. PROCEDURE.

(a) These proposals shall be immediately considered by the Executives of the Trade Unions concerned in the stoppage, who will

E

at once report as to whether they will place their powers in the hands of the General Council and carry out the instructions which the General Council may issue from time to time concerning the necessary action and conduct of the dispute.

(*b*) And, further, that the Executives of all other affiliated Unions are asked to report at once as to whether they will place their powers in the hands of the General Council and carry out the instructions of the General Council from time to time, both regarding the conduct of the dispute and financial assistance.

Meanwhile, the Premier had admitted that a Proclamation under the Emergency Powers Act, declaring a State of Emergency to exist, had already been prepared and signed, though, of course, it had not yet been issued. As early as the previous November the Government had circularized Local Authorities explaining the scheme that had been elaborated for emergency services in case of a great national stoppage. The Government was clearly preparing for all eventualities even before the Samuel Commission had finished its work. The day on which the Trade Union Conference adopted the strike arrangements and handed over the control of the ensuing movements to the General Council saw the issue of the Emergency Proclamation and of Regulations regarding the export of coal and the rationing of gas, electricity, and coal. The Government and the General Council continued negotiations but they prepared for the struggle that would come if no settlement could be reached. Finally, on Sunday, May 2nd, the day before the miners were to be locked out, in which case the national strike called by the General Council would begin on the following Tuesday, a formula was devised which the Government and the General Council could both accept. The miners' acceptance had also to be secured, but while discussions were proceeding between their leaders and the General Council on this issue, the Premier suddenly announced that negotiations were at an end owing to the action of the Unions in declaring a "general strike," and to the "overt act" already committed by printers on the *Daily Mail*, who had, on their own responsibility and without the knowledge of the General Council, refused to set up an article they considered unfair and provocative. The terms of the Government's ultimatum and the General Council's reply were as follows:—[1]

His Majesty's Government believe that no solution of the difficulties in the coal industry which is both practicable and honourable to all concerned can be reached except by sincere acceptance of the Report of the Commission. In the expression "acceptance of the report" is included both the reorganization of the industry which should be put in hand immediately, and pending the results of the reorganization being attained such interim adjustment of wages or hours of work as will make it economically possible to carry on the industry in the meantime. If the miners or the Trade Union Committee on their behalf were prepared to say plainly that they accept this proposal the Government would have been ready to resume the negotiations and to continue the subsidy for a fortnight.

But since the discussions which have taken place between Minis· ters and members of the Trade Union Committee it has come to the knowledge of the Government not only that specific instructions have been sent (under the authority of the Executives of the Trade Unions represented at the Conference convened by the General Council of the Trades Union Congress) directing their members in several of the most vital industries and services of the country to carry out a general strike on Tuesday next, but that overt acts have already taken place, including gross interference with the freedom of the Press. Such action involves a challenge to the constitutional rights and freedom of the nation.

His Majesty's Government, therefore, before it can continue negotiations must require from the Trade Union Committee both the repudiation of the actions referred to that have already taken place, and an immediate and unconditional withdrawal of the instructions for a general strike.

Letter from the General Council of the T.U.C. to the Prime Minister in reply to the Government's decision to break off negotiations, May 3, 1926:—

Your letter of the 3rd inst. announcing the Government's decision to terminate the discussions which had been resumed on Saturday

[1] *Trade Union Documents*, 339 ff.

night was received by the General Council with surprise and regret. The negotiations which had taken place between the Industrial Committee of the General Council and representatives of the Cabinet had been adjourned for a brief period in order to allow the Industrial Committee to confer with the full General Council and representatives of the Miners' Federation who were on your premises, in order to advance the efforts which the Industrial Committee had persistently been making to accomplish a speedy and honourable settlement of the mining dispute.

The Trade Union representatives were astounded to learn that without any warning the renewed conversations which it was hoped might pave the way to the opening up of full and unfettered negotiations had been abruptly terminated by the Government for the reasons stated in your communication. The first reason given is, that specific instructions have been sent under the authority of Trade Unions represented at the Conference convened by the General Council of the Trades Union Congress directing their members in several industries and services to cease work. We are directed to remind you that it is nothing unusual for workmen to cease work in defence of their interests as wage earners, and that the specific reason for the decision in this case is to secure for the mineworkers the same right from the employers as is insisted upon by employers from workers—namely, that negotiations shall be conducted free from the atmosphere of strike or lock-out. This is a principle which Governments have held to be cardinal in the conduct of negotiations.

With regard to the second reason, that overt acts had already taken place, including gross interference with the freedom of the Press, it is regretted that no specific information is contained in your letter. The General Council had no knowledge of any such acts having occurred and the decisions taken by it definitely forbid any such independent and unauthorized action. The Council is not aware of the circumstances under which the alleged acts have taken place. It cannot accept any responsibility for them, and is taking prompt measures to prevent any acts of indiscipline. The Council regrets that it was not given an opportunity to investigate and deal with the alleged incidents before the Government made them an excuse for breaking off the peace discussions which were proceeding.

The public will judge the nature of the Government's intentions by its precipitate and calamitous decision in this matter, and will deplore with the General Council that the sincere work which

the Council has been engaged in to obtain an honourable settlement has been wrecked by the Government's unprecedented
ultimatum.

Retreat was now impossible for either side. The entire
forces of Trade Unionism were marshalled against those of the
Government, in economic, not in military, array. The full
story of the strike is outside the scope of the present volume,
but certain features of it must be described, and the general
character of the conflict must be analysed. The stoppage at
first affected the transport services by rail and road, docks,
power supply for industrial purposes, iron and steel production,
printing (including the Press), and, of course, coal. The response
to the strike call was admitted by all to be remarkably solid.
All the trades affected were entirely stopped, as far as their
regular workers were concerned, and non-unionists went out
as well as members of Unions. As it was desired to cause as
little inconvenience as possible to the general public and to
eliminate all risk to life essential services like gas, water,
electricity for domestic use and street lighting, sanitary services,
supplies to hospitals, etc., were excepted from the instructions
to strike, and in general they continued in operation throughout
the dispute. On May 1st, the General Council had written the
following letter to the Premier:—

Mining Lock-Out: Essential Foodstuffs[1]

I am directed to inform you that in the event of the strike of Unions
affiliated to the Trades Union Congress taking place in support
of the miners who have been locked out, the General Council is
prepared to enter into arrangements for the distribution of essential
foodstuffs.

Should the Government desire to discuss the matter with the
General Council they are available for that purpose. The General
Council will be glad to learn your wishes in this respect.

This offer was not even acknowledged by the Government,

[1] *Trade Union Documents,* 344.

but later, on the last day of the strike in fact, it was referred to as follows:—[1]

His Majesty's Government, with reference to the above, took the view that no one has the right to interfere with the food supplies of the country, and that the Government are responsible for overcoming all such difficulties and for assuring all citizens that their rights and freedom under the law will not be invaded. The offer of the Trades Union Council to assist in distributing supplies after having previously called a general strike was an attempt to usurp the duties of the Government and of Parliament.

It was, in fact, an act of constitutional presumption. The Government have therefore throughout steadily refused to accept any form of co-operation with the Trades Union Council, and have consistently enjoined the same course of action upon all local authorities and private people. All persons who have felt constrained to accept the so-called T.U.C. permits should realize that they are failing to show due confidence in the strength of their country.

Trades Union Congress permits were nevertheless issued and accepted in appropriate cases throughout the strike, though the Government ordered them to be withdrawn.

Many regulations were issued under the Emergency Powers Act for all kinds of purposes, from authorizing arrests for sedition to giving power to commandeer land and vehicles, but many of these powers were very little used. As the Press was practically stopped, the Government issued its own newspaper, the *British Gazette*, and the Trades Union Congress its own daily under the title the *British Worker*. Both engaged in a propaganda war reminiscent of the 1919 Railway strike, and in addition the British Broadcasting Company was used by the Government for disseminating news bulletins. At an early stage the Government raised the cry that the strike was an "attack on the Constitution." The following "Message from the Prime Minister" was issued to the nation:—[2]

Constitutional Government is being attacked. Let all good citizens whose livelihood and labour have thus been put in peril bear with

[1] *British Gazette*, May 12, 1926, 1.   [2] *Ibid.*, May 6, 1926, 1.

fortitude and patience the hardships with which they have been so suddenly confronted. Stand behind the Government, who are doing their part, confident that you will co-operate in the measures they have undertaken to preserve the liberties and privileges of the people of these islands. The laws of England are the people's birthright. The laws are in your keeping. You have made Parliament their guardian. The General Strike is a challenge to Parliament and is the road to anarchy and ruin.

STANLEY BALDWIN

This kind of propaganda was repeated many times and the General Council replied with the constantly repeated statement that the strike was purely an industrial dispute:—[1]

General Council's Policy Constitutional

The General Council does NOT challenge the Constitution.
It is not seeking to substitute unconstitutional government.
Nor is it desirous of undermining our Parliamentary institutions.
The sole aim of the Council is to secure for the miners a decent
　　standard of life.
The Council is engaged in an Industrial dispute.
In any settlement the only issue to be decided will be an industrial
　　issue, not political, not constitutional.
There is no Constitutional crisis.

The General Council also inserted the following "Message to all Workers" in the *British Worker*, on various dates:—[2]

The General Council of the Trades Union Congress wishes to emphasize the fact that this is an industrial dispute. It expects every member taking part to be exemplary in his conduct and not to give any opportunity for police interference. The outbreak of any disturbances would be very damaging to the prospects of a successful termination to the dispute. The Council asks pickets especially to avoid obstruction and to confine themselves strictly to their legitimate duties.

On May 5th the police raided the *British Worker* offices, but allowed the printing to continue, while on May 7th an appeal by the Archbishop of Canterbury and others, for the

[1] *British Worker*, May 9, 1926, 4.　　[2] *Ibid.*, May 5, 1926, 1.

resumption of negotiations, was not allowed to be sent out over the wireless, though it was finally broadcast on May 11th.

Large numbers of special constables had been enrolled by the Local Authorities since the beginning of the strike, for extra police duty, but on May 9th the Government started a new auxiliary force, the Civil Constabulary Reserve, a paid force, equipped with batons and helmets, to assist the police in quelling any disorder that might arise. As a matter of fact there was practically no disorder from start to finish, and a friendly game of football on May 9th, between the police and the strikers, at Plymouth, was typical of the general spirit displayed. Throughout the dispute, however, there were numerous arrests for distributing "seditious" leaflets, making "seditious" speeches, and for breaches of the various Emergency Regulations.

On May 11th the General Council decided that on the following day the "second line" should be called out, and engineering and shipbuilding workers were instructed to cease work. On the same day, *The Times*, which had managed to print emergency issues, said in a leading article, "No one suggests for a moment that any considerable number of men on strike are animated by revolutionary motives." The Government, nevertheless, continued to attack the strike as revolutionary, and as an attack on the Constitution.

On May 12th the strike was called off by the General Council, the miners, however, continuing their stoppage for another six months or more. For several reasons, the chief of which were the lack of a clear, united policy on the part of the Trade Union movement, and the effective organization of road transport and other alternative services by the Government, the strike was a victory for the Government. But it was not an easy victory, and it left the whole community with an uneasy feeling about the future, so strongly had the remarkable solidarity and discipline of the strikers impressed themselves on the public mind.

The Trades Union Congress had, admittedly, made practically no preparation. This was no carefully planned, long-thought-out attack on the Government. The T.U.C. had practically no money, the Unions had to beggar themselves to pay strike benefit, and in the last resort the loyalty of the rank and file worker to his organization was all there was to depend upon for the success of the strike. Against these the Government placed all the resources of the State, and its plan for frustrating the strike had been carefully elaborated and tested over several years. To the worker the Government held up the fear of revolution and unconstitutional conduct, and the reassurance, constantly repeated, that all who remained at work or returned to work would be protected from any subsequent loss of benefits or reprisals in any form.[1] Police authority was strengthened and the military forces were notified as follows:—

All ranks of the armed forces of the Crown are hereby notified that any action which they may find it necessary to take in an honest endeavour to aid the Civil Power will receive, both now and afterwards, the full support of His Majesty's Government.[2]

In addition to the dispatch of troops to South Wales, Lancashire, and other industrial areas, battleships were sent to various ports. According to a well-informed writer, "months in advance the Naval Staff at the Admiralty was directed to prepare plans for assisting the civil power in maintaining essential services."[3] Before the strike was over there were 226,000 special constables, compared with 98,000 before the strike, with a further 18,000 in the newly formed Civil Constabulary Reserve. The Government was thus fully prepared to use all the military, naval, and police power at its disposal to crush the strike. Actually, none of it was needed, as there was almost perfect discipline among the strikers. The Government's

[1] *British Gazette*, May 6, 1926, 1, 4.   [2] *Ibid.*, May 8, 1926, 1.
[3] *The Fighting Forces*, July 1926. Article on the General Strike: the Navy's Aid.

organization for maintaining essential services is worth describing in some detail. It is outlined in the Circular[1] sent to Local Authorities in November 1925:—

Ministry of Health Circular 636, England and Wales, 1925

To Town Councils.
Metropolitan Borough Councils.
Urban District Councils.   MINISTRY OF HEALTH,
Rural District Councils.   WHITEHALL, S.W.I.
        20th Nov., 1925

SIR,

I am directed by the Minister of Health to refer to the Circular Letter which was sent to Local Authorities in May 1922 (See Appendix (A)), in which it was stated that it would be for Local Authorities to make such arrangements for the maintenance of local services as might be thought to be required in the event of need arising.

The events of recent years have shown that an industrial dispute may be so extended as to interfere seriously with communications, the conveyance of food and of other necessities, the supply of light and power and the health and means of livelihood of the population at large. While it is desirable that Government authorities, whether central or local, should keep aloof from any industrial dispute so far as it affects only the employers and the employed in the industry concerned, it is essential that other members of the community should be protected from the dangers and inconveniences of such a situation as is here indicated. This protection can best be supplied by decentralized organization designed to secure the maintenance of services essential to the well-being of the community.

Should such an emergency occur it is to their Local Authorities that the people will naturally turn for help in the difficulties which they may have to meet, and in order that any action initiated locally may harmonize with the national measures which the Government consider it desirable to take they think it necessary now to communicate to Local Authorities the following outline of the organization which would be brought into operation by the Government to deal with essential services which are not purely local in character. This outline will, if it be necessary, be supplemented by further details in a later communication. By "emergency" is meant a state of affairs

[1] *Trade Union Documents*, 352 ff.

necessitating the issue of a Proclamation under the Emergency Powers Act, 1920, as a preliminary to the issue of Regulations "for securing the essentials of life to the country."

The organization which the Government propose is designed to supplement and to assist in an emergency the normal methods of communication, supply and distribution and to give to all those who can help an opportunity of doing so in the manner most required. It is not intended that the Government should substitute new machinery for that ordinarily existing to meet the essential needs of the community.

1. A Minister will in such an emergency act as Civil Commissioner on behalf of the Government in each of ten Divisions covering the whole of England and Wales. He will be assisted by a staff consisting mainly of representatives of the Department of Government concerned and dealing with the following subjects: Transport; Food; Postal Services; Coal. It will be the duty of the Civil Commissioner and his staff during the emergency to keep in touch with the Local Authorities in each Division and to be available for consultation by them; and he will be empowered if necessary to give decisions on behalf of the Government.

The towns in which Civil Commissioners will be stationed and the general outlines of the areas of the Divisions for which they will act are set out in Appendix (B).

The Officers who will act as the Chief Assistants to the Civil Commissioners and those who will act as Technical Representatives for the services mentioned have been appointed, and these Officers will, as requisite, put themselves in touch with representatives of Local Authorities, and provide them with such information as may be practicable in regard to details of the organization.

2. Each Division is divided into suitable areas for administering essential national services and, if considered necessary, for recruiting volunteers for those purposes. In each area there will on an emergency be a local Food Officer, a local Road Officer and a Haulage Committee and a Coal Emergency Officer, besides representatives (where required) for other essential services. There will also be a Chairman selected by the Government to convene and preside over a Volunteer Service Committee in each area for the recruitment of volunteers to assist in maintaining essential national services.

In any town in which the Chairman of the Committee might consider it necessary to open a recruiting centre, it is earnestly hoped that it would be found practicable for the Local Authority concerned to combine with him in making the centre available for recruiting both for national and for local purposes, allocating by arrangement volunteers to local and national services in accordance with their qualifications and the needs of the occasion. Local Authorities are not expected to take any action so far as national services are concerned, unless and until approached by the Chairman.

3. On an emergency arising reliance will be placed to the utmost extent upon normal channels for the supply and distribution of food, and to this end the Divisional Food Representative upon the Civil Commissioner's staff will arrange for consultation with the principal traders as to the stocks of essential food-stuffs in their possession or in transit. In the event of any shortage or delay in the supply of essential food-stuffs to the Division, the Food Representative will be in possession of information as to alternative sources of supply and the means to make them available.

Local distribution and local shortages not affecting national supplies will ordinarily be dealt with by the local Food Officer.

4. Road Transport will be dealt with on similar lines. The Road Commissioner upon the Civil Commissioner's staff will be assisted by Road Officers and Haulage Committees in each of the areas comprised in the Division, who will endeavour by voluntary arrangement to promote the economical use of existing vehicles and where necessary the diversion of vehicles from less to more important services. Road Commissioners and Road Officers will be furnished with powers to this end should the exercise of such powers prove necessary.

5. In an emergency full directions will be sent as to the supply and distribution of coal. These directions may, if necessary, limit the supply of coal obtainable for any household or business, and may also place upon Local Authorities responsibilities for regulating the consumption of gas and electricity within their districts. They would probably necessitate in most cases the allocation of a particular officer or officers by the Local Authority during the period that they were in force.

The Local Authority will have the assistance of a Coal Emergency Officer and of a Committee of Traders within their own district.

6. The maintenance of law and order and the protection of persons and property from violence may be one of the most important services. The organization of the necessary arrangements and the control of the Police and Special Constabulary rest with the Police Authorities and the Chief Constables, but the Local Authorities

might co-operate, for instance, in securing able-bodied citizens of good character to serve as Special Constables. The arrangements for the enrolment of Special Constables will be made by the Police, and any men who come forward as Special Constables, or who offer their services in a general capacity and appear most suited for service as Special Constables should be referred to the Police Station or other place of enrolment appointed for the purpose.

7. While it is impossible to draw any hard and fast line of demarcation between national and local services which is universally applicable the position may be broadly defined as follows: Local Authorities are expected to undertake responsibility for the maintenance of local public utility services; in addition they are asked to co-operate with the national organization in regard to local transport and the local distribution of coal. In the absence of further directions they are not expected to undertake responsibility for the local distribution of food nor are they asked to accept responsibility for shipping, railway or postal communications, or docks and harbours except where the Local Authority are also the Port Authority.

8. It will be realized that in an emergency the burden upon national resources must in any event be considerable and responsibility could not be accepted by the Government for expenditure incurred by Local Authorities in meeting local needs. Where, however, a joint recruiting station is established, the expenditure incurred would have to be allocated between the Government and the Local Authority concerned. Precise instructions on this point would be issued to Chairmen of Volunteer Service Committees.

I am, Sir,

Your obedient Servant,

W. A. ROBINSON

Appendix (A)   *Circular* 312.
                (England and Wales)

MINISTRY OF HEALTH,
WHITEHALL, S.W.1.
May 23, 1922

SIR,

I am directed to refer to the "Memorandum for the Guidance of Local Authorities," which was issued in April of last year and to state that His Majesty's Government have decided that the Memorandum is to be regarded as withdrawn from the present date, and that it will be for Local Authorities to make such arrangements for maintenance of local services as may be thought to be required in the event of need arising. The copies of the memorandum sent to you should be destroyed forthwith as the financial and other provisions will not be applicable on any future occasion.

I am, Sir,

Your obedient servant,

W. A. ROBINSON,

Secretary.

The Clerk
    to the Local Authority.

Appendix (B)

Divisional Headquarters	Area of Division
London	London, Middlesex, Herts, Essex, Kent, Sussex, Surrey.
Reading	Berks, Oxfordshire, Bucks, Hants, Isle of Wight, Wilts.
Bristol	Gloucestershire, Somerset, Dorset, Devon, Cornwall.
Cardiff	Glamorgan, Carmarthen, Pembroke, Cardigan, Radnor, Brecon, Monmouthshire.
Liverpool	Lancashire, Cheshire, Denbighshire, Montgomeryshire, Merioneth, Carnarvonshire, Anglesey, Flintshire, Cumberland, Westmorland.
Newcastle-on-Tyne	Northumberland, Durham.
Leeds	Yorkshire.
Nottingham	Notts, Lincolnshire, Rutland, Leicestershire, Northants, Derbyshire.
Birmingham	Warwickshire, Worcestershire, Herefordshire, Salop, Staffordshire.
Cambridge	Cambridgeshire, Beds, Hunts, Norfolk, Suffolk.

Apart from these measures, committees of traders were set up to work in conjunction with the Government Departments in regard to the supply and distribution of commodities. Only in the case of London's milk was a service run directly by a Government department, in this case the Board of Trade (which incidentally made a profit of £73,000 over the short period the arrangement lasted!). The magnitude of the stoppage may be illustrated by figures of the estimated cost to the workers, in loss of wages, and to industry, the former item being about 11 million pounds to 12 million pounds (excluding the miners, who were locked out), and the latter about 30 million pounds. The total number of workers on strike (excluding the miners as before) was estimated by the Ministry of Labour to be 1,580,000 and the total number of working days lost, 15,000,000 (compared with 76,000,000 lost owing to the coal stoppage which was the cause of the strike, and which lasted for another six or seven months).

The total cost of the Government's organization was £433,000. This included all emergency costs for England and Wales, including the *British Gazette* (£16,000), the Civil Constabulary Reserve (£65,000), and miscellaneous police expenditure (£100,000).

These figures indicate to some extent the view taken by the Government of this challenge to their authority, the greatest ever made in this country by an industrial body. The Trades Union Congress saw the strike as a purely industrial dispute called to bring pressure to bear upon the Government, by perfectly lawful and constitutional means, to bring about a just settlement of the miners' grievances. The Government saw it as an attack on constitutional rule and on Parliamentary democracy, not perhaps in the sense that it was intended to be so, but in the sense that its inevitable result, if successful, would be to undermine the sovereignty of Parliament, and to set up a rival authority to that of the State itself.

The foregoing selection of disputes in which the authority of the State has been denied and challenged by organizations of workers has been made with a twofold object. In the first place it is clear that ever since the opening years of the present century there has been a series of conflicts of this nature in various parts of the world. In almost every industrial country there has been either an open rising of the industrial population against the State with Trade Unions taking an active share in pressing for economic objectives, or there have been strikes and demonstrations either of so extensive and grave a character as to be called "general strikes" or at least directed against the Government and not merely against a private employer. Where Trade Unions have given their support to a revolution, as in Germany, Russia, and Austria, for economic as well as political aims, it is clear that the most unbridgeable chasm must have existed between organized Labour and the political Government.

Where the major part of a country's industry has been brought to a standstill, as in Holland, Denmark, Sweden, Norway, Belgium, France, and Britain itself, it is equally clear that the normal machinery of government has failed in its purpose, if that purpose is conceived to be the reconciliation of conflicting claims within the community. Even where strikes and other forms of pressure have not been "general," but have nevertheless been directed against the Government, it is evident that Governmental authority as such, if ever it did for any long period hold the entire allegiance of all citizens, can be said to do so no longer. The same conclusion must be reached from consideration of such cases as those cited, where international Labour bodies have commanded an allegiance transcending national frontiers and superior to that commanded by individual States.

In the second place, the fact that the most appalling war in history was incapable of destroying loyalties that clashed violently with loyalty to the national State is most significant, for if ever there was a crisis when the sentiment of patriotism, to say nothing of the urge to self-preservation, might have been thought powerful enough to crush completely any allegiance other than that to the State, the war surely provided it.

We had the conflicts between organized Labour and the State in war time as in peace time, though naturally less pronounced in number and severity.

It is, further, most important to observe that there has been an unbroken chain of such conflicts from the early years of the century up to the present time, and that there has been no tendency for the gravity of the disputes to lessen but rather the reverse. They have occurred in practically all industrial countries, whether economically prosperous or depressed, whether in Europe, America, Australasia, or Africa. What is even more significant, the philosophy that has appeared to be responsible for the attitude taken up by organized Labour has varied from period to period, from country to country. Whether Syndicalism, Guild Socialism, I.W.W.-ism, Shop Stewardism, Communism—or simply old-fashioned Socialism —has been the attendant theory, the industrial and social disharmony has taken much the same form and has happened in much the same way. The theoretical construction has been a by-product of the existing circumstances and tendencies rather than their cause and inspiration.

What factors have been present throughout that might account for these facts? The answer appears to be, as already indicated, the growing intensity of industrialization, leading to highly developed organizations of Labour. It is not simply a matter of labour conditions, in any absolute sense, in terms of wages and hours. High wage countries like the United States, Canada, and Australia, have had struggles quite as fierce as those in Italy or Poland. In a wider sense labour conditions may be said to be important, for in that term we may include the status of Labour, the position of the Labour organizations themselves. As they have grown to power (as a consequence, be it noted, of the growth of industrialism), they have developed both the demand for status and the strength to make a bid for it. The evolution of Trade Unionism has resulted in larger and larger units being formed and this has meant an ever-widening area of stoppage in important strikes. Consolidation in all its forms has been necessary to give power and has resulted in that power being used on a

F

large scale and with ever-increasing potentialities for disturb-
ance, as well as with a stronger determination to achieve
recognition and status. That determination may be quite
unconsciously held, or be only half-conscious, but it has been
and still is the primary motive behind the modern tendency
to industrial disharmony and conflict of the kind under examination. Trade Union organizations have themselves become
principalities in their own world and they are no longer content
to be treated as unruly infants, to be alternately scolded and
petted by the all-wise but stern paternal State. Status, a part
in the making and shaping of the industrial society of which
they are a part and which tends more and more to dominate
the political society, the refusal to be a passive factor in the
unceasing adaptation of humanity to economic organization,
these appear to be the springs of action that send wave after
wave of unrest and conflict battering against the citadel of
State authority. There are, and must be, lulls in the struggle,
but it is inconceivable that it will either disappear or diminish
in the future unless the problem of conflicting claims is resolved
to the satisfaction of the rival powers.

II

THE TRADE UNION GROUP

CHAPTER VIII

TRADE UNION AIMS AND PURPOSES

HAVING outlined the problem raised by the recurrent clashes between the State and organized Labour, it becomes necessary to say something of the character and functions of the group organizations through which the workers act. The Trade Union itself, as a separate organization, is nowadays only part of a larger group. It is an association of persons but it is itself a member of a still larger association which may be termed the "Trade Union Movement" or "Organized Labour." We may even discover a "super-group," in the International Trade Union movement. Just as in practice the vague conception of the State crystallizes out into what is theoretically its instrument and agent, the Government, so the tangible form of the Trade Union movement in this country is to be discerned in the Trades Union Congress, or, in the wider international sense, in the International Federation of Trade Unions.

The Trade Union itself may first be considered as a sub-group, before passing on to the larger and more complex associations.

The definition of a Trade Union adopted by Mr. and Mrs. Sidney Webb in their monumental history runs: "A Trade Union . . . is a continuous association of wage-earners for the purpose of maintaining or improving the conditions of their working lives."[1] This is, with a slight alteration, the definition given in the first edition of their work in 1894, but it now requires revision. Its view of Trade Union purpose seems somewhat out of date, too limited, too static. It does not now correspond to the facts of Trade Union function or to the newer ideas of Trade Union direction. It would, perhaps, be more in line with present conditions and tendencies to say

[1] *History of Trade Unionism*, I.

that a Trade Union is an institution having as its purpose
the advancement of the vocational interests of its members.
By their vocational interests is meant their interests as persons
following a specific vocation, whether a trade or profession,
as distinct from their interests as inhabitants of a particular
locality, as believers in a particular religion, as golfers, as
theatre-goers, or as owners of land or capital. Thus, an association of coal miners or of lawyers may be a Trade Union,
but not an association of coal owners as such, for their relation
to coal owning is not a vocational one. Managers, even directors,
may be members of a Trade Union, in so far as they carry
out definite functions in relation to the economic process,
but the ownership of capital or land is not a vocation; it is a
legal and not a functional relationship. In practice the great
majority of Trade Unions have as their members employed
persons, but there are recognized vocational associations of
"independent" workers—medical men, authors, lawyers, and
the like. In the above definition the term institution rather
than association is used to indicate the fact that these bodies,
though associations, and voluntary ones at that, in most cases,
are part of the permanent structure, part of the pattern, of
modern society. They are no longer casual, external, irrelevant
bodies, from the point of view of the community at large,
but institutions playing an active and a vital part in the functioning of society. To maintain or improve the conditions of
the working lives of their members, in the Webbs' phrase,
is an important part of the function of Trade Unions, but not
by any means the whole of it, and still less does it correctly
describe the purpose of Trade Unionism as a larger group.
To secure the highest possible standard in the conditions of
working life is to sell labour on the most advantageous terms,
but a Trade Union is more than a Labour cartel, though it is
that incidentally.

A recent study of organized Labour has suggested that the
primary function of a Trade Union is to secure "control of

the job." "Manual groups" we are told, ". . . have had their economic attitudes basically determined by a consciousness of scarcity of opportunity, which is characteristic of these groups. . . . Starting with this consciousness of scarcity, the 'manualist' groups have been led to practising solidarity, to an insistence upon an 'ownership' by the group as a whole of the totality of economic opportunity extant."[1] Again, "The province of the Union is therefore to assert Labour's collective mastery over job opportunities and employment bargains, leaving the ownership of the business to the employer, and creating for its members an ever-increasing sphere of economic security and opportunity, equal to that which the craft guilds—those superb manifestations of the manual worker's aspirations and power—were able to guarantee to workingmen's communities of an earlier age."[2]

This links Trade Union psychology with that of the mediaeval Guilds in that handicraft economy which "as a system is an economic society based on exchange between free and independent workers, who are animated by the motive of securing a livelihood, who follow traditional methods in their technology, and who act according to rules prescribed by a common organization."[3]

Now, historically all this is very true. With no actual continuity in structure between the mediaeval Guild and the modern Trade Union there was nevertheless a psychological affinity, based on a traditional attitude towards the entire economic environment. Underlying all the superficial philosophies that have been imposed on the workers' movement by "intellectuals," or that the workers' leaders themselves have formulated, there has been this fundamental economic pessimism, this insistence on job control arising out of a "scarcity conscious-

[1] Perlman, S., *A Theory of the Labor Movement* (1928), 6.
[2] *Ibid.*, 253.
[3] Sombart, W., *Der Moderne Kapitalismus*, I, 1–188, cited Perlman, 238.

ness." But it is suggested here that this largely negative attitude is no longer the sole determinant of Trade Union policy.

To begin with, the consciousness of scarcity has in recent years grown much weaker and now tends to disappear altogether.[1] The problem now is to organize production and distribution so that the abundance of wealth scientifically possible becomes an actuality. It is therefore becoming quite common for all parties in an industry to display a certain solidarity. No longer can the psychology of scarcity be said to mark off Trade Unions as separate groups.

Further, the handicraft system was static, while the machine system is essentially dynamic. There can be no question of traditional methods in technology. A static society, a limited market, a traditional technology—all these will tend to create a very rigid institutionalism, an outlook based on custom, and a social ethic founded on habit. As is suggested later, in another connection, it is these traditional attitudes which, crystallized in a kind of social heritage, give rise to the conceptions of "natural rights" held in succeeding ages. Those "rights" that survive do so because the conditions that have changed do not affect these specific ways in which man reacts to his environment. Where changed conditions are relevant, as in the case under consideration, mental attitudes and reactions change accordingly. So at first the scarcity consciousness and its mental consequences, its conception of the "right to the job," its fixed idea of a limited market, and its passionate adherence to craft distinctions, were carried over to the new and quite different industrial conditions of the machine age. Stubborn, as one would expect of the traditions of centuries, they have been compelled to abdicate in modern times and we are witnessing the re-orientation of ideas and practices that has been made necessary.

One sign of this is the great growth in Trade Unionism among professionals. Perlman's statements, cited above,

[1] See Chapter XXVII.

refer explicitly to manual workers' groups. The professional groups have never had a similar psychology, but they now organize as Trade Unions because the entire conception of Trade Unionism has changed or, at any rate, is changing. "The essence of a profession," says Tawney, "is . . . that its members organize themselves for the performance of function."[1] While it would be an exaggeration to say that this is the outlook that now dominates the organized Labour movement, it is in this direction that events are tending. The reasons for this change, as well as the concrete evidences for it, will be described at a later stage, but in brief it may be said that the changes in the structure and working of industry itself are responsible. The more modern conception has even triumphed to such an extent in some countries that the Trade Union is recognized as representing the trade or profession as a whole and as having the right to protect the interests of the trade or profession in general, and not merely the economic welfare of its members, in the narrow sense. This is expressly laid down by statute and by the Courts in France, Germany, Poland, and Brazil, for instance.[2] The public character of Trade Unions is apparent even in those countries which do not formally recognize it to the same extent as in the countries just named. In Great Britain, the Courts do not admit that a Trade Union has a public interest at all, while in the United States such a public character has several times been emphatically denied by the Supreme Court.[3] Yet in a number of cases there has been very effective recognition, especially of the Trade Union movement as a whole. In the administration of the Miners' Welfare Fund, set up by statute, the Trade Union is specifically mentioned, for the expenditure of the Fund is vested in a Committee "consisting of five persons, appointed by the Board of Trade, of whom one shall be appointed . . .

---

[1] Tawney, R. H., *The Acquisitive Society* (1921), 139.
[2] *Freedom of Association* (1927), (I.L.O.), I, 40.
[3] E.g. in *Coppage* v. *Kansas* (1915), 236, U.S. 1.

after consultation with the Miners' Federation of Great Britain."[1]

In the appointments to the Railway Rates Tribunal, the public authority responsible for fixing railway freight rates and passenger fares, twelve members of the general panel are nominated by the Minister of Labour, "after consultation with such bodies as he may consider most representative of the interests of labour and of passengers upon the railways."[2] For this purpose the body "representative of the interests of labour"—the phrase is significant—that is actually consulted is the Trades Union Congress, which, moreover, is specifically mentioned in the same Act as one of the four bodies each entitled to nominate one "representative of the users of railways" to the Railway National Wages Board.[3] It will be seen later that in a multitude of cases the Unions individually and the Trades Union Congress as a whole have been, in practice, quite effectively recognized as having a public interest, and even in the United States the war period witnessed developments of a similar kind in relation to the American Federation of Labor.

Governments, as well as employers, have had to be realistic, and have been compelled to recognize the facts of the situation. Thus, the purpose of the Trades Union Congress is wider than the original aim of protecting the trade interests of its constituent Unions, for in order to do that effectively it has had to branch out into a host of new activities and assume functions of a much more far-reaching character in connection with the organization and working of the whole economic system. It has become a semi-public institution, with interests and duties transcending those concerned directly with the vocational side of life, though that aspect is always there in the background. Group interests have in this respect been recognized to the

---

[1] Mining Industry Act, 1920. 10 and 11 Geo. V. c. 50, sec. 20(3).
[2] Railways Act, 1921. 11 and 12 Geo. V. c. 55, sec. 24(1).
[3] Sec. 64(1)(b).

extent that we are able in many cases, even in legislation, to speak of questions having a "Labour interest," in a general sense, and the Trades Union Congress is regarded as the institution representing this point of view.

A Labour interest, in this wider sense, may be interpreted to mean a "class interest," but is a class a group, or rather is it the group we are considering? The interpretation is possible and has actually been adopted by many Labour theorists, but in fact the Labour interest represented by Trade Unionism is not the class interest of the "dispossessed," the "proletariat," the "victims of capitalism." Otherwise how shall we reconcile this view with the continued existence of Trade Union sentiment in Russia, which has abolished Capitalism and economic classes? If we accepted this interpretation we should have to believe, with many Socialists, that Trade Unionism would disappear in a Socialistic community. No Trade Unionist would assent to such a view. The interest represented is not a class interest but a vocational interest, a functional interest. Looking back over the record of general strikes for objectives unconnected with vocational interests, in hardly any case does it appear that there was spontaneous activity, by the Trade Unions, along these lines. The Unions were in some cases requested by their political friends and allies to take action, in others vocational objectives had to be added to secure a solid backing for political or social programmes. Much more is this true of the less emotional activities of organized Labour. Vocational interests can, it is true, be given a very wide interpretation, for in the modern industrial community there are few sides of life that, for the vast majority of citizens, are not bound up, directly or indirectly, with their vocations. A wider interest than the vocational—a class interest, for example—might embrace many non-vocational aspects of life, and we find this in the early history of Trade Unions. In their earliest forms they were organizations for social and recreational, as well as vocational purposes.

The eighteenth-century conditions which produced the movement were characterized by certain features, new to industry, which struck the workers of that period as being peculiarly oppressive and indeed immoral. Capitalism in the modern sense of the term was emerging from the remains of the mediaeval economic system, factories were beginning to multiply, the security of Labour was disappearing, and, worst of all, the fixing of wages by the justices, according to customary standards of living, had given way to the new and strange force of competition. Industrial autocracy, the anarchic destruction of accepted standards, insecurity, and a repudiation of ethical factors in Labour relations gave the workers' movement the character of a moral crusade. This feature, it is true, has never disappeared, though its importance has varied from time to time. In its emotional as well as purely "business" appeal, the early Union was the workers' substitute for the human, paternalistic State that had become transformed by the philosophy of competition into a remote, inhuman monster. Some of the comfortable ideals of the Middle Ages still exercised an influence well into the eighteenth century, and the forms of social organization had not yet become so complex as to make those ideals seem inevitably obsolete. The coming of the factory system and of the new industrial methods must have appeared more menacing and hostile to the workers of that time than we can well imagine. It is often suggested nowadays that the development of the material side of Western civilization has proceeded too quickly for human beings to make use of it in a proper way; that we have not evolved quickly enough an individual and social technique capable of dealing with the problems created by the rapid march of applied science. If such an idea has any significance one can say that the fears felt by the Labour pioneers of the eighteenth century were prophetic. Material civilization passed a turning-point in that period, and their reaction to the menace of the unknown forces sweeping down upon them was different from ours to the new developments of to-day only because they were still in touch with the ideals of a simpler age.

"Fellowship is life and lack of fellowship is death," was the burden of John Ball's teaching, in William Morris's vision. That was a principle familiar enough to the pioneers of Trade Unionism, and when social forms had so changed that fellowship was no longer to be found in existing institutions, they created their own associations to supply the need. So, the early Union was club and social centre, the focus of recreation and fellowship, as well as—even more than—a mechanism for getting higher wages. Therein was a further likeness to the mediaeval Guild. The worker went to his Trade Union branch —which usually, in the early days, held its meetings in a public-house—to chat and smoke with his friends, as well as to devise ways of improving his standard of life and work in an economic sense. All kinds of social adjuncts quickly became attached to the organization which, significantly enough, was on a geographical basis, where a purely vocational function would have suggested an industrial basis. In the literature of the movement this aspect of early Trade Unionism has been rightly stressed, but the impression is often given that it is equally important at the present day. This is by no means so. Not that the social character of the Trade Union branch has vanished altogether, still less the moral appeal of the movement as a whole. The tendency has, however, been all in the direction of emphasizing the purely business objectives, and the wider vocational interests, and naturally so. A great sentimental value attaches to the conception of a many-sided organism, serving its members in social as well as industrial ways, but in actual fact it has to be realized that the modern Trade Union only fits this conception to a very limited extent. For the keen, active members this traditional factor is still a frequent reality, but for the great majority of members it does not exist. Efforts have recently been made to restore some of the earlier features. Many Unions now provide educational facilities, arrange social events and even organize sports. But the great mass of Trade Unionists remain unaffected, and this is seen to be very natural. For one thing there are far too many competing distractions and loyalties for any but a really keen worker to concentrate his social life in a single organization. The very complexity of our industrial civilization which first stimulated the formation of Unions has since provided a bewildering variety of institutions for amusement, recreation, education, and social life generally. The ever-increasing specialization of modern times has abolished the simple conception of an "omnibus" association, which could express all the diverse forms of human fellowship. Differentiation according to function, and not a fusion of different functions, appears to be the principal feature of present-day development, and to this the Trade Union is no exception. The modern citizen does not want to find all his satisfactions through the medium of one organization, nor does he think it possible, whether that organization be a Trade Union or the State itself. Moreover, the increasing size of the Unions has made it almost impossible to maintain the same intimacy and personal touch. Even branches are now, in many cases, huge bodies in which the individual personality is lost. Like all other large organizations of our time they tend to become machines rather than fellowships. A further result of this is that a large part, probably a majority, of the members acquiesce rather than participate in the activities of their Union. Without being in any way hostile they are nevertheless "passive" in their membership, except in times of emergency, and often regard their Union in the same way that they regard their Church or Insurance Society or the State itself, as a matter of course. Their Union is an organization to which they pay their dues but which has normally little meaning for them outside its industrial functions. Keen Trade Unionists may be indignant at this suggestion, but it is foolish to deny what is a perfectly natural thing and even more foolish not to realize that this same lack of enthusiasm and positive co-operation is a feature of all great organizations to-day. The notable fact is that in times of stress and danger to any section, a loyal and active spirit immediately springs to life.

Thus, the "business" side of Trade Unionism tends to become more and more emphasized and its non-vocational functions to fall into the background. This does not mean that it ceases to be idealistic or that it becomes solely concerned with questions of pence and hours. Nor does it mean that the Trade Union ceases to be a genuine group or to display the same essential features that have characterized it through the century and more of its history.

CHAPTER IX

GROUP LIFE OF TRADE UNIONS

WHETHER we consider Unions individually or their wider associations it cannot be doubted that all the characteristics of a typical group are present. The early history of organized Labour is sufficient to prove this, quite apart from its characteristics at the present day. In origin Trade Unions, in this country and many others, were spontaneous growths, depending neither on the fiat of the State nor on the deliberate act of any person or group of persons.[1] They arose out of the needs of the common people, those needs being "for fellowship between craftsmen, for mutual help, for improvement in the remuneration and conditions of labour, for an increasing measure of control over the circumstances of daily life."[2] Born in this way they survived through innumerable efforts to suppress them. The power of the State could not crush them. Their unquenchable spirit not only carried them through but finally compelled the State to recognize them. No clearer example could be imagined of the inherent vitality of a genuine group organization having a common purpose and a vivid group aspiration. A further indication of the independence of this collective life is the natural development, practically unaffected by external forces, of the internal legislative, executive, and judicial machinery whereby the group's activities are carried on and made effective. In so far as Trade Unionism comes into contact with the State or other associations or individuals it is subject to most, though not all, of the laws and regulations made for the community in general. For specifically Trade Union relations inside the Unions or inside the Trade Union movement, there has evolved, by the will of the members

[1] Webb, *History of Trade Unionism*, ch. I.
[2] *Trade Union Documents*, I.

themselves, and with no external sanctions or even legal recognition, all the means of adjustment and decision that any such group requires if it is to live a healthy, independent life. Not only does the Trades Union Congress act as the legislative body for the whole group, and the Conference of delegates of an individual Union for that sub-group, but in each case there is an Executive body, with the requisite power to apply this "domestic law," which has, after all, only a moral sanction in many respects (and especially in respect of industrial policies and principles). Rule 3, subsection 8, of the Transport and General Workers' Union, for instance, lays it down that "The general policy of the Union shall, subject to the Biennial Delegate Conference, be determined by the General Executive Council, but the policy of every area or trade shall, within the powers delegated to an area, or national or area trade group, committee by these rules or by the General Executive Council, be determined by such area, or national or area trade group committee."

"Every decision and order of the Executive Committee," runs subsection 7 of Rule III of the National Union of Railwaymen, "shall be binding on members and branches, subject to appeal to the next succeeding Annual General Meeting; and every member of the Union, both present and future, agrees that this clause shall be of full force and effect, and shall form the essential basis of the contract between the Union and its members and every one of them, and that no order or decision of the Executive Committee whatever shall be questioned, reversed, controlled or suspended except by way of appeal as aforesaid."[1] This "domestic law" is practically always conformed to, even where it overrides the immediate interests of individual members.

Again, Unions have their own domestic tribunals for the settlement of internal disputes, and the Trades Union Congress

[1] For fuller details as to the government of Unions see *Trade Union Documents*, 94–114.

G

similarly has its machinery and procedure for adjudicating between conflicting Unions.

Rule 101 of the Durham Miners' Association, for example, provides that "Should any dispute arise between a member, or a person who has ceased to be a member, or person claiming through such member or person, or under the rules, and the society, or the committee of management, or any officer of the society, it shall be decided by arbitration. Three arbitrators shall be elected by the society at the annual general meeting, none of whom shall be directly or indirectly interested in the funds of the society. In each case of dispute the names of the arbitrators shall be written on pieces of paper and placed in a proper receptacle, and the one whose name is first drawn out by the complaining party, or by someone appointed by him, shall be the Arbitrator to decide on the matter in dispute."

The Trades Union Congress Rule dealing with inter-Union disputes is as follows:—

(a) Where disputes arise, or threaten to arise, between affiliated organizations, the General Council shall use its influence to promote a settlement.

(b) Upon application from an affiliated organization the General Council shall also have the power to investigate cases of dispute or disagreement between affiliated organizations, whether relating to general industrial questions or demarcation of work.

(c) If the parties to a dispute fail to submit the case to the Disputes Committee of the General Council as provided by this Standing Order, it shall not be permissible for such dispute to be raised at the Annual Meeting of Congress.

(d) The General Council shall have power to summon the contending organizations to appear before the Disputes Committee of the General Council and to require such organizations to submit all evidence and information that the Disputes Committee may deem essential to enable them to adjudicate upon the case.

(e) If the result of such an inquiry be that the complaining society fails to prove the charge, it shall bear the whole cost of the investigation, including the expenses incurred by the defending society.

(f) Should any decision of the General Council in connection with such cases under this section be ignored by any organization, the Council may at once issue a report to all the unions. If compliance with the decision of the General Council is still refused, the matter shall be reported to Congress to deal with as may be decided upon.

A significant feature is that the Disputes Committee of the General Council is developing (half unconsciously) a code of principles governing decisions. A specialized jurisprudence is evolving based not on abstract notions nor on any other system, but on their own knowledge and experience of industrial life, and their interpretation of the specific case in the light of this knowledge and experience. In this connection the remarks of the Disputes Committee on inter-Union competition in its Report for 1924 are noteworthy.[1] The Disputes Committee says that, arising out of the cases with which it has had to deal, certain comments may usefully be made. It goes on to suggest principles the observance of which would lead to a diminution in the number of inter-Union disputes, and inferentially it indicates the kind of tests applied to certain classes of disputes.

This development, as it proceeds, must prove enormously important not only to the Trade Union movement itself but to the community at large. Its importance is twofold. In the first place it means that, with the evolution of this judicial machinery and this reliance on a "rule of law," the sphere of such a jurisprudence may legitimately expand to include matters that are now dealt with by the State and the ordinary Courts. While a group is organized solely for struggle no constructive judicial and administrative functions can easily be undertaken, for there is neither the tradition of a judicial process nor the machinery for its exercise. When such machinery and habit have been incorporated into the structure and the very life of the group, for its own purposes, the determination and decision in many classes of cases affecting the community outside may safely be left to it. So, the Unions may in time take over or at least share in the adjudication of claims in

[1] *T.U.C. Annual Report*, 1924, 156, *Trade Union Documents*, 158.

workmen's compensation, social insurance, and other matters of vital public concern. To some extent this process has already begun.

In the second place, as an informed method is evolved for dealing with the peculiar problems of the group, the methods of the outside world, of the political State, or of other groups, may be influenced, and the Union's methods may be copied in special classes of cases.[1] Both developments have already taken place in connection with Unemployment Insurance. Trade Unions have in the great majority of cases paid unemployment benefit out of their own funds long before any State Unemployment Insurance existed. This form of benefit is, in fact, one of the oldest in the history of Trade Unionism. The Unions in consequence evolved an elaborate judicial and administrative code for the determination of claims to such benefit, designed to prevent abuses and safeguard the funds of the society while helping genuine cases. The State was without experience in these matters, and when the national Unemployment Insurance scheme started in 1911 the method adopted by the Unions was followed. "That method," says an official Report,[2] "which was itself for the most part copied from the general practice of the trade unions covering workers insured in the trades insured under the Act of 1911, is . . . the requirement of the attendance of the claimant, in general daily, during ordinary working hours, in order to sign an unemployed register or vacant book as evidence of his unemployment. This method is appropriate to the circumstances of most industries, but it is not the only method in use by trade unions which have experience in the matter of out-of-work payments. In making arrangements, therefore, the Department have regard to the special circumstances of different trades or industries

[1] Cf. "All voluntary societies are seeking to make solutions peculiar to themselves, general solutions accepted by the State." Laski, H. J., *A Grammar of Politics* (1925), 59.

[2] *Report on National Unemployment Insurance* (1923), Ministry of Labour, 137 ff.

and have admitted certain variations." The development
under the Unemployment Insurance Acts of a jurisprudence
different from that recognized by the ordinary Law Courts
would have been necessary in any case by reason of the subject
matter and because of the need for speedy adjudication, but
its actual form has been largely determined by the pre-existing
methods adopted by the Unions.

Arising out of the same set of circumstances the sphere of
the Unions has been extended to include administrative and
judicial functions in connection with the national Unemployment Insurance scheme, e.g. the disbursing of funds, part of
which have been contributed by the Exchequer and the
employers, is in certain cases entrusted to Unions, which also
have the responsibility of adjudicating claims in these cases,
and the State pays the Unions a fee for their services.[1]

This one instance may serve to show how the evolution of
an internal code of law and administration may lead on the one
hand to an extension of the functions of Trade Unions, and
on the other hand to the incorporation of such domestic codes
in the wider mechanism of the State.

Further evidence of the vigorous group life of Trade Unions
is to be seen in the multitude of inter-Union agreements that
are concluded for the safeguarding of mutual interests, the
demarcation of jurisdiction, the avoidance of disputes, and
many other purposes. As a rule these agreements (which,
of course, have no legal force in the majority of cases) are
only concluded after negotiations and "diplomatic" exchanges.
In some instances these inter-Union treaties are "registered,"
so to speak, with the Trades Union Congress, just as international treaties are registered with the League of Nations,
the larger group having often taken a benevolent interest,
or perhaps an active part, in the initiation and conduct of the
discussions leading to the compact. There are many multi-

[1] See, e.g., Unemployment Insurance Act, 1920. 10 and 11 Geo. V.
c. 30, sec. 17.

lateral agreements providing for the free transfer of members and reciprocal recognition of Trade Union cards. A typical agreement for group co-operation in organization may serve to illustrate the manner in which a very long standing dispute was brought to an end by the parties themselves meeting in negotiation and drawing up terms of settlement.

INTER-UNION AGREEMENT

Nat. Union of Railwaymen; Amal. Eng. Union; Electrical T.U.; United Patternmakers Assn.; Nat. Soc. of Coppersmiths, etc.; Nat. Union of Foundry Wkrs.; United Op. Plumbers, etc.; Workers' Union; Amal. Machine, Engine and Iron Grinders, etc.; Fed. of Engin. and Shipbuilding Trades. 1927.

Railway Shopmen

Agreement with a view to securing Efficient Organization of Railway Shopmen throughout Great Britain.

1. MEMBERSHIP.

(*a*) That the membership of the unions, parties to this agreement, catering for shopmen should be regarded as inviolate, and that no member of a union engaged as a railway shopman should be admitted to membership in any other union until after his former union has been consulted and all dues to this union have been met.

(*b*) The membership application form of all the unions concerned in this agreement should contain an inquiry to be answered by the applicant as to whether he is, or has been, a member of any other union, and if so, what his financial relationship is to such union.

(*c*) That for the purpose of providing a uniform method of determining membership, 26 weeks shall constitute the period which should elapse before a man is regarded as having ceased membership in a union.

(*d*) Recognizing the respective constitutions of the unions, parties to this agreement, it is agreed that craftsmen, who are not at present members of any union, should be approached to join a union catering for their occupation, it being distinctly understood that the efforts of all unions, parties to this agreement, shall be directed to the elimination of non-unionists. It is also agreed that periodical consultations between local representatives of the said unions shall take place in the various centres with a view to giving effect to this clause.

2. SUBSCRIPTIONS.

With a view to discouraging the desertions from the unions by the attraction of a cheaper contribution, an endeavour shall be made to secure unification of contribution of each of the unions, parties to this agreement, in so far as Trade Union benefits are concerned.

3. BENEFITS.

Each union will be responsible to its members for the payment of benefits in accordance with the rules of the unions concerned.

4. NATIONAL NEGOTIATIONS.

(a) It is advisable that all national negotiations affecting the interests of railway shopmen shall be conducted jointly by the unions concerned, parties to this agreement.

(b) With respect to purely craft questions each individual union shall have the right of separate negotiations. In the event of national machinery for shopmen being established, each union, party to this agreement, should co-operate to utilize it to the fullest advantage.

5. EXPENSES—LOCAL AND NATIONAL MACHINERY

The expenses of the local and national machinery shall be met by the unions concerned.

Again, the rich variety of forms of inter-Union federation and association may be suggested as evidence of the vitality and spontaneity of Trade Unions as groups. Local branches of Unions, even, federate in Trades Councils, a very early and purely voluntary form of association. This same development is found in most countries, and in France it may be said to be the foundation of Trade Union organization, the local Bourse du Travail being historically the unit, more or less self-contained, the national Union appearing on the scene, if at all, at a much later date.

Federations of Unions exist in almost every industry to provide a means of expression for wider group interests than those covered by the individual societies. In some cases these federations exercise very important functions, including the negotiation of general collective agreements and the control of strikes, on behalf of the entire group. Rule 5(*b*) of the National Federation of Building Trades Operatives, for example, provides that "No Society shall enter into a trade dispute affecting another Union or Unions without the sanction of the Executive Council or Emergency Committee being first obtained." Federations in this way limit the powers of constituent organizations in the interests of the entire group concerned. Amalgamations of Unions within a specific trade or industry are often brought about as a result of the successful working of federations, and even where this does not happen an "industry" solidarity is almost always developed. Thus, the group consciousness in the building industry or the printing trade is probably as keenly felt through the federation, in each case, as in the transport industry, where a former federation led to the amalgamation of a number of Unions into one organization.

The operation of conflicting group loyalties may, as a matter of fact, be studied to perfection in the formation and attempted formation of amalgamations and federations. In the case of business amalgamations there is seldom any feeling of loyalty to a firm in the minds of the shareholders who are invited to ratify an amalgamation project. As a rule it is a matter solely of a remunerative offer in terms of an exchange of shares, etc. The case of a family business may be different, but a joint stock company rarely gives rise to this group feeling. Where a Union is asked to amalgamate with another organization the financial aspect is also important, but there is almost invariably the factor of loyalty to the established body to be considered as well, particularly if there is a long and honourable history behind it. There is a great pride in the very name of the Union which makes members unwilling to see it merged in another Union, with perhaps a new name for the combined body. There is pride in its past achievements, in its rules and constitution, perhaps in its very peculiarities and defects. This sentiment

frequently stands in the way of an amalgamation being successfully negotiated. But it is not merely a matter of sentiment,
either. The very fact that a Trade Union has been formed at
some period postulates a definite vocational area to be safeguarded. A merger with another group may be desirable on
the general ground of efficiency but this implies a merging of
vocational areas also. As a general rule, the wider the boundaries of the group the less intense is the group feeling created,
and members who are invited to merge the identity of their
smaller group in a larger society often feel that their more
immediate vocational interests may be sacrificed, or at any
rate insufficiently recognized. In a Report on Amalgamation[1]
the General Council of the Trades Union Congress made special
reference to this difficulty. "Special provision should be made,"
said the Report, "where definite craft and occupational interests
arise, for the preservation of certain craft or occupational
autonomy. In recent years large organizations have found the
necessity for grouping together workers with common interests,
allowing them to elect a National Committee, and, in addition,
permanent officers have been attached to the groups to attend
solely to their requirements. In some cases, local and district
committees have been set up by the groups, for the consideration of their own peculiar problems. At least part of the executive is elected on a craft or occupational basis. By these means
the interests of certain classes of workers have not been sub-
merged and a measure of autonomy has given them responsibility and preservation of identity which is necessary to induce
certain sections of workers to link up with a larger organization." This powerful consciousness of the interests of the smaller
group is perhaps the most common obstacle encountered in
amalgamation proceedings. At the same time the members of
the Unions concerned are quite alive to the reality of the larger
group interest present. They seldom if ever refuse to look
beyond the confines of their own organization to the wider

[1] *T.U.C. Annual Report*, 1927, 107 ff.

vocational sphere of which they are part, but the conflict of interests impels them to adopt an intermediate form of association in the form of a federation or the even looser form of an "alliance." The establishment of federal organizations is nearly always the easiest method of reconciling claims for autonomy within the narrower vocational group with the needs of the more comprehensive group. Practically every industry has its federations of Trade Unions. They follow no uniform principle in form and functions, but are adapted to the needs of the Unions and the characteristics of the industry concerned.

As the problem of social organization is largely one of the relation of groups to each other and to larger inclusive groups, and of the reconciliation of their conflicting claims, the operation of federal associations in the Trade Union movement is very instructive to the student of political theory. The conflict of group claims is rather one of area than of opposed interests, however; the interests of the International Federation of Trade Unions, of the Trades Union Congress, of a federation of Unions in a particular industry, of a single Union in that industry, are all identical in the long run. The difference, if any, on a short view, is due to the fact that the more comprehensive the organization the more it is concerned with general principles and long-time results rather than with immediate details of the workshop. To express it in another way, the affairs of a craft or section may bound the normal sphere of the small Union, whereas the Federation is interested in the fortunes of the industry as a whole, the T.U.C. in industrial organization and functioning generally, and the International Federation in world industry and its interconnections. Yet the reality of the group interest in each case is unquestionable. It is shown beyond all doubt by the sentiment of solidarity that is evoked at each stage. The term "solidarity" is used here in its ordinary sense of loyalty to a social group or institution, and a consciousness of common interests necessitating common action.

It is the psychological fact, rather than the metaphysical abstraction of Duguit, that concerns us.

Solidarity shows itself in the individual Trade Union in almost every phase of its work. The strong dislike of the "blackleg" shown by all Trade Unionists is not due merely to the feeling that this man is gaining the advantages won by Trade Unionism without paying for them; it is even more the feeling that the non-unionist is an "outsider" as regards this particular social group to which he ought to belong. To break away from the group to form a dissident, rival association is one of the worst sins in the Trade Union calendar. It receives strong official condemnation in a resolution adopted by the Trades Union Congress in 1927: "This Congress pledges itself to discourage in every possible way the formation of new Trade Unions, and directs the General Council to refuse to accept the affiliation of any Trade Union which is composed of members who have broken away from an existing Union affiliated to Congress."

"Breakaway Unions" are accordingly fought bitterly and relentlessly. They have broken the code of loyalty and solidarity which runs strongly through Trade Union ethics. The Miners' Federation of Great Britain, aided to the extent of a campaign costing thousands of pounds, undertaken by the Trades Union Congress, fought unremittingly against the "breakaway" Notts Miners' Industrial Union, formed in 1926, and against the "breakaway" Unions set up in certain of the Scottish coalfields. These latter were "left-wing" revolts, small in size, while the former was a "right-wing" secession of larger proportions, but both were opposed with equal determination. The Union of Post Office Workers allowed the entire Whitley machinery of Joint Councils for the Post Office to be suspended for years, rather than recognize a "breakaway" Union to which the authorities wished to give representation. These revolts, indeed, raise an important problem in the internal government of Trade Union organizations, but the policy adopted in all such cases is impressive evidence of the sense of solidarity that exists. That it is also evidence in many cases of the fear lest a minority become a majority is true enough, but this is essentially part of the sentiment of solidarity, which, as in most institutions, is almost as frequently menaced from within as from without.

It is, however, the threat from without that usually brings out manifestations of solidarity in the most spectacular form. Above all, the sentiment is displayed most impressively in strikes. The mere existence of a strike is evidence of group loyalty, for a number of workers—it may be a hundred or a hundred thousand—have given up their wages with their jobs, risked their futures and those of their families, and thereby faced suffering and distress at the call of their organization. Individually they may, and usually do, have little conception of the issues at stake. Collectively they engage in a struggle about the real causes and significance of which only their leaders are fully informed. But the initiation of a strike is seldom, if ever, blind obedience to an order or instruction from leaders. The motive force is usually a deeply felt, though perhaps inarticulate or semi-articulate, resentment of some injury or desire for improved conditions. If such a feeling is evoked and, owing to the circumstances, it bursts through all efforts to find a peaceful settlement, a strike may occur without any "leadership" being involved. Or when it is a duly authorized strike the leaders may be, and usually are, merely registering the wish, or more accurately the vehement demand, of their members. Such emotional solidarity may often be regarded psychologically as a form of mass suggestion, to the extent that many persons are influenced to a course of action for which they have not formulated rational grounds. Suggestibility in general has been ascribed to the gregarious system of instincts,[1] and certainly opinions and feelings that are due to herd-sug-

[1] Rivers, W. H. R., *Instinct and the Unconscious* (1920).

gestion are commonly held with an exceptional degree of conviction and strength. "Opinions formed more individually by weighing evidence and coming to conclusions are held more tentatively. . . . Emotions communicated from a group often lead to action of a more whole-hearted and uncontrolled kind than those originated individually."[1] Thus, strikes frequently begin with the powerful feeling generated in the minds of members of the group affected by some unsatisfactory element in their working conditions or environment; this spreads by "sympathy"—the emotional aspect of suggestion—to the generality of members of the group, and then the leaders formalize and systematize it in strike instructions.

That is often, but not always, the mechanism of group solidarity in strikes. If a stoppage is prolonged, loyalty becomes more difficult to maintain. "The first burst of enthusiasm," as one writer has put it, "is usually not sufficient to enable the strikers to endure losses and sufferings which frequently follow. Therefore, efficient collective conduct requires that group success be placed above immediate personal advantages; for when each reflects upon his own immediate interests, *rapport* lessens until the strike suddenly goes to pieces."[2] This is where the formal organization of the group becomes important, for without it the sentiment of solidarity will probably evaporate in the way suggested. A vital factor in the creation of group feeling in all cases is the complex of rules and regulations, funds and financial arrangements, ancillary services of education and recreation, commissariat arrangements, and so on. Hobhouse has well expressed this truth: "The behaviour of the group will be affected not only by the character of all its members but by the nature of its organization. The courage of an army is not a simple product of the bravery of individual soldiers, for each soldier will be affected in action

[1] Thouless, R. H., *Social Psychology* (1925), 169.
[2] Hiller, E. T., *The Strike* (1928), 79.

by the confidence he feels in his comrades, his leaders, the supply of munitions behind the lines, and so forth."[1] Thus, it is beside the point to criticize the action of a Trade Union in devising means whereby the enthusiasm and solidarity of strikers are maintained and even increased. Strikes are rarely planned by the leaders, but once this form of group protest is undertaken, however spontaneous its beginnings may have been, the executive body of the Union must thereafter do everything in its power to utilize a technique of solidarity and loyalty. Accordingly, we find Unions arranging sports and entertainments for strikers, organizing food supplies in some cases, carrying on educational classes for their members temporarily idle, making provision through sympathisers in other districts for the children of strikers to be cared for while the conflict lasts, and so on, in addition to the usual speeches, processions, and demonstrations designed to fan enthusiasm to the highest pitch.[2] Such procedure is followed with armies, and even, nowadays, with football teams, public schools, boy scouts, and similar groups, though the details vary to suit the circumstances. The Church itself does not disdain, in America at any rate, to heighten group fervour with histrionics, fancy dress, and displays of bathing beauties.

More remarkable than the solidarity shown by strikers in conflicts where their own Union is involved is the loyalty displayed to the Trade Union movement generally in "sympathetic" strikes, "general strikes," and international strike action. A sympathetic strike is sometimes called because the workers in a trade or industry feel that their own immediate interests are menaced by the action of the employers in another

---

[1] Hobhouse, L. T., *Social Development* (1924), 189.

[2] The conditions of *morale* in such group conflicts are analysed in detail in Hiller's study of strikes, already quoted, and the practical side is admirably illustrated in the various accounts of the great Steel strike in U.S.A. in 1919, e.g. Foster, W. Z., *The Great Steel Strike* (1920).

trade or industry where there is a stoppage. This is not always the case, however. The majority of sympathetic strikes are called "in sympathy" with another striking group, or in loyalty to the larger body of workers of which they are part. Carried to extremes this last feeling may lead to a "general" strike, in which case the entire body of workers is fired, not by the prospect of immediate gains for their own craft or industry, but by a more ideal kind of hope for the future of the whole working class. The "general strike" that occurred in this country in 1926 was not, of course, a true "general strike" at all in this sense; it was essentially a sympathetic strike. The million and a half workers who ceased work did so out of a feeling of solidarity with the miners, whose standards were being attacked, and out of loyalty to the Trades Union Congress representing the working-class as a whole. From the brief account already given of this strike it will be clear that the solidarity and loyalty displayed were nothing short of amazing. With nothing whatever to gain for themselves, with everything to lose, in fact—their agreements, their standards, their very jobs—practically 100 per cent. of those called out responded, remained out for nine days, and then only went back on being instructed to do so. Such an exhibition of loyalty and group feeling is only unique in its large scale; similar examples on a smaller scale could be cited for nearly every industry and every industrial nation. It is remarkable, and worthy of very earnest thought, that there was greater loyalty and solidarity in the Trade Union group in 1926 than in the State group in 1914 on the outbreak of war, a comparable testing time. The critic might retort that loyalty to the State in 1914 was sufficiently powerful to wipe out the loyalty of the workers to their own international organization and its pacifist programme. That is true in the main, but even international Trade Union solidarity has its impressive instances, some of which have been described in the preceding pages. One need only refer to the action of the French Trade Union movement in 1923 in opposing its own Government and allying itself with the international movement against the French occupation of the Ruhr. The entire British Trade Union movement, to take a further instance already cited, prepared for direct action in 1920 against the Government's supposed intention to help Poland's war against Soviet Russia; this was an international gesture of some importance, and was linked up with the campaign of the International Federation of Trade Unions to stop the transport of munitions to Poland.

Even during the war, internationalism was sufficiently alive among the Unions to make the Government exceedingly cautious in regard to war aims, and the inter-allied Labour Conferences that were held showed that the Trade Union movements of the allied nations were by no means in the grip of an exclusive nationalism. The new "Amsterdam" International of Trade Unions (I.F.T.U.) was successful in forcing the Inter-Allied Supreme Council to admit the German and Austrian Trade Unions to the Washington Conference of the International Labour Organization of the League of Nations in 1919. It was announced that not a single workers' delegate would go to Washington if Germany and Austria were excluded. The Governments capitulated and invitations were sent, though in the event neither country was able to send delegates. The International Federation of Trade Unions and its affiliated members scored a great success at Washington and their spokesmen and delegates displayed "a degree of discipline and solidarity among themselves which 'aroused the astonishment of the government delegates and the envy of the employers.' "[1]

The solidarity of the "international group" was further shown in the seven weeks' boycott of Hungary in 1920, following an appeal by the Hungarian workers. Another impressive example was in the financial and other support given by the various Trade Union movements, through the I.F.T.U.,

[1] Lorwin, L. L., *Labor and Internationalism* (1929), 204.

to the British Trades Union Congress in the National strike of 1926. "In Holland, 25 cent 'stamps of solidarity' were put on sale; the Danish trade unions offered to make weekly payments for the duration of the strike; the Swiss trade unions called upon their members to levy themselves not less than one franc per head; in France, the printers of Paris, who had just obtained a wage increase, handed over the amount of the increase to the British strikers. In Germany, big mass meetings were held at which collections were taken up."[1] In addition, steps were taken in nearly every country to stop the transport of coal to England. In a sense more significant still, the International Federation of Christian Trade Unions, normally an opponent of the Amsterdam International, offered help, and in the Ruhr coalfield the Christian Trade Unions, which are strong in this area, co-operated with the Unions affiliated to the I.F.T.U. to stop coal going to England.

These are only a few recent instances of the very real solidarity that unifies the Trade Unions of different countries into an international group, which has a distinct outlook of its own, identical neither with that of its component national associations, nor with that of other international bodies. All these facts illustrate convincingly the extension of group interests to wider group interests in which the central vocational character is retained, but at the same time is transfused with the more liberal definition and meaning of a common vocation that come from a more extensive contact between groups and between individuals.

So we return to a question already raised. Is this group life having a common aim and purpose the life of the Trade Union, or of the federation of Unions in a specific trade or industry, or of the national Trade Union movement as a whole, or of a world organization? The answer is that it is all these things. Each of these groups is real, each has its loyalties, each commands allegiance within its own sphere. In the vocational

[1] Lorwin, L. L., *Labor and Internationalism*, 326.

H

world, as elsewhere, group life and group relations are highly complex. At every stage they have been called into existence by real needs, and there are no few simple principles or assumptions by virtue of which a solution can be found to the problems thereby created.

CHAPTER X

INTERNAL GROUP PROBLEMS

LIKE other groups, Trade Unions have their own internal problems. In so far as they are of purely domestic concern they need not be dealt with here, but a surprisingly large number of them are of direct concern to other groups, including the State, and are of paramount importance in any consideration of the place of vocational associations in the society of to-day or of the future. Broadly speaking, these problems are in essence the same that confront every human association; they relate either to the freedom of the individual member or to the efficiency of the group, and as a particular case which is relevant to both classes, they include that of the individual member's relation to the government of the group.

It will therefore be unnecessary, and it would indeed be out of place, to enter into any theoretical discussion of these general problems. Their special application to Trade Union practice is all that can be attempted. Theoretically and legally every member of a Trade Union is a member of a voluntary association. The State, says Professor Laski, "differs from every other association in that it is, in the first place, an association in which membership is compulsory."[1] In fact, as distinct from law, this is by no means always a correct statement of the case. In many instances expulsion from a Trade Union is recognized as being equivalent to vocational death. It is so with the medical and legal professions. It is so, effectively, with many manual workers' organizations in this and other countries. For all practical purposes it is so in nearly all vocations in Russia and Italy, owing to the legal position of Unions in those countries.

For many years there has existed a collective agreement in the dyeing trade, in Yorkshire, whereby every employee of

[1] Laski, H. J., *A Grammar of Politics*, 69.

the largest combine in the trade must be or become a member of one of the signatory Unions. The clause of the agreement runs: "Any employee ceasing to be a member of any of the Unions shall be required by the Association (the employer) to resume membership of one or other of the Unions."[1] In the Birmingham brassfounding trade an old-standing agreement, revised in 1926, provides that workmen are to be members of the National Union of Brass and Metal Mechanics.[2] The Co-operative Wholesale Society passed a resolution in 1924, "That in the case of all other eligible employés, continuing membership of one or other of the Trade Unions eligible for affiliation to the Trades Union Congress shall be a condition of employment by this Society and dismissal shall follow non-compliance therewith accordingly."[3]

Where membership of a Union is not enforced by the employer—and there are not many such cases of compulsory Trade Unionism—the Unions themselves try to maintain the same restriction in the interests of their wage and other standards. Strikes for the purpose of forcing one or more workers to join the Union are not uncommon, but, of course, the actual degree of moral coercion thus exerted depends upon the strength of organization in the trade or establishment concerned. Throughout the printing trade, at any rate in the large centres, Trade Union membership has been in practice compulsory for the skilled craftsmen, not through any rule of the employers but through the strength of the workers' organizations. In agriculture, on the other hand, there is the individual freedom in practice that exists in theory. Where Trade Unionism is strong and well established, as in printing, an employer will take care to employ only Union members, even though there is no formal agreement to that effect. Where it is very weak he may go to the other extreme and employ only non-Unionists. Most large employers in this country would probably say they make no discrimination either for or

---

[1] *Trade Union Documents*, 238.   [2] *Ibid.*, 246.   [3] *Ibid.*, 202.

against Trade Unionists, and this is frequently so in practice, though over a considerable area there is in fact discrimination against non-Unionists. Where the habit of organization has become settled and accepted this is bound to be the case. As Mr. Baldwin said in his famous "Peace in our Time" speech, referring to the employers' association, "We cannot lose sight of the fact that in that organization, just as much as in the men's organization, the mere fact of organizing involves a certain amount of sacrifice of personal liberty. That cannot be helped. Everybody knows that perfectly well, both employers and employees. . . . The workmen's organization is formed to see that under the conditions a workman cannot get his living in a particular trade unless he belongs to that union. An employers' organization is formed in that particular trade for the protection of the trade, and it has the result of effectively preventing any new man starting in that trade."[1] The organization of human beings in groups for specific ends does involve in some cases compulsory membership. The political ends served by the State and the economic ends served by the Trade Unions are too vital, too close to the very existence of man as a civilized being, and too easily menaced by weakness of organization to allow membership to be genuinely voluntary for those coming within their respective spheres. It is futile to pretend that the freedom of the individual is not limited in this way. No amount of metaphysical word spinning will alter this very real fact. It is regrettable, but it has to be accepted as one of the penalties of living in a complex society, the countervailing benefits of which are so obvious in our daily environment.

Freedom within the Union is another matter. Its realization presents the same problems that are familiar in discussions of political liberty, and their solution has been sought along similar lines. Democracy as a political device has in fact, as well as in theory, been realized more thoroughly in the Trade

[1] Parl. Debates, March 6, 1925.

Union movement than in most societies. The democratic State itself has, perhaps, something to learn from the older "industrial democracy," as the Webbs happily termed Trade Unionism. With their elaborate constitutions designed to safeguard the rights and powers of every individual member their delegate meetings, periodical conferences, and democratic methods of electing leaders, the workers' organizations can claim to carry out to a quite unique degree the wishes of the general membership.

The traditional attitude towards leadership, in the Unions, is instructive, and a remarkable system has in consequence developed which maintains a high degree of stability and continuity without abridging the rights of the rank and file. Theoretically the leaders are elected in the ordinary democratic fashion and are subject to recall at specified intervals, in most cases. In this they do not differ from leaders in other democratic organizations, including the State. Political leaders, however, though frequently followed, are as frequently thrown over: Trade Union leaders are not. This difference has had a profound influence on the entire history of Trade Unionism and goes a long way to explain both its virtues and its defects.

With the newer conceptions of its functions and aims, the Trade Union movement is now changing its traditional outlook on the problem of democratic organization and government. It will be seen later that a very significant change has taken place in the current ideas of "workers' control" and other theories of the workers' relation to industry, and this is reflected in the more realistic approach now made by Trade Unions to their own internal arrangements. For many years the rival schools of "industrial unionism" and "craft unionism" fought bitterly over the question of the most efficient form of organization of the workers. Should they be organized on the basis of their industry or their craft? Ought all the workers engaged in building houses, for instance, to be in one Union, or all bricklayers, whether on house building or in a coal mine or anywhere else? These were not the only possibilities. Some theorists advocated the organization of all workers in one Union, irrespective of craft or industry, while still different proposals were advanced by others. Practically, it was found on examination that all such discussions were academic in character, for the existing organizations had grown up in an entirely spontaneous unplanned way and they could not be swept out of existence in order to rebuild the structure according to theoretical conceptions.[1] But apart from this practical difficulty, the correct basis of internal organization of the group depends upon the purpose of the group. So long as Trade Unions conceived their function as one merely of fighting against employers for higher wages and shorter hours, the craft basis seemed not only adequate but in every way the most suitable. When Unions embraced the doctrine that their purpose was to overthrow Capitalism and (according to the belief of many Trade Unionists) to control and manage their own industry, through an organization of all the workers in the industry (Guild Socialism), they felt a craft basis was quite inadequate and they eagerly advocated "industrial unionism."[2] Full-blooded Syndicalists, with their teaching of "the mines for the miners," "the railways for the railwaymen," etc., naturally had to uphold industrial unionism, too, for this meant that ownership of each industry, as well as its management, was to be in the hands of its workers.[3] On the other hand, to those who saw how, in modern times especially, one industry merges into another, how one industry dies and a new one arises as a result of technological advances, how fluid and indefinite in form are most industries to-day, both "craft" and "industrial" unionism seemed equally futile, and only One Big Union—the organization of all workers in one association—appeared capable of meeting the employer class on equal terms.

[1] *T.U.C. Annual Report*, 1927, 99.
[2] See Cole, G. D. H., *Self Government in Industry* (1917).
[3] See Chapter XXIV.

While all these ideas are still current and controversy still continues over the organization issue, the more modern conception of the functions of Trade Unionism and its place in the community is throwing a new light on the whole problem. It is realized that just as business organization itself has no one standard form, but a variety of forms according to the circumstances of different industrial processes, so Trade Unions must adapt their own forms of group organization to the circumstances of their own work. Meanwhile, the organization of the movement as a whole, the Trades Union Congress, becomes better defined, less tentative, more confident and complete, as it actually performs more and more functions and advances to a new status in the community. It tends to deal more and more with general economic issues affecting the entire working class, and less and less with sectional industrial affairs (unless there is a dispute in which its aid is invoked). In other words, it becomes not so much a federation—a piece of machinery—for pressing forward the industrial programmes and rectifying the industrial grievances of its constituent Unions, but rather a more generalized group, to correspond with the conception of a general vocational interest.

The adaptation of Union organization to the particular industrial spheres covered is admirably shown in the case of the Transport and General Workers' Union. Being a "general labour" Union it has sections in almost every industry in the country, and a comparative study is possible without going outside the one organization. Being of recent formation and therefore hampered by no old-established forms of organization or outworn traditions, it has been able to view its problems and tasks realistically. The rules of this Union provide for a division of the membership in both territorial and trade groups. There are at present six national trade groups comprising respectively the principal occupations covered by the Union, and in some cases there are sub-sections of trade groups providing for a further vocational division.

So far there appears to be uniformity rather than diversity. But Rule 3(8) lays it down that while the general policy of the Union is to be determined by the Biennial Delegate Conference and the General Executive Council, "the policy of every area or trade shall, within the powers delegated to an area or national or area trade group committee by these rules or by the General Executive Council, be determined by such area, or national or area trade group committee." Rule 6(4) provides that "Each national trade group committee shall transact and overlook for its membership the Union's business as affecting movements relating to pay, hours, and working conditions, and other questions pertaining thereto." Each trade group is thus able to work out its own methods of dealing with the problems that confront it. Consider, for instance, the trade group covering passenger transport by road. A very important part of its sphere concerns the omnibus service in London which has a wages staff of over 27,000. The London General Omnibus Company[1] organizes its administration in three divisions, each of which comprises a number of districts, each district again comprising a number of garages. "In each garage there is a branch of the Union, with its Branch Secretary. Each branch elects one representative to the divisional committee. The divisional committees, of which there are three corresponding to the three divisions into which the Company is organized for operation, each elect two members to the Central Bus Committee."[2] Machinery has been set up for discussing and settling points in dispute concerning working conditions. There are three divisional officers working under the Central Bus Committee and also a Schedules Officer. Complaints regarding schedules and rates are discussed by the Schedules Officer and the Chief Depot Inspector of the

[1] Now part of the publicly owned London Passenger Transport Service.

[2] Johnston, G. A., and Spates, T. G., "Industrial Relations in the London Traffic Combine," *International Labour Review*, April 1930, 495.

Company, if the Branch Secretary and the Inspector cannot settle them directly. If a settlement is still found to be out of reach the matter is discussed by the Joint Secretaries of a Joint Committee representing both sides, and if these cannot agree it goes to the Joint Committee itself. General complaints are similarly taken up by the Divisional Superintendent of the Company and the Divisional Officer of the Union if the attempt to settle directly has failed. It will be noted that for the operating section of the service the Branch, based on the garage, is the unit of Trade Union organization, and that administrative divisions of the Union correspond to those of the Company. At the Company's Repair Works other Unions of engineering craftsmen, etc., are involved, and this machinery is therefore not suitable. Here there is a Works Committee which is recognized by the Transport and General Workers' Union as well as by the other Unions.

In the other trade groups, similarly, the Union has developed its special methods and organization to fit the circumstances of the industry concerned. Moreover, it has evolved a new form of amalgamation which is proving very successful. Where another Union wishes to amalgamate with it, the fusion may be complete (the normal type of amalgamation), or on the other hand the circumstances of the case may dictate a looser form of association, the fusion being complete in respect of finance, the new constituent retaining, however, a certain independence in administration, and a degree of autonomy in trade policy. This flexibility in organization and administrative machinery and methods is a source of great strength in view of the changing conditions in modern industry, the changing forms of business organization, and the varying circumstances of different trades. It indicates a realistic approach to the problem and illustrates the futility of viewing questions of Trade Union structure and methods from one angle merely, and that a purely theoretical one having no relation to the facts of industrial experience. While this experimental attitude cannot as yet be said to be typical of Trade Unionism, for the forces of tradition and old-established methods are very strong in the workers' organizations, it is by no means as uncommon as is often supposed, and it will undoubtedly be the predominant attitude in the future.

CHAPTER XI

DISCIPLINE IN TRADE UNIONS

A FREQUENT criticism urged against Trade Unions is that they are unable to guarantee the obedience of their own members to the decrees of the organization. This is a problem of every group, including the State itself, as we have already seen. Trade Unions have at least as good a record in this respect as any other organization which has not the power to inflict punishment on those who violate its laws. It is well known that collective agreements, which in this country have no legal force, are in practically all cases adhered to by the workers, even when this course involves wage reductions or other unwelcome changes.[1] The high degree of solidarity and loyalty displayed in the workers' movement has already been noted, but there is naturally no means of coercing members into compliance with the decisions of the governing body of the organization. Pressure can be brought to bear in various ways, but in the last resort a Trade Union can only expel a member who refuses to abide by the decisions reached, though it must not be forgotten that the threat of expulsion is very frequently such an effective form of pressure that it is equivalent to coercion. The right of private judgment, the right to revolt, in fact, must be regarded as an inalienable possession of the individual member of a Union in relation to his organization as it is of the citizen, or any group of citizens, in relation to the State.

The Trade Union is after all only a means to the welfare and happiness of the individual member. "To exhaust the associations to which a man belongs," as Professor Laski says, "is not to exhaust the man himself."[2] The major part of every

[1] For testimony to the general observance of agreements see *Trade Union Documents*, 228.

[2] *A Grammar of Politics*, 67.

human being remains after all such relations with organized groups have been accounted for, and every human being keeps intact his privilege of disagreeing with any association to which he belongs, even to the point of open rebellion. A state of "contingent anarchy" must be accepted as a characteristic of Trade Unions as of other organizations and of the State itself. It is, in fact, a healthy sign. When the machine is so perfect that private judgment is never exercised, or never becomes vocal and leads to revolt, there is something wrong. There is equally something wrong if the margin of insurgence increases to such a pitch that the efficient working of the organization is prevented. So, if a Trade Union organization has to devote the greater part of its energies over a long period to the maintenance of internal peace, its elective machinery and its system of government are clearly defective.

But if such an organization is able to exist for a long period without even the fear of an eruption in this or that quarter, its membership is probably lacking in "public spirit," is apathetic, or cowed into unwilling acquiescence.

A successful democracy must always be in a state of uneasy equilibrium, but it must never topple over into positive disequilibrium. For, after all, it exists to get something done. A Trade Union is only justified in the eyes of its members if it is able to perform efficiently the functions for which it exists. When its functions were confined to fighting, in a somewhat primitive fashion at that, indiscipline mattered relatively little. In the crises of struggle solidarity could always be relied upon and if the intervals were enlivened by revolts little harm was done. Such an easy attitude is not possible to-day, when the major part of a Trade Union's work consists in the negotiation of agreements that have to be observed and the formulation of policies that have to be loyally followed. With the assumption of still more important duties in the community the necessity for substantial unity of action and continuity of policy becomes even more urgent. If, as indicated in a later chapter, Trade

Unionism becomes legally recognized as an essential factor in industrial government, revolt must become as rare as in the political State, even though internal criticism and independence of judgment are not stilled.

We find accordingly that as the Unions have grown in power and responsibility the former easy acquiescence in indiscipline has tended to disappear. Not that members are often expelled for acts of revolt. Expulsion is usually the result of failure, without sound reason, to pay contributions as laid down in the rules. Apart from the possible effect on the member's employment, expulsion is in many cases a very grave penalty because it involves the loss of rights to superannuation or other forms of financial benefit towards which he may have contributed for years. It is for this reason that the Courts will scrutinize the circumstances in which expulsion has taken place, if an aggrieved ex-member of a Trade Union applies for relief. A member must be given a fair trial, in accordance with the provisions laid down in the rules or, if there are no special provisions, in accordance with the accepted principles of "natural justice."

The care taken to treat offenders fairly is illustrated in the rules which most Unions have for the regulation of this ultimate punishment, and as an example the rule of the National Amalgamated Union of Shop Assistants may be cited:—

Rule 27.

1. It shall be competent for the Executive Committee to suspend from all Benefits or expel any member from the Union upon proof satisfactory to the Executive Committee being given, that such member has refused to comply with their decision or ruling, or broken the rules for the time being of the Union, or by his conduct has in the opinion of the Executive Committee brought the Union into discredit, or has fraudulently received or misapplied the funds of the Union or the monies of any member entrusted to him for payment to the Union, or has received monies on behalf of the Union and has wilfully withheld or not duly accounted for the same or has knowingly received any benefit from the Union not being entitled thereto, or has practised any fraud on the Union, and on

suspension or expulsion of any member who has committed any one or more of the offences aforesaid, he shall refund any monies he may have received as aforesaid, and shall forfeit all contributions paid by him but without prejudice to any liability to prosecution.

All such members shall be supplied with particulars of the charges made against them and have an opportunity of presenting their defence to the Executive Committee.

2. Prosecutions shall be instituted and expulsions effected only by the Executive Committee.

The Durham Miners' Association has a system of arbitration for the settlement of members' grievances and complaints, as already mentioned,[1] and similarly nearly every Union has its appropriate machinery of appeal to safeguard the rights of the individual member. Apart from what may be called "financial" offences, the type of conduct most likely to lead to expulsion is that of the "blackleg," the member who works when he is supposed to be on strike or locked-out, or who takes the place of a striker. In short, conduct directly striking at the very existence of Trade Unionism, treachery to accepted Trade Union principles, this is the behaviour viewed most gravely by organized Labour. Political or religious principles, or indeed any beliefs or conduct not directly connected with vocational interests, will not, in this country at any rate, be visited with penalties. Even the Trade Unions that have in recent years most strongly condemned and opposed Communist propaganda have not expelled known Communists merely for their political faith. Communists have certainly been forbidden to hold official positions in a number of Unions, but they have not been expelled. Only when propaganda or conduct impinges directly on the efficient functioning of the organization is there retaliation to this extent. It is a remarkable tribute to the entire movement that very seldom indeed is it alleged that Trade Unions unfairly use their power to punish offending members. If fairness and discretion in the dispensing of internal justice are criteria, Trade Unions are at least as

[1] P. 98 *supra*.

fit as any professional associations or other voluntary bodies
to exercise still wider powers in their own sphere. They have
indeed used their present powers with remarkable freedom
from excess in either direction. It cannot be said that every
manifestation of independence of opinion or even of revolt
has been ruthlessly suppressed and punished by the exclusion
of the rebels, though there are always "die-hards" in any
society who, lacking psychological insight, would hasten to
apply this "remedy" in all such cases. Nor, on the other hand,
can it be said that revolt and anarchy have been encouraged by
the existence of machinery that could be easily manipulated
by malcontents or of officials who could be easily swayed. The
local machinery of most Trade Unions can indeed by "captured"
much too easily by small groups of energetic and determined
members intent on gaining control, but these tactics can seldom
penetrate as far as the national machinery, which tends to
represent fairly faithfully the policy and desires of the mass
of the membership. The leadership, again, if faulty in any
way, has been defective rather in its unwillingness to speak
unpalatable truths of which uninformed members were sorely
in need, than in any propensity to be stampeded by sectional
interests.

Whatever may be said in general of the possible tyranny of
"domestic" tribunals and the defenceless position of individual
members of voluntary associations, it cannot fairly be said
that there is any case for conferring upon members of Trade
Unions the statutory right to appeal to the ordinary Courts
of Law against decisions of the tribunals provided by their
organizations. The Courts will not normally interfere with
the decisions of "domestic" tribunals. Only when the
principles of "natural justice" have been violated (e.g.
decision to expel a member without first giving him a
fair hearing), or the tribunal has acted beyond the scope of its
authority, will the Courts hold themselves competent to set
aside the decision of which complaint is made.

It has been urged by certain writers that, in view of the power often possessed by "domestic" tribunals, the Courts should be given the power to review and set aside their decisions on appeal by aggrieved members of the voluntary associations in question.[1] Such general transference of these judicial functions of "domestic" tribunals to the Law Courts is almost certainly impracticable, merely on the ground of the additional burden of work that would be placed on the Courts, for it must be remembered that there is an enormous number of voluntary associations apart from Trade Unions, but in any case the remedy would be far worse than the disease. There is, indeed, very little disease to be cured, as far as Trade Unions are concerned. The Courts cannot possibly know the peculiar circumstances in which voluntary associations carry on their work, nor can they appreciate the weight that is given, and rightly given, to all the factors arising out of the member's relation to the organization. In no case could a Trade Union admit that a Court of Law ought to have the power to interfere in the purely internal relations of a voluntary association and its members. If dissatisfaction is felt, the sound line of advance would seem to be in the provision of some further appeal machinery within the Trade Union movement itself. But, in fact, serious breaches of discipline by individual members are relatively infrequent and the necessity for further appeal tribunals has not yet arisen.

One of the most difficult forms of indiscipline to deal with, and at certain periods the most common, is the "unofficial" strike. It is usually over strikes of this kind that outside interests are apt to criticize the "failure" of Trade Union leaders to carry their own members with them. The theoretical issue this question raises is one of the most complicated and delicate in the sphere of Trade Unionism; and there is a comparable problem in every democratic organization. In practice it is usually not so difficult to solve, for an open defiance of the

[1] See Robson, W. A., *Justice and Administrative Law* (1928), 312.

I

considered ruling of the organization cannot be countenanced, and drastic measures are as a rule promptly taken if milder persuasion fails. There have been many cases, however, where the Union has considered it wise to adopt an unofficial strike and make it official; defective staff work, lack of co-ordination between local and central machinery, or weak leadership, seem to be indicated in many of these instances. Where an unofficial strike is deliberately fomented and organized by sections of the membership (or in some cases by persons outside the Trade Union) simply in order to embarrass the leadership and strike at the organization, the line of action to be pursued is clear enough. The more difficult case is that of the sincere and perhaps sorely provoked resistance of a group of workers to some demand made by employers, a resistance that the Union would in some circumstances have sponsored, but which is considered tactically inopportune at the time in question. It is absolutely necessary to have unity of action, it is necessary to maintain efficient organization, discipline, and direction, if the Union is to attain its aims, and even though the leaders may privately sympathize with the insurgents it may be, and often is, their imperative duty to decide against what seems to many of the rank and file the obvious policy. This, of course, is where leadership has its opportunity to accomplish the difficult task of impressing the "long view" on members who have only been accustomed to take "short views," and if the "long view" is to prevail the leadership must be of a high order. Many of the well-known leaders of Trade Unionism have had this gift of persuasion. Those that have not have either never been out of trouble with their members or more commonly they have taken the line of least resistance and have followed rather than led. Nearly every large Union, however well led, has nevertheless experienced minor waves of unofficial strikes. Where the organization is in a healthy condition they are easily dealt with, if they arise at all, and it is only in very exceptional cases that they lead to serious trouble. Their occurrence is often to be regarded as the expression of those somewhat vague feelings of dissatisfaction and impatience that periodically sweep over all democracies. At any rate economic conditions do not appear to explain such outbreaks, nor do local circumstances, nor the type of organization adopted by the Union. There have been national as well as local unofficial strikes, and industrial Unions as well as craft Unions have been affected.[1] Periods of prosperity as well as of depression have witnessed such outbreaks, and apart from movements deliberately organized by "disruptionists" it seems difficult to isolate any common feature which would explain why certain groups of members feel they have to revolt against their own organizations. Accusations of treachery, cowardice, autocracy, and so on, are of course always made against the officials of the Union by the "outlaw" strikers, but these epithets must be taken as the conventional small change of controversy rather than as serious charges.

The "unofficial" movements that took place during and immediately after the war in many countries, and that were represented in Britain by the strikes associated with the "shop stewards" organizations, fall in a different category from most "outlaw" strikes. The official machinery of the Unions during that period was practically debarred from launching wage and other movements that would have been taken up in normal times, and unofficial action was perhaps inevitable. These were cases in which one could often say that both official and unofficial elements were right from their respective points of view. Normally, the public problem raised by unofficial action is not a serious one. It is very seldom that collective agreements are violated in this way. There is the possibility, however, that the increase in the size of Unions as a result of amalgamation may increase the likelihood of this kind of indiscipline. With

[1] See Kopald, S., *Rebellion in Labor Unions* (1924), 261 ff. But this study of unofficial strikes, though interesting and useful, is one-sided and uncritical.

the formation of very large bodies possessing half a million members or more the chances of separate action on the part of more or less isolated sections may well seem greater.[1] On the whole this development need not be feared, for as Unions grow in size and complexity they also evolve new techniques of administration and control. The new form of amalgamation designed by the Transport and General Workers' Union to allow of considerable sectional autonomy will be recalled in this connection. There is, moreover, a steady growth among the members themselves of an appreciation of the need for orderly and constitutional methods. This results from the very practical demonstrations they have had of the superiority of such methods in attaining tangible results. Even now one occasionally finds remarkable instances of this rank and file feeling, as when the "unofficial" strikers in the New York printing trade in 1919 went on individual vacations in order to avoid violating the official order not to strike![2] This technical obedience to the Union's instructions is very interesting as showing the extent to which, even in a movement like this, the desire to follow constitutional procedure was dominant.

The problem of dissentient groups occurs in the wider Trade Union movement as well as in individual Unions. The case of the National Union of Seamen was some years ago an outstanding one. For many years this Union had under the leadership of Mr. Havelock Wilson pursued a policy which was quite out of harmony with the accepted policy of the Trades Union Congress to which it was still affiliated. The decisions of Congress were flouted and no opportunity was lost of displaying the lack of sympathy that existed between this group and the movement in general, yet Congress had no power to expel any member. The climax was reached in 1927 when the Seamen's Union gave active support to a "breakaway" Union, the miners' non-political Union in Nottinghamshire which was formed of miners who had broken away from the Miners'

[1] See Hiller, E. T., *op. cit.*, 77.   [2] Kopald, *op. cit.*, 186.

Federation. To aid a rival organization that has broken away from an established, recognized Union is regarded with the same detestation as the act of breaking away itself. That a Union affiliated to Congress should thus help a dissident body was quite intolerable. Not even the virtual refusal of the Seamen's Union to join in the National strike in 1926 and its open hostility to that movement aroused so much resentment. The result was that in 1928 a new Standing Order was adopted by Congress giving power to expel any Union found guilty of anti-Trade Union practices. Under this rule the Seamen's Union was expelled in the same year, after an opportunity had been given of rebutting the charge. After Mr. Havelock Wilson's death in 1929 the Union was readmitted to Congress on giving undertakings regarding the conduct of which complaint had been made. The new Standing Order is as follows:—

12(*g*) If at any time there appears to the General Council to be justification for an investigation into the conduct of any Union, on the grounds that the activities of such Union are detrimental to the interests of the Trade Union movement, or contrary to the declared principles and policy of the Trades Union Congress, the General Council shall summon such Union to appear before it or its appropriate Committee in order that such activities may be investigated. In the event of the Union refusing to attend, the investigation shall proceed in its absence.

(*h*) If as the result of such investigation the General Council is convinced that the activities of the Union concerned are detrimental to the interests of the Trade Union Movement, or contrary to the declared principles and policy of the Trades Union Congress, the General Council shall have power

(i) to call upon the Union to cease forthwith such activities, and to undertake not to engage in such activities in future;
(ii) to suspend forthwith the Union from membership of Congress until the next annual Trades Union Congress, and shall submit a report of the case to the next Congress.

(*i*) Any Union which has been suspended shall have the right to appeal to Congress, and shall be entitled to appoint delegates for this purpose in accordance with Standing Orders Nos. 16 and 17.

(j) Congress shall have the final authority to deal with the case, whether by way of re-admission, further suspension, or exclusion from membership of Congress.

In a sense this rule completes the disciplinary powers possessed by Trade Union organizations and makes the whole movement more of an ordered unity and an effective self-governing group capable of protecting itself against disintegration by sectional revolt.

CHAPTER XII

TRADE UNION FUNCTIONS

THE general aims and purposes of Trade Unionism have
already been described, and some account has been given of
its more important functions. It would be out of place in this
study to give any detailed description of the multifarious
activities of Trade Union organizations, but it is necessary to
mention certain parts of their work in order to illustrate the
extent to which they already live up to the wider definition of
Trade Union purpose that has here been adopted.

Many people still think of Trade Unions as being concerned
mainly with strikes and friendly benefits. If such a view was
ever justified in the past, it is no longer so. Strikes are
surprisingly infrequent, notwithstanding the spectacular conflicts that take place from time to time (particularly spectacular
when they are clashes between organized Labour as a whole and
the State). The menace of the struggles described earlier is rather
on account of their great size, their grave character, and their
deplorable results than because the Trade Union world is
constantly preoccupied with this kind of activity and policy.

The functions and activities stressed here may be classed
under two heads; first, those of a technical kind connected with
the industrial process, and second, those of a public kind
connected with the process of national government. The former
are mainly, though not entirely, the concern of individual
Unions, while the latter are mainly, though again not entirely,
the province of the movement as a whole acting through the
Trades Union Congress.

Trade Unions and Industry

The extent to which Unions now help to regulate the way
in which the labour of their members is utilized is very

considerable in some industries, smaller in others. In many cases this control is provided by collective agreements, in others it is embodied in customs that are not recognized but which are nevertheless effectively in operation. An interesting example of regulation by collective agreement exists in the textile dyeing, bleaching, and finishing trades. Here all workers are engaged through the Unions, or, if these are unable to supply the required labour, the employers may then engage workers, who, however, must join the Union at once. The Unions are also entitled to be consulted regarding overtime after 6 p.m., and no such overtime is worked except by arrangement with the Unions. The transference of labour from one works to another under the same firm is only carried out by agreement with the Unions. Much of the work is paid for by a system of collective piecework based on collective payment for collective work, the fixing of rates and the arrangement of sets being agreed upon between the employers and the Unions. No rate or set may be altered except with the consent of the Unions.

In the metal trades, on the other hand, it is by custom rather than by agreement that the Unions are able to affect working conditions. The same is true of shipbuilding, while in the transport industries and to some extent in building and woodworking there are agreements covering these questions. In coal, as indeed in many industries, there are both agreements providing for Union regulation and also customs extending the field of control.

As has often been pointed out, however, the control exercised by the Unions in this way is largely negative in character; it is a form of control which enables the Unions to say that certain things shall *not* be done rather than a constructive control for positive improvements. Such a situation is psychologically bad, and is due mainly to the traditional attitude of employers to Trade Unions.

The engagement of workers through the Unions is an

example of constructive control, and this is, or has been, in operation in many trades, including certain branches of textiles and shipping. No seaman can be engaged in Britain except through the joint machinery of the employers and the Union, and a man must possess a Union card.

The sharing out of available work among the men employed in the trade has been secured by a number of Unions in the printing, glass, clothing, and other industries. The guaranteed day or week has been won by a large number of Unions also; these are chiefly in the railway, boot and shoe, printing, glass, and transport industries.

In a few cases, mainly small monopolistic crafts, the workers have the right to nominate their foreman, and in other instances the shop stewards, elected by the workers, are to a large extent employed in foremen's duties. The miners' checkweighmen, appointed by the workers at every pit, not only perform their statutory duty[1] of checking the weights of coal sent up, but they are practically the men's agents in general matters and are able to exercise considerable influence. In addition, the miners are entitled by statute[2] to appoint examiners to inspect the pits and to see that all necessary safety devices are in operation.

In the building and other industries the Unions have jointly with the employers drawn up codes of safety regulations.

The Transport and General Workers' Union has accomplished a great deal in the way of control; it arranges the allocation of work schedules in certain sections of the industry; it has helped to draw up a decasualization scheme for dockers; it has concluded agreements for health and safety in the docking and flour milling industries.

These are but a few of the cases in which Unions have

---

[1] Coal Mines Regulation Act, 1887, 50 & 51 Vict. c. 58; Coal Mines (Checkweigher) Act, 1894, 57 & 58 Vict. c. 52; Coal Mines (Weighing of Minerals) Act, 1905, 5 Edw. VII. c. 9,

[2] Coal Mines Act, 1911, 1 & 2 Geo. V. c. 50

succeeded in establishing the right to some measure of regulation of the conditions of work by collective agreements with employers.

If we turn to unwritten rules and customs, there is a vast field over which some measure of control is exercised.

The limitation of the number of apprentices is one of the oldest Trade Union functions, although in most cases the employers absolutely refuse to recognize the right of the Unions to interfere. Nevertheless, there is a good deal of effective regulation exercised in this direction.

The engineering "shop stewards" during the war managed to gain a very large share of control over their working conditions, but this has mostly disappeared since. Either by Union rules, or by unwritten understandings, the workers in individual establishments in all the large basic industries are able to prevent the employer from acting in a purely autocratic manner in engaging new workers, in distributing work, in appointing foremen, in working on piece rates or time rates, in fixing starting times and meal times, and in introducing new machinery and processes. The consultation secured, though often informal, is undoubtedly effective in innumerable cases.

In badly organized trades, and trades where a large proportion of women are employed, there is naturally much less of this detailed control, either formal or otherwise. As there are Trade Boards for most of these industries, the Unions being represented equally with the employers, the workers do not suffer as they otherwise would from their lack of bargaining strength. The Trade Boards have the power to compel the employers throughout the industry to observe minimum wage standards. Their work in this direction has unquestionably raised the wages and improved the conditions of workers in sweated and badly organized trades. The Trade Board system has fully justified itself in the twenty years of its existence, and as in every case there are equal numbers of employers' and workers' members on the Boards, together with "independent" members appointed by the Minister of Labour, the experience gained by the Trade Union representatives and the insight they have obtained into the working of their industries have proved of immense value in bringing organized Labour into closer relation with the industrial process.[1]

Some critics hold that the system of Trade Boards and their success in operation have weakened Trade Unionism or prevented its full development in the industries concerned. A diametrically opposite view is taken, however, by many observers. It seems probable, in any case, that Trade Boards will remain a permanent feature of British industrial organization.

The system of Joint Industrial Councils for industries, known as Whitleyism,[2] has become neither as important nor as widespread as its authors hoped. Comparatively few industries set up Whitley Councils, these including wool, printing and building, among others. Coal, cotton, steel, engineering, shipbuilding, and transport refused to have anything to do with the proposals. In those cases where Whitley Councils were appointed the intentions of their authors were hardly ever carried out, though of course the proposed constitution was adopted, there being equal numbers of representatives of employers' associations and Trade Unions respectively. The idea was that they should concern themselves with the general state and policy of the industry, its economic aspects, and its all-round efficiency. It was only because there was this chance of participating to some extent in the management of industry that any Trade Union leaders were induced to favour the scheme. In practice, however, the Unions were not as a rule allowed to share in the control of the economic factors affecting

[1] See Sells, D., *The British Trade Boards System* (1923).
[2] The more important sections of the Whitley Reports are given in *Trade Union Documents*, 487–495. See also Seymour, J. B., *The Whitley Councils Scheme* (1932).

industrial conditions in their trade. In only a few instances were Unions given access to the necessary statistical facts relating to production, prices, profits, etc. In all but these few cases the Whitley Councils soon degenerated into negotiating bodies of the ordinary kind, useful indeed, but concerned almost entirely with questions of wages and hours.

The flour milling industry has been more fortunate in possessing a Whitley Council and a group of employers that have taken their responsibilities and opportunities more seriously. With a university lecturer in philosophy as secretary, this Council has done a great deal of valuable work on matters quite outside wages and hours, and all with the active co-operation of the Unions, who constitute, of course, half the membership of the Council.[1] The Whitley Council for the pottery industry has also been enlightened and progressive. The Civil Service Whitley Council started well, producing a Report on the reorganization of the Civil Service which the Government adopted, the entire administrative machinery of the State departments now being organized on the lines suggested by the Council. Latterly, however, it has become ineffective. In short, the Whitley system has, with a few exceptions, proved a disappointment to all who hoped that a way might be found to bring the Unions into some kind of organic relation with the administration of industry and public services. These exceptions are, however, very important as illustrations of what may be done in favourable cases.

The Whitley Report suggested the setting up of district councils and works councils as well as councils for individual industries as a whole, the conception being that all industry should be covered by a network of joint bodies, the employers and Unions being represented in equal numbers, with a view to evolving some kind of constitutional government in the

---

[1] Green, L. H., "A Success of Whitleyism," *Manchester Guardian Supp.*, November 30, 1927, 22. See *Trade Union Documents*, 496.

economic sphere.[1] This part of the scheme, also, was not carried out. The entire set of proposals was put forward for voluntary adoption, there being no question of legislative sanction, and nothing was done by either side in industry to appoint district councils or, except in a few isolated cases having no connection with Whitley Councils, to set up works councils. Works councils exist, therefore, in comparatively few undertakings in Great Britain, and they are in most cases nothing but joint committees for supervising such matters as welfare, accident prevention, etc., though a few deal with allocation of work and even with appeals against dismissals. Moreover, the Whitley scheme was based on representation of the workers through their Trade Unions, and the co-operation of the Unions in the setting up of works councils was expressly laid down. In the works councils that exist in this country at present the co-operation of the Unions is not always obtained. The scheme recently adopted by Imperial Chemical Industries, Lord Melchett's great chemical combine, is interesting because it not only provides for works councils in all the establishments of the company and for a central works council for the concern as a whole, but there is also an advisory committee to the central works council, and on this sit the national officers of the Unions concerned.

A large number of employers now state openly that they prefer their employees to be Trade Unionists. The convenience of being able to negotiate with one or two organizations on wage and other conditions affecting thousands of men in many different grades has become obvious. Thus, the posting of notices by employers stating their preference for Trade Unionists is occasionally found.[2]

A statutory seal has in many cases been placed upon Trade Union participation in the conduct of industry, and this may

[1] For Whitley Report on Works Committees see *Trade Union Documents*, 492.

[2] See examples in *Trade Union Documents*, 459.

be regarded as one of the most significant developments in the history of organized Labour. One of the oldest instances of this is in the provisions of the various Acts regarding checkweighmen, already noted, and these have been followed up by Acts giving the miners power to appoint examiners to inspect coal mines,[1] and the right to representation equally with coal owners on the national advisory committee on coal and the coal industry, and on the committee which allocates the proceeds of the Miners' Welfare Fund raised by a compulsory levy on the output of coal.[2] Under the Unemployment Insurance Acts which have been passed from 1911 onwards, Trade Unions which comply with certain conditions regarding payment of out-of-work benefit are empowered to make arrangements with the Ministry of Labour whereby they administer the payment of State benefit on behalf of the Government. They act as agents of the State in this respect, and they are paid a fee for their services in administering the scheme.[3] Trade Unions also, in many cases, function (through subsidiary organizations) as Approved Societies under the National Health Insurance Acts, and they administer the Act on behalf of the State in precisely the same way as other Approved Societies which are subsidiaries of insurance companies, friendly societies, etc.

During the war the Trade Unions in the cotton trade participated, with the employers, in the scheme for the government of the industry through the Cotton Control Board. This was a remarkably successful experiment, the control of the trade being left almost entirely in the hands of the Board, the majority of the members of which represented the industry itself. The payment of unemployment benefit on behalf of the Board was handed over to the Trade Unions themselves, and we are told that "the Board placed implicit confidence in the

[1] Coal Mines Act, 1911, 1 & 2 Geo. V. c. 50.
[2] Mining Industry Act, 1920, 10 & 11 Geo. V. c. 50.
[3] Ministry of Labour *Report on Unemployment Insurance*, 1923.

unions and in their officials, trusted them to pay out its money in accordance with the spirit as well as with the letter of its rules, and deemed it unnecessary to exercise any supervision to see that they actually did so . . . the proportion of wrongful payments under the Control Board's scheme was not a fraction of that which occurred under the Government Out-of-Work Donation scheme, with all its provisions for repeated signings-on at the Labour Exchange and the rest of its elaborate machinery."[1] This is very significant, coming as it does from the Secretary of the Board itself.

Many important judicial or quasi-judicial functions, as well as administrative duties, are now entrusted to Trade Unions, especially in connection with the fixing of wages and other conditions. The Courts of Referees, which are the first courts of appeal in disputed cases of unemployment benefit, under the State scheme of unemployment insurance, have equal numbers of workers' and employers' representatives among their members, while there is a similar equality of representation on each of the forty-three Trade Boards which, as already mentioned, fix legal minimum wage rates and frequently other rates for low-paid or badly organized trades. The National Union of General and Municipal Workers has 83 representatives on Trade Boards, the Tailors and Garment Workers Union 112, the National Union of Distributive and Allied Workers 61, Transport and General Workers' Union 84, and so on. In all, 26 Unions affiliated to the Trades Union Congress are represented on Trade Boards, the aggregate number of representatives being no less than 467.[1] The number of Trade Union representatives on Courts of Referees is also very large.

On the Industrial Court and on many Conciliation Boards the workers are naturally represented, the function of conciliation and arbitration being one in which organized Labour is especially concerned, since it is the corollary of the daily negotiations that form the main part of Trade Union activities.

[1] Henderson, H. D., *The Cotton Control Board* (1922).

While in all these ways the individual Trade Unions become more and more involved in the smooth working of the industrial machine, and in some cases the State machine itself, the workers' movement as a whole has also become closely associated with the functioning of the State, especially on the industrial side. The Trades Union Congress is represented, for instance, as is the consumers' Co-operative movement, on the National Wages Board for the railways, the final court of appeal on questions of railway wages; this is, however, a body without legal power to enforce decisions. Provision is made for a representative of the workers on the Railway Rates Tribunal, which fixes freight and passenger rates on the railways; on the Central Electricity Board, which supervises the carrying out of the national scheme of electric power generation and distribution; on the British Broadcasting Corporation, which conducts the national monopoly of wireless broadcasting; and on a number of other bodies.

One recent development is sufficiently important, in this connection, for special mention. The creation by the Prime Minister of an "economic staff" with an Economic Advisory Council, to advise the Government on economic affairs, is a step of considerable importance in its theoretical implications even if, as is generally thought, it has in practice degenerated into futility. It is a recognition of the vital part played by economic forces in the functioning of the modern State and an admission that the political Government needs specialized advice as well as special knowledge in this sphere. The General Council of the Trades Union Congress is represented on this Council, and in this representation the fact is recognized that the Trade Union movement is directly concerned and directly participates in the economic functions of government.[1] A very important recognition of a similar kind is seen in the inter-

---

[1] Though it should be noted that all the members of the Economic Advisory Council are appointed as individuals and not in a representative capacity.

national sphere, under the provisions of Part XIII of the Treaty of Versailles whereby an International Labour Organization was set up as an integral part of the League of Nations. Of the four delegates from each country to the General Conference each year, one is a workers' representative and one an employers' representative. There are six workers' representatives and six employers' representatives out of the twenty-four members of the governing body of the organization. The British workers' delegate is nominated by the Trades Union Congress, as are his "technical advisers," who are allowed to accompany the delegate to the Conference. The British workers' delegate is also at present a member of the governing body. It is not necessary to stress the significance of this representation of Trade Unionism upon the International Labour Organization, which is performing such remarkable work in the levelling up of international labour standards.

A member of the Trades Union Congress General Council was also a delegate to the World Economic Conference convened by the League of Nations in 1927, and is a member of the Consultative Committee set up by the Economic section of the League as a result of the Conference. At the Imperial Economic Conference at Ottawa in 1932, and again at the World Monetary and Economic Conference in London in 1933, two members of the General Council of the T.U.C. were appointed by the Government to its panel of industrial advisers. On Government commissions and enquiries (to return to the national sphere) there is invariably Labour representation whenever the subject is one of concern to the workers. As it is usual in this country to set up bodies of this kind before any new legislative measure of importance is drafted, representation on them is of considerable value. The Trade Union members are often able to influence the other members, and to secure part if not all the movement desires. In addition, it is customary for the Government departments to consult the Trades Union

K

Congress, or in suitable cases the Unions individually, when a Bill affecting the workers' interests has been drafted. The employers are also consulted, of course, and changes may be made in the measure before it is discussed in Parliament. The consultation may be either by correspondence or by verbal interchange of views. There is often similar consultation on administrative matters. Further, several Ministries (e.g. Education, Health) have Consultative Committees on which the workers are represented. These are permanent bodies, meeting regularly for the purpose of advising the department and the Minister. The method of appointment of workers' representatives to these various bodies is not uniform. In some cases the General Council of the T.U.C. is asked to nominate the member(s). It has five nominees, for instance, on the National Advisory Council for Juvenile Employment, a Government body for co-ordinating and developing work in connection with the education and industrial placing of juveniles.[1] The usual plan, however, is for the Government to ask the Trades Union Congress to submit a list of names from which the Minister selects the required number of representatives. The entire question of the appointment of representatives on Commissions, Administrative Boards, etc., has recently been under consideration by the General Council of the T.U.C., as there is at present no recognized method, and no formal obligation even, to give the workers representation at all. Public and semi-public administrative bodies and consultative bodies are becoming more and more important in modern times, and the Unions wish to get some binding principle adopted by Governments.

In the sphere of local government there is not the same scope for Labour representation, as such. Most local governing bodies have, however, some advisory or even executive com-

[1] The General Council also nominated the members who served as industrial advisers at the Imperial Economic Conference, 1932, and at the World Monetary and Economic Conference, 1933.

mittees to which members not on the elected Municipal Council are "co-opted."

Education authorities, for example, have such committees for various purposes, and there is always a Juvenile Advisory Committee, a Pensions Committee, an Insurance Committee, and so on, though not all of these are committees of the local governing body. On most of these committees the workers are represented, though not necessarily through their Trade Unions directly.

There remains to be mentioned one of the most interesting and significant movements of recent years in the direction of Trade Union consultation on national industrial questions. Just as the Government has recognized the right of organized Labour to be consulted, by its appointment of two members of the General Council of the T.U.C. to the Economic Advisory Council, so the organized employers have recognized the same right. In 1927, Sir A. Mond and a group of influential employers invited the Trades Union Congress to confer with them on a wide variety of questions relating to industrial reorganization and industrial relations. A series of conferences followed (usually termed the Mond–Turner conferences), and a number of agreed statements were issued dealing with a variety of topics. One of these suggested the setting up of a National Industrial Council, representing the Trades Union Congress on the one side, and on the other the two national organizations of employers, the National Confederation of Employers' Organizations and the Federation of British Industries. These two organizations, with whom organized Labour as a whole had not hitherto had relations of any kind, were unable because of constitutional difficulties and for other reasons to join in this scheme, but instead they suggested that other means of consultation between the three organizations should be devised as a substitute both for the proposed National Industrial Council and for the conferences with Sir A. Mond's group. After some negotiation, a satisfactory scheme of joint consultation and co-operation was agreed upon early in 1930 as follows:—

(1) The T.U.C., Confederation or F.B.I., can propose as subjects for discussion any matter within their respective provinces which is of common interest to British Industry, it being understood that these discussions will not invade the provinces or trespass upon the functions of the individual constituents of the T.U.C., Confederation or F.B.I.

(2) Having regard to the separate spheres and functions of the Confederation and the F.B.I., and the necessity for the T.U.C. knowing which of these two Organizations will be responsible for the Employers' Side of any question proposed for discussion, the Confederation and the F.B.I. will set up an Allocation Committee, whose sole function will be to say whether any given subject proposed by the T.U.C. or which the Confederation or F.B.I. proposes to raise with the T.U.C. is one which concerns the responsibility of the Confederation or the F.B.I. or both.

(3) The question of allocation having been settled, the future procedure will be carried through direct between the T.U.C. on the one hand, and the Confederation or F.B.I. or both on the other hand, without further reference to the Allocation Committee.

(4) When the T.U.C. on the one hand, or the Confederation or F.B.I. or both on the other hand, accept a subject for discussion, the Organization so accepting shall take up with the Organization which proposed that subject the question of the size of the Committee for the purpose and the other arrangements of procedure for its discussion.

(5) If the T.U.C. on the one hand, or the Confederation or F.B.I. on the other hand, considers itself unable to discuss a subject it is understood that the Organization declining will explain its reasons therefor to the Organization proposing.

(6) All discussions at Meetings, and correspondence arising out of the procedure proposed, shall, unless otherwise mutually agreed, be confidential to the T.U.C., Confederation and F.B.I., and when a subject proposed for discussion has been accepted and discussed no action shall be taken on any conclusions reached until these conclusions have been specifically approved by the Organizations concerned.

(7) These proposals provide the practical machinery for the selection of subjects and their discussion, but the Joint Committee

considers that, for the purpose of examining these proposals they should be accompanied by way of illustration by some indication of the types of subjects in regard to which the machinery could operate and the following list has been drawn up by the Joint Committee for that purpose:—

1. UNEMPLOYMENT.
2. INDUSTRY AND FINANCE—Macmillan Committee.
3. TAXATION OF INDUSTRY:
   (a) General effect of Taxation on Industry.
   (b) Inadequate allowances for Obsolescence and Depreciation, Taxation of wasting assets, taxation of moneys put to reserve and similar points.
4. SOCIAL SERVICES—Co-ordination.
5. EDUCATION AND INDUSTRY—"Shaftesbury" and "Elgin" Councils.
6. DELEGATED POWERS OF GOVERNMENT DEPARTMENTS—Donoughmore Committee.
7. INTER-EMPIRE TRADE—Imperial Conference and Imperial Economic Conference.
8. INTERNATIONAL TRADE:
   (a) Tariff Truce Proposals;
   (b) Proposals for Multilateral Customs Agreements;
   (c) Most Favoured Nations Treatment;
   (d) Import and Export Restrictions Convention and similar problems.
9. TRADE FACILITIES.
10. INSURANCE OF EXPORT CREDITS.
11. GENERAL INTERNATIONAL LABOUR QUESTIONS.
12. INDUSTRIAL AND COMMERCIAL STATISTICS.

This arrangement has been put into operation, and represents the farthest point yet reached by the Trade Union movement in establishing the right to be consulted by organized employers as a whole in matters relating to the functioning of the industrial system.

Thus, as will be clear from this brief summary, Trade Unionism has already succeeded to a remarkable extent in attaining a position of influence in the economic sphere, and even in securing some share in the direction of industrial policy. In individual undertakings and industries, in the working of Capitalist industry as a whole, and in the economic mechanism of the State itself, the Trade Union movement is now, through organized consultation and even in some cases through administrative or controlling bodies, fulfilling definite, constructive functions.

III

TRADE UNIONS, THE STATE, AND THE LAW

CHAPTER XIII

LAW AND ECONOMICS

IN the preceding section we have been concerned with the
nature of the Trade Union group as it is, or as, under the
pressure of current tendencies, it is becoming. Legally, however,
the position of the Trade Unions is very different from what
might be anticipated from a study of their actual functions and
powers. The relation between a changing law and a changing
public opinion has been shown many times since Dicey's
classical exposition,[1] but what is not always realized is that in
modern times more particularly, economic forces and institutions, the problems of which occupy more and more of the
time of the legislature, themselves change far too rapidly for
public opinion to keep pace. That is to say, the currently
accepted ideas of economic and social organization are usually
well behind current practice. But law is usually behind even
the current public opinion in matters of general principle. As
Dicey says in a famous passage: "The judges . . . are men
advanced in life; they are for the most part persons of a
conservative disposition. . . . The ideas of expediency or
policy accepted by the Courts may differ considerably from
the ideas which at a given time . . . guide Parliamentary
legislation. . . . If a statute, as already stated, is apt to
reproduce the public opinion not so much of to-day as of
yesterday, judge made law occasionally represents the opinion
of the day before yesterday."[2]

The result is a strange jumble of ancient and modern. Parts
of the law governing Trade Unions are fully in line with

[1] Dicey, A. V., *Law and Public Opinion in England* (1905). See also
Commons, J. R., *Legal Foundations of Capitalism* (1924), and Keezer,
D. M., and May, S., *The Public Control of Business* (1930).

[2] Dicey, A. V., *op. cit.*, Lecture II.

present-day requirements, because the sheer pressure of events has forced a jump in legislation, while other parts (constituting unfortunately the bulk of the law) creak and groan under the inadequacy of their response to modern needs. Progressive jurists and political philosophers have always insisted on the necessity for an evolutionary outlook in jurisprudence. The law exists to serve and not to bind mankind. The changing needs and beliefs of peoples must find an appropriate vehicle in a changing law. The framework of the legal system, its courts and procedure, its rules and regulations for making justice accessible, swift, and within the reach of all citizens, may have to change too, but the content of the law has to be in a state of flux at all times if it is to serve the commonwealth. It is a misconception to think that this means the introduction of uncertainty and caprice into the law. There is a stability and constancy underlying change when the development is ordered and not haphazard, when it is an adaptation to social forces and needs and not an arbitrary or chance variation.

This attitude towards law has been taken by enlightened lawyers and laymen alike, and it is more than ever important in modern times if only because Parliament and Courts tend to become more and more preoccupied with problems of economic organization and industrial changes. The law of England is the growth of centuries; the economic system as we know it to-day is of very recent growth, and its changes are amazingly rapid. Hence the necessity for law to be regarded as living, flexible, and in a state of continuous development. The interaction between economics and law is a fascinating subject of study, but this work is only concerned with it incidentally. The adaptation of the content of law to modern industrial development has been admirably shown in one of its aspects by Professor Commons.[1] But, to take a matter having more direct relevance to Trade Union functions, the evolution of the doctrine of "restraint of trade" is no less instructive

[1] Commons, J. R., *op. cit.*

than the changes in the legal conception of "property." In this country as in most others the Courts have from time to time revised their attitude towards restrictions on freedom of trading; not until the march of events made the old views unworkable did the judges bow to public opinion, but inevitably the changes had to be made. It is only in the occasional case of an enlightened and progressive judge that this need is consciously and freely recognized.

In this connection, Lord Sankey's words in a recent case are notable for their modern, realistic tone:[1] in considering contracts in restraint of trade, he said, the Court had to take into account not only the interest of the parties but also the interests of the public, and these were always susceptible to the influence of current views of public policy. The needs of large-scale business have compelled the Courts to take a more realistic view than they formerly took, but in many fields where development is equally necessary, but is not supported with the same degree of pressure, the law has lagged behind.

If we wish to trace the extent to which the law has become adapted to the needs of present-day society, we shall have to look to both legislation and Court decisions. Progress may be made or hampered by either means. Legislation may often seem to mark the important stages in the evolution of public opinion, and in Trade Union law, for example, we may tend to think of the Acts of 1824-25, 1859, 1871, 1876, 1906, 1913, 1917, and 1927 as constituting the entire body of significant change. Actually, the development of important general principles of jurisprudence, of special concern to Trade Unionism, is to be found rather in the judgments of the Courts than in these Acts. Legislation often reflects the momentary passions of Parliamentary forces, and from the point of view of ordered change part, at least, of the statute law governing Trade Unions must appear to be quite out of harmony with current tendencies in the economic world. Certainly a changing

[1] *English Hop Growers* v. *Dering*, [1928] 2 K.B. 174.

public opinion and a changing economic environment may be reflected in the succession of statutes passed by Parliament, but the character of party politics is such that these laws may equally well represent only the momentary state of political forces and alignments. They may be quite out of touch with the real forces operating in the economic world, and even with the existing form of economic institutions.

To take only one or two instances of this: by Section 6 of the Trade Disputes and Trade Unions Act, 1927, local and public authorities were forbidden to make membership or non-membership of a Trade Union a condition of employment or to discriminate either in favour of or against their employees in respect of their Trade Union membership, and membership or non-membership of a Union was not to be made a condition of any contract made or proposed to be made with such authorities. This restriction quite ignored the fact that there are now very many industrialists, some of them among the largest employers of labour in the country, who voluntarily and for their own advantage openly declare their preference for Trade Union employees. They find it more convenient to have their workers organized. Yet public authorities may not give effect to such a view in their own service or in contracts.

As a further instance, consider the Combination Acts of 1799–1800. These Acts, it is true, represented a dominant public opinion at the time.[1] "The combination law as it stood at the beginning of the nineteenth century," says Dicey, "may be thus broadly summed up: Any artizan who organized a strike or joined a trade union was a criminal and liable on conviction to imprisonment; the strike was a crime, the trade union was an unlawful association."[2] The dread of "clubs," the fear of revolutionary activities inspired by the then recent Reign of Terror in France, accounted largely for the attitude taken up by powerful elements among the public, while relics also remained of the Tory paternalist outlook of the seventeenth

[1] Dicey, A. V., *op. cit.*, 95 ff.   [2] *Ibid.*, 99.

and early eighteenth centuries. The statement that "The Combination Act, then, of 1800, represented the public opinion of 1800"[1] is quite justified. Yet at this very time, as throughout the greater part of the eighteenth century, Trade Unions existed and even flourished. Hatters, tailors, wool textile operatives, curriers, printers, brushmakers, basket makers, shipwrights, farriers, smiths, coachmakers, carpenters, joiners, dyers, bricklayers, cordwainers, and bookbinders were among the trades that formed Unions in the eighteenth century, despite a series of statutes making such bodies illegal. The 1799–1800 legislation, more severe and repressive than any previous Acts, was in operation until 1824, yet some of the Unions were accepted and recognized by employers, and collective agreements were actually concluded in the printing and brushmaking trades in London in 1805, and in the coopering trade in 1813. Even at that early period the economic interests of employers made repressive legislation futile and out of date.

The failure of Parliament to keep abreast of modern economic developments is shown even more by the absence of legislation in certain important fields than by the positive law that exists in statute form. We have for some time been in a world of combination among businesses as well as among workmen, yet the attitude of the law towards cartels and combines is completely undefined by Parliament. As has already been pointed out, the Courts have to try to give practical judgments on the basis of the very old and very vague common law conceptions of conspiracy, restraint of trade, and so forth, and some judges may take a view diametrically opposed to that adopted by other equally eminent judges.[2]

Turning, then, from statute law to case law we find that the

[1] Dicey, A. V., *op. cit.*, 102.
[2] As for instance in the famous cases of *R. v. Denyer*, [1926] 2 K.B. 258, and *Hardie and Lane Ltd. v. Chilton*, [1928] 2 K.B. 306, with the irreconcilable judgments of the Court of Criminal Appeal and the Appeal Court.

Courts, so far from having acted on Lord Sankey's view already cited, that the interests of the public are really whatever the public at the time think sound policy, have consistently tried to impose upon Trade Unions a mass of restrictions and disabilities that reflected the "public policy" of a previous age. Thus, Dicey writes, "The best and wisest of the judges who administered the law of England during the fifty years which followed 1825 were thoroughly imbued with Benthamite liberalism. They believed that the attempt of Trade Unions to raise the rate of wages was something like an attempt to oppose a law of nature."[1] More precise corroboration of this statement is to be found in the history of the judicial attempts during the nineteenth century to make entirely new departures in law and even to nullify statutes that were actually passed to protect Trade Unions. If this seems to be too strong an observation, reference need only be made to any standard history of English law.

So we read the following impartial judgments:[2] "The prosecutions of 1851 went further still, and procured the ruling of Mr. Justice Erle[3] to the effect that, quite independently of statute or the use of illegal means, a combination of workmen, for the purpose of 'obstructing' an employer in his business, and so of forcing him to agree to a certain schedule of prices, by 'persuading' 'free men' to leave the employer's service, would be 'a violation in point of law.' Thus was born the doctrine of 'common law conspiracy' in its criminal aspect. . . . For such a doctrine it is difficult to find historical warrant. . . . Indeed, it is a little difficult to see how such a crime could have existed."[4]

Again, "In the case of *Temperton* v. *Russell*[5] the Court of Appeal, in spite of the decision of the House of Lords in the

---

[1] Dicey, A. V., *Law and Opinion*, 199.
[2] Jenks, E., *Short History of English Law* (1920 Ed.), chap. XVII.
[3] *R. v. Rowlands* (1851), 5 Cox 462.
[4] Jenks, E., *op. cit.*, 328–9.
[5] [1893] 1 Q.B. 715, C.A.

previous year,[1] boldly adopted the doctrine, hitherto unknown to English tribunals, that a combination of persons, if not a single person, who knowingly induced others not to enter into contracts with A, would be liable to an action by A, if the latter actually suffered loss in consequence of the Defendants' conduct."[2] "Thus came into existence the new doctrine of 'civil conspiracy,'" continues Professor Jenks, this doctrine being "fully upheld by the leading decision of *Quinn* v. *Leathem*[3] (the Belfast Butchers' Case), in spite of the fact that two of the learned Lords who decided that case had taken part in the unanimous judgment in the *Mogul Case*," in which, not being a Trade Union case, a diametrically opposite decision had been given, the defendant's action being said to be in the pursuit of legitimate trade competition.

The next comment is on the famous Taff Vale Case,[4] which, we are told, "really worked a revolution in English Law,"[5] at the expense of the Trade Unions, be it noted. For the proposition advanced by the employers and adopted by the House of Lords "there was no historical authority," says Professor Jenks. "The House of Lords had first invented a new civil offence ('civil conspiracy'), and had then created a new kind of defendant against whom it could be alleged."

Other instances could be cited, but sufficient has been said to illustrate the contention that in the past the Courts have used considerable ingenuity in order to restrict Trade Union activities in ways that did not in the least reflect current public opinion, much less current practice. Trade Unions Acts were passed in 1906 and 1913 for the express purpose of nullifying judicial decisions, made in 1901 and 1910 respectively, which were entirely new departures in law and which evidently did not in the least commend themselves to public opinion. Not only Benthamite Liberalism, but active hostility to Trade

[1] In *Mogul Steamship Co.* v. *McGregor*, [1892] A.C. 25.
[2] Jenks, E., *op. cit.*, 334. [3] [1901] A.C. 495.
[4] [1901] A.C. 426. [5] Jenks, E., *op. cit.*, 336.

Unionism, a hostility based on the judges' ignorance and fear of the working-class movement, marked many important judicial decisions in the nineteenth and early twentieth centuries. *Laissez-faire* doctrines succumbed on the "restraint of trade" exercised by business firms in the Mogul Case, but an almost identical restraint was forbidden to Trade Unions in the following year!

Consideration of such cases as have been cited invites discussion upon the nature of the "common law" and its constant expansion and adaptation by the Courts, and hence upon the development of case law as we know it in England. Few people will be disposed to quarrel with Geldart's statement,[1] "No one can seriously imagine that the Common Law of five hundred years ago would have had an intelligible answer to many of the legal questions of modern life." How, then, do the Courts cope with the problems of to-day in the absence of statute law? There is nothing especially scientific in the procedure adopted. In so far as precedents exist, or can be presumed by a little stretching to apply, judgment follows accordingly. The binding force of precedent, however, has been held so rigidly in England that the healthy growth of the common law has been gravely hampered. The late Mr. Justice McCardie said:[2] "My own view is that this slavery of case law is doing infinite hurt to English law. To my mind, principles and decisions should change with the times. I am more and more convinced of it as I look at the appalling chaos of case law by which Judges are governed by decisions given in the sixteenth and seventeenth centuries."

In an interesting paper[3] on "Case Law in England and America," Professor Goodhart has shown how much more flexible is the American practice, due to a definite movement away from the doctrine of *stare decisis*, and the student of

---

[1] Geldart, W. M., *Elements of English Law* (1914), 22.

[2] *The Times*, May 23, 1930.

[3] 15 *Cornell Law Quarterly* (1930), 173.

American conditions will probably conclude that the result has been wholly advantageous. A standard English work[1] says, "A judicial precedent speaks in England with authority; it is not merely evidence of the law but a source of it; and the courts are bound to follow the law that is so established." Goodhart points out that in six cases reported in the Law Reports (King's Bench, vol. I) for 1926, "one or more of the judges state that they might have decided the case before them differently if they had not been bound by a prior decided case." In the United States, on the other hand, the "Supreme Court and the highest courts of the various States have never held themselves to be absolutely bound by their own decisions,"[2] and in the twentieth century especially departures from precedent have been fairly frequent. "Courts exist," said Mr. Justice Crane,[3] "for the purpose of ameliorating the harshness of ancient laws inconsistent with modern progress, when it can be done without interfering with vested rights."

It was formerly thought that the system of case law really had the advantage of flexibility, and so of keeping abreast with changes in social and economic life, but it is now generally accepted, as Geldart put it, that "the binding force of precedent is a fetter on the discretion of the judge; but for precedent he would have a much freer hand."[4] This "binding force of precedent" has been held to be necessary in the interests of certainty in the administration of the law. "*Interest rei publicae*," said Lord Halsbury,[5] "that there should be *finis litium* at some time, and there could be no *finis litium* if it were possible to suggest in each case that it might be re-argued, because it is 'not an ordinary case,' whatever that may mean." But, as Dean Wigmore says,[6] "*Stare decisis*, as an absolute dogma, has seemed to me an unreal fetish. The French Civil Code expressly

---

[1] Salmond, J., *Jurisprudence* (7th Ed.).   [2] Goodhart, *loc. cit.*
[3] *Oppenheim* v. *Kridel*, 236, N.Y. 156, 165 (1923).
[4] Geldart, W. M., *Elements of English Law*, 28.
[5] *London Street Tramways Co.* v. *London County Council*, [1898] A.C. 375, 380.   [6] *Problems of Law* (1920), 79.

L

repudiates it; and, though French and other continental judges do follow precedents to some extent, they do so presumably only to the extent that justice requires it for safety's sake. *Stare decisis* is said to be indispensable for securing certainty in the application of the law. But the sufficient answer is that it has not in fact secured it. Our judicial law is as uncertain as any law could well be. We possess all the detriment of uncertainty, which *stare decisis* was supposed to avoid, and also all the detriment of ancient law-lumber, which *stare decisis* concededly involves—the government of the living by the dead, as Herbert Spencer has called it."

Professor Goodhart suggests[1] that the admitted departure from the strict supremacy of precedent in the United States Courts has been necessitated by the rapid changes in social and economic conditions in that country. With this there will be general agreement, but we must strongly dissent from the further statement that the case system "satisfies the needs of a country such as England, where conditions are more or less static." More or less static! No student of contemporary economics and politics could agree that such a description is accurate. Certainly the history of Trade Union law shows very conclusively that kaleidoscopic changes in social and industrial life are by no means confined to America, and that the case law system, with its rigid interpretation of *stare decisis*, has been a powerful barrier in the way of progress. Given a more elastic application of the doctrine of judicial precedent, the system of case law could certainly become that flexible and sensitive instrument that it was once supposed to be, and the response of the law to the vital needs of modern conditions would be more adequate.

Even so, this would not necessarily mean a more satisfactory state of Trade Union law, for, as has been pointed out, the Courts have in the past been guilty more than once of inventing entirely new principles of law, to apply to Trade Unions, and

[1] *Loc. cit.*

of ignoring the doctrine of *stare decisis* when the interests of the workers' organizations were concerned, while adhering to it for Capitalist aggregations. The living must not be governed by the dead, but that is a problem of personnel as well as of the doctrines of jurisprudence. Rightly or wrongly, the Trade Union world has come to regard the judges with the deepest suspicion, and to attribute to them not only ignorance of working-class institutions and conditions but even active prejudice and hostility. Dicey's aphorism already cited is significant enough, coming from one whose conservatism was as unimpeachable as his juristic authority. Certainly the bias of the judiciary has been hardly concealed in Trade Union cases for the past hundred years. There has been an initial assumption, almost, that strikes and cognate activities were, if not completely unlawful, at any rate in the highest degree reprehensible, and that Trade Unions were merely organizations of agitators and revolutionaries. It will be granted that this attitude has been less pronounced in the past twenty years, but there is by no means the same confidence in the impartiality of the judges in such cases as there is, with every justification, in those cases which do not involve political and economic issues. Perhaps the main reason why Mr. Justice Holmes is regarded by liberal-minded people all over the world with such veneration is that he has consistently refused to judge such issues by the standard of his own personal views of what is or is not desirable in the economic sphere.

It must be conceded that to fill the judicial bench with persons who are sufficiently philosophical in their own attitude and sensitive to major changes in public opinion, while at the same time completely immune against the influence of temporary aberrations of the mob, is a matter of supreme difficulty. To make judges elective, as in some of the American States, is the worst course of all, but our own method is very far from being perfect. The traditional British connection between politics and the higher judicial appointments cannot be defended. "The habits you are trained in, the people with whom you mix," says Lord Justice Scrutton,[1] "lead to your having a certain class of ideas of such a nature that, when you have to deal with other ideas, you do not give as sound and accurate judgments as you would wish." Everyone must agree with Professor Hughes Parry when he says that "in so far as a political office is treated as a preliminary qualification for a judicial appointment, the Bench must naturally tend to be influenced by definite economic and political outlooks."[2]

One obvious line of progress is to include some study of economics and of history in the normal curriculum of legal education. Lawyers and judges would then at least be aware that the crudities of clubland and the naïveties of country-house parties do not constitute the body of modern knowledge and thought upon the economic issues with which the Courts are now so much concerned. If the service of law, in the widest sense, is to be a "continually more efficacious social engineering,"[3] the engineers had better know something of the strains and stresses in the structure of society.

A change in legal education, though necessary, is not enough to give the desired result. The principle of selection needs to be in all cases as high and disinterested as it is already in some instances. The judge who has been trained in the social sciences as well as in the law, who has not been tied too rigidly to a party political career, who is sceptical enough in temper to be detached from most of the bitter political controversies, and who is yet not so fossilized as to be intolerant of new theories and experiments—this is the primary need of the judicial bench in the modern community, with its complex socio-legal problems. It is one of the major tasks of statesmanship to secure the appointment of this type of person to the judicial bench.

[1] 1 *Camb. Law Journal*, 6, 8.

[2] "Economic Theories in English Case Law," 186 *Law Quarterly Review*, 184.

[3] Pound, R., *Introduction to the Philosophy of Law* (1924), 99, and see also Dean Pound's *Interpretations of Legal History* (1923).

CHAPTER XIV

FREEDOM OF ASSOCIATION BEFORE THE
NINETEENTH CENTURY

IF a lawyer were to be asked, "Which branches of English law
are most obscure and doubtful, most difficult and unsettled?"
he would probably say that among the worst from this point
of view are the law of conspiracy, the law relating to restraint
of trade, and the law governing unincorporated associations.
The law affecting Trade Unions may be said to be compounded
of these three branches together with a few special statutes.
It is therefore somewhat chaotic and illogical and unsatisfactory.
For historical reasons no clear-cut body of law has developed
which will show, with certainty and lucidity, what is the legal
relationship of Trade Unions to the State. The law has been
pieced together, very largely from obsolete doctrines, from
superstitions that have no relevance to the modern world, and
attempts to modernize it have been half-hearted and scrappy.
It is not intended here to give an exposition of Trade Union
law; there is neither the space nor the need, and excellent
works on the subject already exist.[1] All that will be attempted
is a survey of those parts of the law that illustrate the main
theme of this work, and especially the position regarding
freedom of association and the status of voluntary bodies, and
the exercise of Trade Union powers in conflicts with the State.

Many foreign observers appear to be under the impression
that freedom of association is something that was unknown to
English law until the legislation of 1824–25 freed Trade Unions
from the taint of criminality. It is imagined by some people
that whereas in many continental countries the freedom of

---

[1] E.g., Slesser, H. H., and Baker, C., *Trade Union Law* (1927);
Sophian, T. J., *Trade Union Law and Practice* (1927); Henderson, A.,
Trade Unions and the Law (1927).

individual citizens to combine and associate for lawful purposes
has never had to be specifically enacted because it was inherent
in their constitutions, in Britain it was necessary to pass
legislation creating this freedom. That notion is, of course,
quite baseless. "Freedom of association" is not a term in
common use in this country, as it is on the Continent, but the
fact of such freedom is deeply rooted in our common law.
Legislation freeing workers' combinations had to be passed in
1824–25 only because legislation had previously been passed
making them illegal. Neither associations nor strikes were
originally illegal at common law.

In order to understand how freedom of association has been
regarded in Britain, it is necessary to give an outline of historical
developments in relation to the conception of the State and to
the growth of voluntary associations. Voluntary societies of
various kinds have always been a notable feature of British life;
they have existed in large numbers and for a bewildering
variety of purposes. Dicey has drawn a distinction between the
English and French attitudes in this respect.[1] Voluntary
associations within the State have, as such, always been
tolerated in this country, he says, whereas in France they were
for long looked upon with hostility and suppressed as far as
possible as being a menace to the central authority. The French
suspicion of "intermediate" groups arising between the individual and the State was perfectly general, and included
religious and literary as well as political and professional bodies.
Trade Unions were merely one variety of association, neither
better nor worse than any other from this point of view. While
industrial associations were singled out for attack by the famous
Le Chapelier law of 1791 and political associations by a further
law of 1798, a more comprehensive Act of 1834 extended the
ban to all associations. Not until 1901 was general freedom of
association restored in France. In England there was no such
hostility to groups in general. Individual citizens could associate

[1] *Law and Public Opinion*. Appendix on Freedom of Association.

and combine and pursue common activities as much as they pleased, provided they did not pursue unlawful objects or use unlawful methods. If they strayed outside the bounds of legality in respect either of objects or of methods, they became conspiracies. Thus Trade Unions were outlawed at an early stage in their history, not because they were voluntary associations which might some time set up a rival authority to that of the State, but because their purpose was frequently held to be illegal, their main object as a rule being to raise wages in defiance of the statutory wage-fixing machinery. Freedom of association in general has never been forbidden in England. The widest measure of suppression was that embodied in the panic legislation of 1799–1817. The Combination Acts of 1799–1800[1] prohibited combinations either of workmen or employers, for trade purposes; the Unlawful Societies Act of 1799[2] prohibited associations for seditious purposes; and the Seditious Meetings Act of 1817[3] banned societies and clubs appointing delegates, etc. Even this legislation was less sweeping than the 1834 Act in France, and its practical operation was limited to a short period of time. Although there had been one other case of a general prohibition of workers' combinations— an Act of 1549[4]—the legislation of 1799 to 1817 represented the only attempt to suppress trade associations because of the fear that they menaced the State. Every association, it was thought at that time, might be a disguise for a revolutionary conspiracy, and to this widespread fear must be attributed the savage legislation of 1799–1800 against Trade Unions. After the repeal of the Combination Acts in 1824 there was no further attempt to prohibit Trade Unionism by statute, though the Courts and the legislature continued for a long period to

[1] 39 Geo. III. c. 81 and 39, and 40 Geo. III. c. 106.
[2] 39 Geo. III. c. 79.
[3] 57 Geo. III. c. 19. Curiously enough, this Act and 39 Geo. III. c. 79 are still unrepealed, though they are, in practice, of no effect.
[4] 2 & 3 Ed. VI. c. 15. This was aimed primarily at combinations for keeping up prices.

hamper the growth and activity of the Unions. On the other hand there were, before the Combination Acts, many statutes prohibiting Trade Unions in specific trades. The fact that such Acts were passed is in itself an indication that freedom of association in general was not questioned. To understand why and how these prohibitions were enacted it is necessary to consider briefly the history of the State regulation of wages which was a feature of English economic life from the middle of the fourteenth to the middle of the eighteenth century. The Black Death of 1348 and succeeding years created an acute shortage of labour, and the immediate result of this novel situation was that there was a widespread demand for the commutation of labour services for money payment, where this had not already taken place, and a general demand for higher wages on the part of the "free" workers. In order to avert a complete breakdown of the economic system legislation was necessary, and this took the form of the stabilization of pre-existing wages and conditions, together with the control of prices. The Ordinance of Labourers[1] led the way by making it compulsory for agricultural labourers to work for the wage customary, prior to the Black Death, in the places where they were employed. The better-known Statute of Labourers[2] was passed later applying the same principle to carpenters, masons, and other craftsmen, as well as to farm workers. The Justices were empowered to enforce the Act. In succeeding years other Acts were passed to strengthen the law, which was proving unworkable, and in 1389[3] a new statute made provision for variations in wages, to be fixed by the Justices, so as to take into account changes in the cost of living.

The next great step was taken in the reign of Elizabeth, when the Statute of Artificers[4] repealed the earlier laws but re-enacted their principles and carried them a stage further. Section 4 of this Act provided that the Justices should meet each year to

[1] (1349 or 1350) 23 Ed. III.
[2] (1351) 25 Ed. III. stat. I.
[3] 13 Ric. II. c. 8.
[4] (1562) 5 Eliz. c. 4.

fix the wages of all artificers covered by the Act and of all other such workers as the Justices in their discretion might decide to rate in this way. There is some dispute as to the success of this system,[1] but it is clear enough that the wages "assessments" were made in respect of many classes of craftsmen and farm workers until well into the eighteenth century. Assessments under later statutes applying similar principles to specific trades were in fact made as late as 1801,[2] though the cases occurring after the end of the seventeenth century were very few and were quite exceptional. Thus the entire course of wage legislation from the time of Edward III up to the middle of the eighteenth century was in the direction of emphasizing the State's prerogative, exercised through the Justices, of fixing wages for nearly all classes of workers. Parts of this legislation were in existence until the nineteenth century, the wages sections of the Elizabethan statute not being repealed until 1813, while part of the Act remained on the Statute Book until 1875.

Thus, throughout part of the fourteenth and all of the fifteenth, sixteenth, and seventeenth centuries State regulation of wages was a reality, and it existed theoretically throughout the eighteenth century. During this period any combination of workers for the purpose of raising wages above the legal rates was therefore attempting to act in defiance of the law, and it was mainly for this reason that statutes were passed from time to time prohibiting such combinations in specific trades. Before the era of State regulation there was apparently one instance of such a statute; an Act of 1303 prohibited workers in cordwainery from holding any meeting or making any provision whch might be "to the prejudice of the trade and the detriment of the common people."[3] This does not affect

[1] See Cunningham, W., 4 *Econ. J.*, 515, and McArthur, 15 *Eng. Hist. Rev.*, 452.

[2] Smart, W., 1 *Econ. Ann.*, 23, 369.

[3] Cunningham, W., *Growth of English Industry and Commerce*, 1, 443.

the general argument, however, that the legal suppression of Trade Unions prior to the Combination Acts was due mainly to the fact that they were usually encroaching upon the sphere of wage fixing, which the State had reserved to itself by the series of statutes beginning with the Ordinance of Labourers in 1349 or 1350 and ending with the Spitalfields Silk Weavers' Act in 1773.[1] Trade Unions having as their object the enforcement of these statutes were in no case suppressed,[2] but were on the contrary applauded by the Courts.[3] Trade Unions setting the wage-fixing statutes at defiance, however, were forbidden both by statutes and by the common law.

The statutory prohibition of workmen's combinations was contained in a series of Acts applying to specific trades from the fourteenth century onwards.[4] In 1360, for instance, all "alliances and covines" of masons and carpenters were declared null and void.[5] In 1425 an Act declared that "by the yearly congregations and confederacies made by the masons in their general chapiters and assemblies, the good course and effect of the Statutes of Labourers be openly violated and broken."[6] The Bill of Conspiracies of Victuallers and Craftsmen, passed in 1549,[7] has already been referred to as the only example prior to the Combination Acts of a general prohibition of combinations of workmen. It dealt primarily with combinations to keep up prices, but it also enacted that "if any artificers, workmen or labourers do conspire, covenant or promise together, or make any oaths, that they shall not make or do their work but at a certain price or rate, or shall not enterprise or take upon them to finish that another has begun, or shall

---

[1] 13 Geo. III. c. 68 (confirmed in 1801 by 41 Geo. III. c. 38). For other important Acts of the fourteenth, fifteenth, sixteenth, and seventeenth centuries see Slesser and Baker, *op. cit.*, 13 n.

[2] Webb, S. and B., *History*, 65 ff.

[3] See Galton, F. W., *The Tailoring Trade* (1923 Ed.), 1, where examples are given.

[4] See list in Slesser, H. H., *Trade Unionism* (1913).

[5] 34 Ed. III. c. 10.   [6] 3 Hen. VI. c. 1.   [7] 2 & 3 Ed. VI. c. 15.

do but a certain work in a day, or shall not work but at certain hours and times," they should be liable to heavy penalties. There were many other Acts forbidding combinations, but after the seventeenth century they usually took the form of statutes fixing wages and sometimes hours in a specific trade, and prohibiting combinations and agreements aiming at the violation of these statutory conditions. Tailors, weavers, hatters, paper workers, silk workers, and other classes of labour were affected by legislation of this kind. In the reign of George III there were fifteen or sixteen Acts of this kind passed prior to the Combination Acts.[1]

The common law attack on Trade Unionism before the end of the eighteenth century was a more subtle matter, being dependent on the law of conspiracy. This doctrine, which has played such an important part in the legal history of Trade Unionism, has never been and is not now at all clearly defined. Trade Unions have been from time to time suppressed, however, on the ground that they were criminal conspiracies, either because they were combinations to violate a statute or because they were combinations in restraint of trade. At a fairly early period in our history the principle that a combination to commit a statutory offence is a criminal conspiracy was generally accepted, and when statutes were in force prohibiting combinations in specific trades or legally fixing rates of wages, any association having as its object the violation of such a statute could be and often was indicted as a conspiracy. The doctrine that a combination in restraint of trade is a criminal conspiracy at common law was at one time held, but this has long been considered unsound law. According to the best authorities such combinations were never criminal at common law, though the contrary view was at one period the basis of a number of decisions.

A brief survey of the development of the doctrine of conspiracy may throw some light on this important branch of

[1] Slesser and Baker, op. cit., 180.

the law and on the attitude of the Courts towards Trade Unions. The crime of conspiracy remained for long as it was defined in the *Ordinatio de Conspiratoribus*,[1] which, following earlier statutes on the subject, made it clear that this offence was essentially "a consultation or agreement, between two or more, to appeal or indict an innocent falsely and maliciously of felony."[2] It is now accepted that there never was a crime of conspiracy at common law,[3] but that the offence owed its origin to this legislation of Edward I's reign. The perversion of justice remained for several centuries the vital factor in the offence, but after Coke's judgment in the Poulterer's Case[4] the "Seventeenth Century Rule of Conspiracy" developed, according to which a combination to commit any crime constituted a criminal conspiracy. Later still the doctrine was extended to cover combinations to raise wages or otherwise act in restraint of trade, and the idea of "common law conspiracy" was evolved as mentioned above. By 1721[5] a Court was declaring that any conspiracy was illegal even though the action which the parties conspired to do would have been lawful for them to do apart from the combination. Thus arose the highly complicated theory of conspiracy that was so effective in suppressing Trade Union activities in the years between the repeal of the Combination Acts (and thus of all statutory prohibition of workers' combinations) and the Conspiracy and Protection of Property Act, 1875, and that even now, despite Acts passed to limit its operations, produces some odd results. Before the nineteenth century, then, combinations were attacked as conspiracies at common law either because their purpose was to violate a statute or because their objects were in restraint of trade. On the latter ground, however, the Courts were divided even in the eighteenth century. While in certain cases combinations to raise wages and improve conditions were

---

[1] 33 Ed. I. stat. 2 (1305).   [2] Coke, 3 Inst. 142–3.
[3] See Slesser and Baker, *op. cit.*, 178 ff.   [4] (1611) 9 Co. Rep. 55.
[5] E.g. see *R. v. Journeymen Tailors of Cambridge* (1721), 8 Mod. 10.

held to be criminal conspiracies at common law, because they were in restraint of trade, in other cases the Courts ruled that there was no such criminal element (unless the combination was directed against the State).[1] A clear distinction was drawn by Holt, C.J., between combinations directed against the State and those having no such objects.[2] This distinction was ignored in the later development of conspiracy, but up to the end of the eighteenth century, at any rate, there was no general condemnation of Unions by the Courts on the ground that they were conspiracies at common law since their objects were in restraint of trade. This does not mean that restraint of trade in itself was at that time considered harmless. On the contrary, the freedom of an individual to exercise any lawful trade as and where he will is a very old principle of the common law, and the Courts at a very early date looked unfavourably on contracts imposing a restraint of trade. As far back as 1300 a "ring" of chandlers at Norwich, which held up the price of candles, was condemned by the Courts.[3] In the fifteenth century it was decided that a "contract imposing a general or even partial restraint of trade was void," and Justice Hull "swore that had the plaintiff been present" who was suing on such a contract, "he would have sent him to prison."[4] Many decisions are reported, during succeeding centuries, declaring contracts void if they imposed restraints on the free course of trade, but the doctrine was not developed greatly until the eighteenth century, when State restrictions on trade were relaxed and the new philosophy of individualism began to make headway. It is important to notice that by no means all Trade Unions had (or have) objects in restraint of trade, and thus not all Trade Unions would be unlawful associations at

[1] Compare *R.* v. *Journeymen Tailors of Cambridge* (1721), 8 Mod. 10, with *R.* v. *Daniell* (1704), 6 Mod. 99.

[2] In *R.* v. *Daniell.*

[3] Cited by Batt, F. T., *Law of Master and Servant* (1929), 81.

[4] Per Hull, J., in 2 Hen. V. fol. 5. pl. 26; cited by Slesser and Baker, *op. cit.,* 8, 15.

common law, on the ground of having this type of unlawful purpose. Even where a Union was "unlawful" at common law for this reason, it was not until the law of conspiracy was erroneously applied, as mentioned above, that the association could be indicted as a criminal conspiracy. Apart from this, to be "unlawful" only meant that its agreements could not be legally enforced.

As far as the legal history of Trade Unionism is concerned before the nineteenth century, then, the position may be summed up as follows. Freedom of association in general was recognized. Statutes existed fixing wages in industry and agriculture, through the mechanism originally set up in the Elizabethan Statute of Artificers and extended or confirmed in successive Acts. This system was effective up to the middle of the eighteenth century, to some extent at any rate. Combinations violating these statutes were prohibited by special Acts passed throughout the period, but especially in the eighteenth century. Trade Unions were usually but not always in this category, and were often suppressed for this reason. In addition, the law of conspiracy was developed from the fourteenth century onwards, and under this doctrine, as extended, Trade Unions could be and often were suppressed as criminal conspiracies, in that they were combinations for the purpose of contravening statute law (the Acts regulating wages and the Acts prohibiting combinations). Further, the doctrine of the unlawfulness of restraint of trade was held throughout this period, and combinations in restraint of trade were sometimes held to be criminal conspiracies at common law; but this doctrine was disputed at the time.

CHAPTER XV

FREEDOM OF ASSOCIATION IN THE NINETEENTH CENTURY

THE Combination Acts of 1799 and 1800 remained on the Statute Book until 1824, and during these twenty-five years the State definitely and unequivocally took up the position that all combinations designed to improve wages or other conditions of labour were criminal conspiracies. Contracts and agreements made by such combinations were declared void, meetings in support of the prohibited objects were made illegal, and attendance at them was made a crime. All Trade Unions, all strikes in all trades, were thus made criminal in these comprehensive enactments.

There were two main reasons for this notable change in policy. First, as already stated, was the general fear of revolutionary conspiracies. The ruling class was horrified and fear-stricken at the events across the Channel. The French Revolution was not a proletarian revolution, not a Socialist rising, and it certainly did not represent the triumph of workers' organizations in France. On the contrary, occupational groups in France were suppressed at an early stage in the development of the Revolution. In March 1791, trade Guilds were suppressed, and in April of the same year the Paris Commune prohibited all combinations of craftsmen to obtain better conditions. In June the famous *Loi Chapelier* was passed, declaring a comprehensive ban on all industrial combinations.

It was not because of any idea that Trade Unionism itself was the revolutionary force in France and might become so in England that the Combination Acts were passed. The fear was rather lest the Unions should cloak revolutionary propaganda under the guise of trade activities. It was felt that any elements of political revolution would be able to use the name and form of trade organization for their purpose. The political unrest and uncertainty prevalent at the time must be borne in mind in any attempt to assess the motives behind the enactment of these exceptionally severe laws.

In addition, throughout the eighteenth century the rapid development of industry, which had finally broken down the old system of State regulation, had inevitably replaced the semi-paternalistic philosophy that had survived since the Middle Ages, by the new *laissez-faire* doctrine.[1] Long before the appearance of Adam Smith's *Wealth of Nations* in 1776, the growing complexity of the industrial structure and the new importance of the entrepreneur had emphasized the role of personal initiative and the value, in that stage of economic development, of individual freedom. It was no accident that the theory of restraint of trade, although five hundred years old at least, only began to be worked out in detail in the eighteenth century, the case of *Mitchell* v. *Reynolds*[2] in 1711 being the first occasion on which a coherent body of principles was laid down. Not only had the industrial structure been so much simpler in preceding centuries, but the rightness of State regulation had been generally recognized. Now this belief was disappearing, freedom of trade and freedom of contract became the dominant though hardly conscious motives. The reactions of the new philosophy on the position of combinations to interfere with the free course of trade were finally shown in the Combination Acts. What had hitherto been forbidden on the ground of non-interference with the functions of the State was now forbidden on the principle of non-interference with the rights of the individual to dispose of his capital or his labour as he chose. Even the State was denied positive functions of regulation and supervision,[3] and combinations were assailed, not for encroaching on the sphere of the State but for trying

---

[1] See Webb, S. and B., *History*, 50 ff.   [2] 1. P. Wms., 181.
[3] The wages clauses of the Statute of Artificers were repealed in 1813 by 53 Geo. III. c. 40.

to override the freedom of the individual. That this was an important element in the 1799–1800 legislation is shown by the fact that the Act of 1800 provided, in Section 17, that combinations of employers to reduce wages, to increase hours, or to increase the amount of work, should be equally prohibited. Certainly, this prohibition was much less general and the penalties imposed were lighter than in the case of workers' combinations, and, moreover, no case is known of any employer having been punished under the Section, although violations were not unknown. Nevertheless, the Act did apply to employers, whereas no previous statute had done so.[1]

The "restraint of trade" aspect of Trade Unionism thus received much more emphasis as the doctrine of *laissez-faire* gained ground. It will be seen that when the fear of revolutionary conspiracies had died down, and the statutory prohibition of Trade Unions had been removed, this aspect continued to be important and was largely responsible for the paradoxical situation from 1824–1875, the period when Trade Unions could exist but could not effectively act.

In passing the Combination Acts, the Government of the day was doubtless actuated largely by class hostility, but it was not influenced to any great extent by general opposition to groups within the State. This feeling came much later in England as Benthamite Liberalism, with its belief in individual freedom, gradually retreated before the onward march of the omnipotent State. In France, on the other hand, the fear of

[1] The statutes passed in preceding centuries had applied only to workers' combinations. This was quite logical, since the Statute of Artificers and most of the later Acts had fixed, or provided for the fixing of, *maximum* wages, and therefore it was only combinations to violate these provisions that were illegal. In a few cases where wages were fixed and *higher or lower* rates were forbidden (e.g. 7 Geo. I. c. 13 in 1720 and 13 Geo. III. c. 68 in 1773), combinations of employers to pay lower rates were doubtless as illegal as combinations of workers to secure higher rates, though no prosecutions of employers on this ground are on record.

M

groups was prominent among the motives that led to the Revolutionary legislation against associations.

Le Chapelier, in supporting his Bill before the Constituent Assembly in June 1791, not only said that free agreements between individual and individual must fix the day's work for each worker, and not only condemned Unions for forcing workers "to leave their shops even when they are content with the wages they are receiving," but in a significant passage he declared that "there must be no more guilds in the State, but only the individual interest of each citizen and the general interest. No one shall be allowed to arouse in any citizen any kind of intermediate interest and to separate him from the public weal through the medium of corporate interests."[1] This kind of attitude does not appear to have influenced Trade Union legislation in England until the enactment of the Trade Disputes and Trade Unions Act of 1927.

Repeal of the Combination Acts

The repressive legislation of 1799–1800 was repealed in 1824–25, but it is instructive to notice that prosecutions between 1799 and 1824 were not so numerous as might have been anticipated, and that in a number of cases Trade Unions not only continued to exist and function, with the connivance of employers, but collective agreements were actually concluded in the printing and brush-making trades in 1805, and in the coopering trade in 1813.[2] The Act of 1824[3] marked a turning-point in the legal history of Trade Unionism, despite the subsequent weakening of its provisions. It lifted the worker "from a status to a contract system";[4] it denoted, in other words, the end of the long period in which custom and status fixed the remuneration of workpeople and ushered in the

---

[1] Cited in 2 *Freedom of Association*, 89.
[2] Webb, S. and B., *History*, 74.
[3] 5 Geo. IV. c. 95.
[4] Jenks, E., *Short History of English Law*, 325.

modern period in which wages and conditions are matters of bargaining and contract.

The new Act laid it down that workers should not be "subject or liable to any indictment or prosecution for conspiracy, or to any other criminal information or punishment whatever, under the common or statute law," for entering into "any combination to obtain an advance, or to fix the rate of wages, or to lessen or alter the hours or duration of the time of working, or to decrease the quantity of work, or to induce another to depart from his service before the end of the time or term for which he is hired, or to quit or return to his work before the same shall be finished or, not being hired, to refuse to enter into work or employment, or to regulate the mode of carrying on any manufacture, trade, or business, or the management thereof."

The Act of 1825,[1] while in effect re-enacting the 1824 Act in many of its provisions, made certain amendments, the most vital of which was to remove from the 1824 law the immunity of Unions from prosecution under the common law. In other words, statutory prohibitions were removed, but combinations were still exposed to the rigours of the common law as interpreted by the Courts. The force of this change was felt later when the Unions found that their activities were proscribed under the doctrine of "common law conspiracy," which was now developed to a high degree of subtlety and ingenuity. The 1825 Act had prohibited the use of violence and intimidation in the conduct of trade activities,[2] and combinations of workers were now convicted of conspiracy to violate this section. Even where no violence or threats were involved, it was ruled that a combination to "obstruct" an employer in his business, by persuading workers to leave his service, so forcing him to pay a certain scale of wages, was unlawful.[3] Strikes for

[1] 6 Geo. IV. c. 129.   [2] Sec. 3.
[3] Per Erle, J., in *R.* v. *Rowlands* (1851), 5 Cox 462, and in *R.* v. *Duffield* (1851), 5 Cox 431.

perfectly lawful objects were thus rendered illegal. "For such a doctrine," says a high authority,[1] "it is difficult to find historical warrant. . . . It is true that the English Courts refuse, and have long refused, to enforce contracts made 'in restraint of trade,' but, as Lord Halsbury carefully pointed out . . . such contracts were never 'unlawful' in the sense that they were 'contrary to law,' i.e. punishable either criminally or civilly." So from 1825 until 1871 the Courts still succeeded in hampering Trade Union activities, even though statutory restrictions had been removed. The Unions were still liable to attack on the ground that they were conspiracies at common law, being combinations in restraint of trade. This was a doctrine having its origin no earlier than the eighteenth century, and it is easy to see its genesis in the new economic conditions with their accompanying *laissez-faire* philosophy. Complete freedom of competition was never more than an abstraction, but actual interference with the "free" course of trade went on for a long time before the law reluctantly recognized "restraints" of certain types, including even some general restraints, as lawful, and contracts embodying them as enforceable. Freedom of contract was held sacred by the Courts for many years before they made possible "the equality of position between the parties, in which liberty of contract begins," to quote Justice Holmes's well-known phrase.[2]

Restraint of trade has generally been condemned as being contrary to public policy, but "public policy" does not mean necessarily the welfare of the community, the public weal. Throughout the greater part of the nineteenth century it meant, in this connection, whatever contributed to the freedom of the individual citizen. It was not "public policy" to allow the "rights" of the individual to be curtailed. The concept of public policy is a vague and fluctuating one, and depends really on the interpretation adopted by the Courts. Well might Campbell, C.J., in a restraint of trade case nearly a century

[1] Jenks, *op. cit.*, 328–9.   [2] In *Coppage* v. *Kansas.* 236 U.S.1.

ago,[1] deplore the fact that "so much should depend on the presiding judge's opinions on political economy and other non-legal topics."

In any case, "it does not follow that because rules may be against public policy they are therefore criminal,"[2] and in 1871 the Trade Union Act[3] declared that "the purposes of any trade union shall not, by reason merely that they are in restraint of trade, be deemed to be unlawful so as to render any member of such trade union liable to criminal prosecution for conspiracy or otherwise." It should not be supposed that this Act, the "Charter of Trade Unionism," as it is sometimes called, finally defeated the supporters of the "rights" of individual employers to conclude wage bargains without Trade Union interference. Having been deprived of all statutory weapons aimed at the existence of Trade Unions, and robbed of their common law weapon against combinations in restraint of trade, they proceeded to develop an attack along a line already indicated in Court decisions during the middle years of the nineteenth century. In 1851, Erle, J., had ruled[4] that a combination could not induce workers to leave their employer as a means of compelling him to observe better conditions, such an action being forbidden as an "obstruction" of the employer, at common law and under Section 3 of the Act of 1825. In order to overrule this judicial view, the Molestation of Workmen Act was passed in 1859.[5] Like the 1825 Act, it confined its formal removal of prohibition to Trade Union activities relating solely to wages and hours, but it defined more precisely the freedom given by that enactment and extended it in certain directions. Although picketing and peaceful persuasion were to some extent legalized, the Act therefore left it open to the Courts to say that the inclusion of any object outside wages and hours would

[1] *Hilton* v. *Eckersley* (1855), 106 R.R. 507.
[2] Per Cockburn, C.J., in *R.* v. *Stainer* (1870), 11 Cox 483.
[3] 34 & 35 Vict. c. 31.
[4] In *R.* v. *Duffield*, 5 Cox 404, and *R.* v. *Rowlands*, 5 Cox 404.
[5] 22 Vict. c. 34.

render such action illegal. However, it is unlikely that purely peaceful persuasion for such other purposes would have been condemned. In the event a controversy arose over the distinction between peaceful persuasion on the one hand, and intimidation and threats on the other. The threat to call a strike was considered illegal, even though the strike itself would have been perfectly lawful.[1] The 1871 Act did nothing to remedy this situation, and the Criminal Law Amendment Act,[2] which was passed in the same year, and which repealed both the 1825 Act and the 1859 Act, left a way open for this kind of attack to be continued.

In a case that came before the Courts in the following year,[3] Mr. Justice Brett said that "if there was an agreement among the defendants by improper molestation to control the will of the employers, then I tell you that that would be an illegal conspiracy at common law, and that such an offence is not abrogated by the Criminal Law Amendment Act." "Improper molestation" was defined by the judge as "anything done with an improper intent, which the jury should think was an unjustifiable annoyance and interference with the masters in the conduct of their business, and which in any business would be such annoyance and interference as would be likely to have a deterring effect upon masters of ordinary nerve."

The result was that after considerable agitation a further Act was passed in 1875, the Conspiracy and Protection of Property Act,[4] which repealed the 1871 measure. Incidentally, the judgment in the Bunn Case was severely criticized and its validity rejected in subsequent cases, the Court holding that the threat of a strike was not indictable either by statute or at common law.[5] The 1875 Act freed strikes and other combinations from criminality (either under statute or at common

---

[1] *Walsby* v. *Anley* (1861); 3 Ell. & Ell. 516; *O'Neill* v. *Longman* (1867), 9 Cox 360.
[2] 34 & 35 Vict. c. 32.   [3] *R.* v. *Bunn* (1872), 12 Cox 316.
[4] 38 & 39 Vict. c. 86.   [5] *Gibson* v. *Lawson*, [1891] 2 Q.B. 545.

law) provided that they were in contemplation or furtherance of a trade dispute between employers and workmen, that they were for the commission of some act which would not be a crime apart from the combination, that they did not involve a conspiracy punishable by statute, and that they were not breaches of the law relating to riot, unlawful assembly, breach of the peace, sedition, or any offence against the State or the Sovereign. Section 4 of the Act made it a crime for workers in gas or water supply services maliciously to break their contract of service if the probable result was to deprive the inhabitants of the area wholly or to a great extent of gas or water. This was extended to electricity supply by the Electricity (Supply) Act, 1919.[1]

Section 5 of the 1875 Act made malicious breach of contract of service criminal if the probable consequence was to endanger human life, cause serious bodily injury, or expose valuable property to destruction or serious injury, and the Trade Disputes and Trade Unions Act of 1927[2] further enacted that employees of local or public authorities wilfully breaking their contract of service should be liable to fine or imprisonment if the probable result was to cause injury or danger or grave inconvenience to the community.

The purpose of the 1875 Act, and the subsequent measures that followed the same line of thought, was to free ordinary strikes and combinations from the continuous efforts of the Courts to find them criminal at common law, while at the same time making criminal a number of acts, whether committed by individuals or combinations, that might take place in connection with trade disputes. Some of these offences related to the use of violence, and one would normally expect them to be offences whether committed in connection with trade disputes or not. Others touched on the difficult border-line between persuasion and coercion. But others—and these are more interesting from the point of view of this work—were offences because of their

---

[1] 9 & 10 Geo. V. c. 100.   [2] 17 & 18 Geo. V. c. 22.

results to the community. The conception was emerging of the "right" of the community to receive uninterrupted supplies of "essential services." The subsequent history of this doctrine is best studied in connection with "general" strikes, and particularly in connection with the wide extension given to the principle in the Act of 1927.

Although criminal liability was removed by the 1875 Act, the Courts set to work and developed the doctrine of civil conspiracy, by which the Trade Unions were left exposed to actions for damages in respect of certain acts committed in contemplation or furtherance of trade disputes. The new attack also had its origin in the judgments already referred to[1] about the middle of the century, Mr. Justice Erle suggesting that there would be a right of action for damages in the case of a common law conspiracy to interfere with an employer's relations with his workers by inducing them to break their contract of service. The proposition that it is an actionable wrong for a combination of persons to induce another person to break a contract, with the result that damage is sustained by the aggrieved party, was thereafter elaborated and applied not only to trade disputes and Trade Union cases, but to many other classes of case, involving breaches of all kinds of contract. This principle was clearly laid down in a case decided before the 1875 Act was passed[2]—not a Trade Union case incidentally— but after 1875 it was applied to cases involving Trade Union interference with the contractual relations of workers, and even extended to cover combinations to induce a person not to enter into a contract with another person.[3] This extension was quite novel; in fact, a parallel case in 1892,[4] in which the parties were both commercial firms, had been decided in the opposite sense. But after 1893 the principle that it was actionable not

---

[1] See p. 181, footnote 4.
[2] *Lumley* v. *Gye* (1853), 2 E. and B. 224.
[3] *Temperton* v. *Russell*, [1893] 1 Q.B. 715 (C.A.)
[4] *Mogul S.S. Co.* v. *McGregor Gow*, [1892] A.C. 25.

merely to induce breach of contract, but to persuade persons not to enter into a contract was accepted, at any rate in Trade Union cases, by a number of decisions.[1] The law governing "interference" with another person's business, and with the contractual relations of other persons, has since been elaborated and expanded in a number of "restraint of trade" and "conspiracy" cases, but as far as the application of such principles to Trade Unions is concerned the process was stopped by the Trade Disputes Act of 1906.[2]

Section 1 of that Act laid it down that "an act done in pursuance of an agreement or combination by two or more persons shall, if done in contemplation or furtherance of a trade dispute, not be actionable unless the act, if done without any such agreement or combination, would be actionable." Section 3 provides that "an act done by a person in contemplation or furtherance of a trade dispute is not actionable on the ground only that it induces some other person to break a contract of employment or that it is an interference with the trade, business, or employment of some other person, or with the right of some other person to dispose of his capital or his labour as he wills." Finally, Section 4 declares that "an action against a Trade Union, whether of workmen or masters, or against any members or officials thereof on behalf of themselves and all other members of the trade union in respect of any tortious act alleged to have been committed by or on behalf of the trade union, shall not be entertained by any Court."

This drastic and comprehensive statute represents the high-water mark of Trade Union freedom, and it remains in full force to-day except in so far as the Trade Disputes and Trade Unions Act, 1927, has removed from its protection certain types of strikes and lock-outs. The Act of 1906, it is often said,[3] places Trade Unions above the law by freeing them

---

[1] E.g. *Reed* v. *Operative Stonemasons*, [1902] 2 K.B. 732; *Giblan* v. *National Labourers*, [1903] 2 K.B. 600.   [2] 6 Edw. VII. c. 47.

[3] E.g. Dicey, A. V., *Law and Public Opinion.*

from all liability in respect of torts committed by or on behalf of the Unions, not merely in connection with trade disputes but in all connections. This question will be discussed when the legal status of Trade Unions is examined in a later chapter, but here it may be pointed out that the real reason why the legislature went so far is to be found in the history, outlined above, of the Courts' unwearied attempts to restrict Trade Unions first by criminal and then by civil process. Time after time Parliament intervened to overrule judicial decisions. After the repeal of the Combination Laws the Courts developed the doctrine of criminal conspiracy in restraint of trade. When this was nullified they elaborated a new doctrine of criminal conspiracy to coerce employers. As soon as this was checkmated and Trade Unions were set free from special treatment under the criminal law, the Courts evolved the doctrine of civil conspiracy and other harassing limitations on freedom of action. The legislature, in the 1906 Act, apparently determined to make it clear once and for all that Unions as such were not to be suppressed, or hampered in their work, by the ingenuity of the judges in discovering new offences.

Thus, throughout the period 1824–1906 the legal history of Trade Unions records a succession of conflicts between Parliament and the Courts, the former attempting belatedly to translate industrial practice into law, the latter using every possible expedient to uphold the principle of *laissez-faire* in industrial relations. As always, economic forces triumphed, and the freedom of combinations to exist and to act was successfully established with the progressive weakening of *laissez-faire* in other aspects of our economic life.

CHAPTER XVI

FREEDOM OF ASSOCIATION SINCE 1906

SINCE the Trade Disputes Act of 1906, important changes in Trade Union law have taken place in regard to freedom of association and the legality of strikes. These developments have, so far, affected only a section of the Trade Union movement, and, apart from the statutory exceptions to be described, combinations of workers enjoy the same immunities to-day that were given by the 1906 Act. In its application to other spheres than that of Trade Unionism and trade disputes, the law governing interference with the contractual relations of other persons, and with the trade or business of other persons, has been greatly expanded. It is still far from clear, however, though it seems to be established, that while a combination wilfully to injure another in his trade is unlawful, and is actionable if damage actually results,[1] a combination to forward the trade interests of its members is not unlawful even though other persons sustain damage.[2] By some authorities conspiracy is in itself regarded as a tort, if the intention of the combination is to injure another, but this doctrine does not receive unanimous assent.[3]

Trade disputes and Trade Unions to which the 1906 Act applies are not subject to the operation of these principles. Nevertheless, since 1906 there has been a definite change in the attitude of the State towards workers' and employers' combinations and disputes. The philosophy of *laissez-faire* has fallen more and more into disrepute, and partly as a result of

[1] *Sorrell* v. *Smith*, [1925] A.C. 700.
[2] *Ware and De Freville* v. *Motor Trade Association*, [1921] 3 K.B. 40; *Mogul S.S. Co.* v. *McGregor Gow*, [1892] A.C. 25.
[3] For a full discussion of this controversy see Haslam, A. L., and Stallybrass, W. T. S., *The Law Relating to Trade Combinations* (1931), 20 ff.

industrial developments, partly owing to the war, State sovereignty has been exalted and group rights have been curtailed. The State tends more than ever to exercise positive functions in the regulation of industry, and as a corollary the rights of industrial groups are more frequently questioned in all matters where the public interest is affected. Industrial disputes are, if on a large scale, once more frowned upon; not, however, as in the nineteenth century, because they interfere with individual freedom; not, as in earlier centuries, because they contravene statutes regulating trades; but because they are held to be inconvenient or detrimental to the welfare and comfort of the community at large.

The concept of "essential services," already present in the Conspiracy and Protection of Property Act, 1875, has been emphasized and extended and has even come to dominate the discussions and enactments of the legislature in matters of industrial relations and organization.

No very detailed description need be given of the emergency war-time legislation dealing with Trade Unionism, since the Munitions of War Acts and other measures were in force only during the war period, and have left no permanent mark on the legal treatment of trade combinations. Freedom of association was in no way interfered with by these Acts, but freedom of action was considerably curtailed, since strikes or lock-outs coming within their scope could be "proclaimed," after which the act of striking was illegal, heavy penalties being prescribed for violation. At the same time, compulsory arbitration was provided in the munition trades, through special Munitions Tribunals. Workers were thus legally compelled to forgo the use of their power to strike and were obliged to continue to work under conditions laid down by these special Courts. As already recorded, this system did not in fact prevent strikes.[1] The Acts were occasionally violated, and it was found impossible to enforce the penalties against large bodies of workers. On

[1] P. 41.

the other hand, many workers were punished under these provisions.

Since the war, freedom of association itself has been legally curtailed as far as certain classes of labour are concerned. The Trade Union Act (1871) Amendment Act of 1876[1] had laid it down that any person above the age of sixteen could be a member of a Trade Union (unless the rules of the Union provided otherwise), but no member under twenty-one could be a member of the committee of management, a trustee, or the treasurer of the Union. This unimportant limitation was the only statutory restriction of any kind upon actual freedom to combine.

In 1919, after a series of police strikes, the Police Act was passed[2] whereby freedom of association was effectively restricted for members of police forces. A Police Federation was established for such members, and it was enacted that "The Police Federation and every branch thereof shall be entirely independent of and unassociated with any body or person outside the police service." All matters of "welfare and efficiency, other than questions of discipline and promotion affecting individuals," were to be within the purview of this Federation, and no member of a police force was thenceforth to be a "member of any trade union or of any association having for its objects, or one of its objects, to control or influence the pay, pensions, or conditions of service of any police force." The penalty for violation of this provision was to be dismissal, with loss of pension rights. A man who was a member of a Trade Union prior to becoming a constable might, with the consent of the chief officer of police, continue his membership. Since 1919, then, members of police forces have been denied freedom of association, except through the official Police Federation.

Freedom to combine was next restricted in the case of Civil Servants. The Trade Disputes and Trade Unions Act, 1927,[3]

[1] 39 & 40 Vict. c. 22.   [2] 9 & 10 Geo. V. c. 46.
[3] 17 & 18 Geo. V. c. 22.

laid it down that the Treasury should make regulations "prohibiting established civil servants from being members, delegates or representatives of any organization of which the primary object is to influence or affect the remuneration and conditions of employment of its members, unless the organization is an organization of which the membership is confined to persons employed by or under the Crown and is an organization which complies with such provisions as may be contained in the regulations for securing that it is in all respects independent of, and not affiliated to any such organization as aforesaid the membership of which is not confined to persons employed by or under the Crown, or any federation comprising such organizations, that its objects do not include political objects, and that it is not associated directly or indirectly with any political party or organization." There was a provision that any Civil Servant already a member of a forbidden Trade Union should be entitled to continue his membership, if he had been a member for more than six months and had acquired benefit rights. The effect of these provisions and the regulations based upon them was to make it impossible for Civil Servants to become members of a Trade Union other than one confined to employees of the Crown, or to become allied either industrially or politically with workers outside Government service.

Although not a violation of freedom of association, a further provision of the same Act is worth notice as affecting employees of local or public authorities. Such authorities were forbidden to make membership or non-membership of a Trade Union a condition of employment, and were forbidden to discriminate in any way against employees because of their membership or non-membership. Similarly, a local or public authority was forbidden to make it a condition of any contract made or proposed to be made with the authority that any person to be employed by any party to the contract should or should not be a member of a Trade Union. The purpose of these limitations was obviously to make it more difficult for the allegiance of a public servant to be divided. The public employee may still be a member of a vocational group, it is true, but his allegiance to the wider and more powerful group is forbidden in the case of Civil Servants, while in the service of local and public authorities the restriction means that employees shall not, at any rate, be compelled to have an allegiance to a vocational group.

As regards the activities of associations, restrictions have greatly increased during the past twelve years. Between 1906 and 1920, limitations on ordinary Trade Union and strike activities were practically non-existent (apart from stoppages of work in breach of contract, where danger to life or property or certain essential services would result). Partly as a result of the modern growth in the power of Trade Union organizations, and partly because of the war-time revival of the sentiment of State unity, the uninterrupted operation of services deemed essential to the existence or welfare of the community has become a major objective of certain sections of opinion. Parliament has passed legislation on this problem twice in the last twelve years. Apart from the causes just mentioned, it will doubtless be agreed that this tendency is linked up with the wider movement towards the assumption by the State of greater powers of regulation over industry, and with the continuously increasing degree of interference with the working of the *laissez-faire* principle in the economic system.

In 1920 the Emergency Powers Act[1] was passed, giving the Government power to declare a state of emergency in the event of action taken or threatened "by any persons or body of persons of such a nature and on so extensive a scale as to be calculated, by interfering with the supply and distribution of food, water, fuel, or light, or with the means of locomotion, to deprive the community or any substantial portion of the community, of the essentials of life." In such a case regulations

[1] 10 & 11 Geo. V. c. 55.

may be issued, by Order in Council, "for securing the essentials of life to the community," and practically unlimited power may be exercised under these provisions.[1] But it is provided that "no such regulation shall make it an offence for any person or persons to take part in a strike, or peacefully to persuade any other person or persons to take part in a strike." While this proviso safeguards the "right to strike" and the right of "peaceful persuasion," the Act does not forbid the framing of regulations allowing interference with or prohibition of many other forms of Trade Union activity incidental to strikes.

Even these powers to restrict Trade Union action were evidently considered inadequate, for in 1927 the drastic provisions of the Trade Disputes and Trade Unions Act made sweeping changes in the law and severely curtailed the freedom of Trade Unions to undertake strike activities. The main innovation was the definition of a category of illegal strikes. Designed ostensibly to prohibit "general strikes," the Act, passed largely as a consequence of the National strike of 1926,[2] did not attempt to define a "general strike," but proceeded to declare illegal any strike that

(i) has any object other than or in addition to the furtherance of a trade dispute within the trade or industry in which the strikers are engaged; and

(ii) is a strike designed or calculated to coerce the Government either directly or by inflicting hardship upon the community.

With the appropriate change of wording an illegal lock-out was defined in similar terms. It was further declared illegal "to commence, or continue, or to apply any sums in furtherance or support of, any such illegal strike or lock-out." The pro-

[1] For the permanent machinery established by the Government to facilitate the application of this Act in large-scale stoppages of work, see p. 74ff.

[2] See p. 60.

tection of the Trade Disputes Act, 1906, is withdrawn from illegal strikes, and the proviso in the Emergency Powers Act, 1920, safeguarding the right of peaceful persuasion under regulations made under the Act, is likewise not applicable to illegal strikes. But it is still no offence under any of these statutes or at common law for the workers to cease work, or for them to refuse to continue to work or to accept employment; the mere act of striking, even if the strike is illegal, is not an offence.[1]

A further section of the 1927 Act imposed new restrictions on picketing in ordinary strikes, and, in prohibiting intimidation, extended the meaning of this term · to cover any conduct causing in the mind of a person a reasonable apprehension of injury, the term "injury" including injury to a person in respect of his business, occupation, employment, or other source of income, and including "any actionable wrong."[2] To return to the ban on "illegal" strikes, the intention to protect essential services emerges more clearly than ever in this statute. It is evident from the Act itself, and from the debates in Parliament, that the aim was to prevent any stoppage of work which had become, or was likely to be, so effective as to interfere with transport, food supplies, gas, coal, electricity, etc. Even so, there is still one type of stoppage where such interference may be legal: a primary dispute may hold up coal or railways or any other essential service and not come under the ban, provided its object is purely industrial. Only where it is "sympathetic" or secondary, or where it has a non-industrial object, is such a stoppage to be held illegal (though the wording of the Act is so ambiguous that it is doubtful whether this can be affirmed with any certainty). Apparently, the Government of the day was not prepared to deny the right to organize a strike, however serious its results might be to the community, where the sole object was to improve the conditions of the strikers themselves.

[1] Trade Disputes and Trade Unions Act, 1927, sec.1.   [2] Sec. 3.

By 1930 there was a stronger, or at any rate a more vocal, section of opinion that was unwilling to go so far in the toleration of primary strikes. The Labour Government's Bill in that year aimed at the drastic amendment of the 1927 Act, and proposed to redefine the category of illegal strikes in such a way as to prohibit only revolutionary strikes, or strikes with a definitely political object. Stoppages with genuinely industrial objects would have been, by this Bill, perfectly legal, whether primary or sympathetic, and whatever their effects on the community, through interruption of essential services. The Bill was finally defeated on this proposal, and it was evident from the discussions at the time that there was a strong current of opinion, hostile to the claims of Trade Unions, that was anxious to prohibit *all* stoppages, whether primary or sympathetic, whether industrial or political, that would be likely to endanger or inconvenience the public by cutting off transport, fuel, or other such necessities. This current of opinion appears to be growing stronger, and due weight must be given to it in any examination of the problem. It is no longer a matter of prohibiting only "general strikes," in the traditional sense; i.e. strikes aiming at the overthrow of the existing economic system. Nor is it only political strikes (for example, to enforce the resignation of a Government) that tend to be banned. Stoppages interfering with any essential service must now be regarded as certain to invite strong opposition and counter-measures on the part of the civil power. This is perhaps the most significant development in the recent history of the relations between Trade Unions and the State, and, for once, legislation has rather led than followed changes in public opinion.

Whether "general strikes" of the 1926 type were legal or illegal before the 1927 Act is an interesting academic question that now, however, has no practical bearing. Revolutionary general strikes used as a pretext for or encouragement to the forcible overthrow of established institutions have doubtless always been illegal, but the view of the highest authorities is that a stoppage of the kind that occurred in 1926 was not in any way illegal prior to the 1927 Act, even if its aim was to compel the Government to adopt certain measures.[1] Parliament has now made such stoppages illegal, and has thus taken the biggest step for more than a century in the direction of asserting the subordination of Trade Unions to the political State. Should the tendency continue, there will be demands in future for still more far-reaching legislation making any interference with essential services illegal and curtailing still more strictly the powers of Trade Unions.

Another aspect of "general strikes" is raised when we return to a consideration of their objects. The series of Acts from 1824 to 1906, referred to above, freed strike activities from criminality and later from civil disabilities only so long as they were in contemplation or furtherance of a "trade dispute" as that term was statutorily defined. A concerted stoppage of work having an object unconnected with a trade dispute would not be entitled to the protection of the Acts of 1875 and 1906. Whether, losing this protection, a strike which aimed, for instance, at the prevention of an unpopular war would be illegal at common law remains uncertain. As far back as 1843 Erskine, J., suggested that a general stoppage to secure the adoption of the Charter would, if peaceably conducted, be legal, but Patteson, J., in the same case considered that such an act would be treasonable.[2] This latter opinion would seem, however, to be erroneous.[3] Strikes having so-called "political" objects, as distinct from the industrial objects of the normal strike, would certainly appear to be outside the protection of the Acts of 1875 and 1906, but they would not necessarily be illegal. Moreover, it would often be extremely difficult to disentangle political from industrial objects. Suppose, for

[1] This is the conclusion reached in the most detailed examination yet made of the legal position of the 1926 strike. Goodhart, A. L., "The Legality of the General Strike," 36 *Yale Law Journal* (1927), 464.

[2] *R. v. Cooper.* 4 St. Tr. N.S. 1248.   [3] See Goodhart, *loc. cit.*

example, that miners, finding it impossible to obtain from their employers what they consider to be satisfactory conditions, declare a strike in order to compel the Government to nationalize the coal industry, believing the desired conditions will thus be obtained. Is this a political object? Such a strike may certainly be said to be "in furtherance of" a trade dispute, the object being really to secure the conditions about which the dispute occurred. Under the 1927 Act such a strike would doubtless be declared illegal, as would, even more clearly, any strike having a purely political object, provided it was calculated to coerce the Government by interfering with essential services.

In short, any strikes causing serious interruption of these services will now be held illegal under the 1927 Act, unless they are primary strikes for purely industrial objects. "Political" strikes not involving such interference with essential services may not be illegal, though they are not in any case protected by the Acts of 1875 and 1906.

In the new statutory limitations embodied tentatively in the Emergency Powers Act, 1920, and more definitely in the Trade Disputes and Trade Unions Act, 1927, the criterion of the State's toleration of large-scale strikes has tended to be their effects and not their objects.[1] If this criterion is permanently adopted and full legal effect given to it, the step thus taken may have vital consequences to the future of Trade Union functions. The main object of the Emergency Powers Act was to give the Government power to organize alternative services where essential supplies were held up by industrial disputes. The superior resources at the disposal of the Government must in any case make a contest between itself and any industrial group very one-sided, but at least the right of a group to organize a stoppage of work in order to secure its objectives was not denied by that Act. To declare that it is the duty—a duty that will be enforced by the Courts—of workers in public

[1] See, for example, speeches made against the Labour Government's Bill in 1930 in Standing Committee C.

utility services to continue to work, whatever the conditions of labour may be, is a very different proposition, but this is the tendency of the 1927 Act. This measure thus brings into sharp relief the legal aspect of the root problems of State sovereignty discussed in later chapters.

CHAPTER XVII

THE STATUS OF VOLUNTARY ASSOCIATIONS
UP TO 1876

THE legal relationship of Trade Unions to the State is not comprehensively described if we confine ourselves to the law governing freedom of combination and regulating the activities of men and women in association for vocational purposes. As soon as people associate in permanent organizations they constitute groups, the very existence of which creates juridical and political problems for the State, quite apart from their acts as affecting other individuals. Although the two aspects cannot really be separated, the activities of persons in association, and the status and legal rights of the associations themselves, are conveniently discussed as separate problems. Broadly speaking, the former deals with the State's toleration or suppression of individual activities arising out of the pursuit of common aims in associations, while the latter deals with the State's recognition of the purposes of vocational groups and of the place of these groups in society.

The law of voluntary associations—their legal status, their power to own property, their liability in contract or in tort—is even more uncertain than the law of conspiracy and the law dealing with restraint of trade, but, such as it is, it can be described more briefly. Historically, English law has turned a blind eye towards spontaneous groupings of citizens within the State. Thousands of associations have existed, their life springing out of the will of their members to combine for common ends. The State has not suppressed them, but it has not brought them into any organic relationship with itself. At the same time, associations intermediate between the individual citizen and the State have been officially created by formal act of the State and under strict regulation. Organizations of a

voluntary kind, created by no act of the State but by the will
of their individual members, have not been "recognized"—or
only very grudgingly and half-heartedly. The result of this, as
we shall see, has been to make the law quite inadequate, in
some respects, to modern needs. The Continental legal systems,
on the other hand, make provision in their Codes for a
Law of Associations, which governs the status and activities of groups in general. There is practically no such thing in
England, although important organizations like the Church
of England, the London Stock Exchange, the Inns of
Court, and the Trades Union Congress are bodies of this
voluntary kind.

Certain types of voluntary association are, however, recognized and regulated to some extent by statute, so that there
are now three types of organization intermediate between the
individual and the State. These are (*a*) Corporate bodies,
created by act of the State and strictly regulated; (*b*) Quasi-
corporate bodies, or voluntary associations to some extent
regulated by statute; and (*c*) Unincorporated bodies, or
voluntary associations not regulated by special statutes.
Registered Trade Unions are in the class of quasi-corporate
bodies, as are Friendly Societies. Such diverse organizations as
the Bank of England; the Great Western Railway Company;
the Dean and Chapter of St Paul's; Trinity College, Cambridge;
the University of Oxford; the London County Council; and
the General Electric Company, Ltd., are corporate bodies.
The Inner Temple, the Athenaeum Club, and the London
Stock Exchange are examples of unincorporate bodies. Quasi-
corporate associations are in some respects treated as though
they were corporate and in other respects as though they
were unincorporate, but the limits are not at all clearly
defined, certainly so far as unregistered Trade Unions are
concerned.

"Prior to the Act of 1871 a trade union, as such, had no
legal status," said Lord Justice Farwell in the famous Osborne

case;[1] and Lord Halsbury, in an earlier, equally famous case,[2] said that "By the 1871 Act the Legislature has created a thing which can own property, which can employ servants, and which can inflict injury." The Trade Union Act of 1871 clearly marked a turning-point in the history of workers' associations, though it left them with the peculiar and anomalous status that they have retained ever since. Before the 1871 Act, Trade Unions were simply unincorporate bodies, which might be lawful or unlawful at common law. If their purposes were in restraint of trade they were unlawful combinations at common law, but this did not mean that they were criminal in any way or that they had no right to exist. It meant that they had no positive legal rights; the Courts would not enforce agreements or contracts they entered into, and in fact the aid of the law could not be sought for any purpose, apart from any special statutes. They could not own property effectively, even through trustees, for the Courts would not enforce the rights of the associations on the trusts. A society which was lawful at common law would not be in this position, but though some few Trade Unions would come in this category the great majority would not. It should be pointed out that the provident and friendly society purposes of a Trade Union have never been regarded as objects in restraint of trade, and a society that confined itself to such objects would have been regarded before 1871 as a lawful combination whose agreements and contracts would be enforced.

A Trade Union in the full sense of the term, having restrictive objects, could not sue or be sued in its own name, but could only appear in the Courts through all its members.[3] If all the members took action, for example, in defence of their joint

[1] *Osborne* v. *Amal. Soc. of Railway Servants*, [1909] 1 Ch. 163.

[2] *Taff Vale Railway Co.* v. *Amal. Soc. of Railway Servants*, [1901] A.C. 426.

[3] Or through several members suing or being sued on behalf of themselves and all other members, i.e. a "representative action" (under Order 16, Rule 9, of the Supreme Court). But see p. 215.

property (the property of the Union, in the realistic sense but not in the legal sense), they could appeal to the Courts, but the association, as a collective entity, could not. As a practical method this was, as a rule, out of the question. Membership was constantly fluctuating, and it was usually impossible to be certain that all those concerned were included in the action. Moreover, since the property of an unincorporated society was regarded as the joint property of the individual members, the Courts considered that it was impossible for a member to steal such property, since he was only taking what belonged to him jointly with other members. Thus, embezzlement of the funds by an official or member of a Union could take place, and there was no legal remedy. Partnerships and similar unincorporated groups were in the same position.

The Friendly Societies Act[1] of 1855 removed this legal disability as far as Friendly Societies were concerned, and Trade Unions made an attempt to register under this Act so as to get the same protection for their funds. The Courts held, however,[2] that as the objects of a Trade Union having purposes in restraint of trade were unlawful it could not register, since it was not, in the words of the Act, "for any purpose which is not illegal."

Finally, a special Act was passed in 1868, the Larceny and Embezzlement Act,[3] providing that "if any person being a member of any co-partnership, or being one of two or more beneficial owners of any money, goods, or effects, bills, notes, securities, or other property, shall steal or embezzle any such money . . . or other property, of or belonging to any such co-partnership or to such beneficial owners, every such person shall be liable to be dealt with, tried, convicted and punished for the same as if such person had not been or was not a member of such co-partnership or one of such beneficial owners."

[1] 18 & 19 Vict. c. 63.
[2] *Hornby* v. *Close* (1867), 2 Q.B. 153; *Farrer* v. *Close* (1869), 4 Q.B. 602.   [3] 31 & 32 Vict. c. 116.

In the following year a further Act was passed giving a summary remedy in these cases. The Trades Unions Funds Protection Act, 1869,[1] provided that an association having objects in restraint of trade should not on that account be deemed, for the purpose of the Friendly Societies Act, 1855, to be a society having an illegal object, or not to be a Friendly Society. This special protection became unnecessary when the Trade Union Act, 1871, was passed, but until then it gave Unions a remedy in cases where funds were embezzled or stolen.[2] It would appear that these statutes of 1868 and 1869 would not have protected the funds of any Union that the Courts declared to be a criminal conspiracy, since a criminal association would be deemed not to have a good title to its property.

The Trade Union Act of 1871 made sweeping changes in the position of Trade Unions in regard to their status, powers, and liabilities. A Royal Commission had been appointed in 1867 to enquire into the legal position of Trade Unions, and the 1871 measure was largely based upon its Minority Report. In view of the quasi-corporate status created by this Act, it is of interest to cite the appropriate passage from the Minority Report signed by Thomas Hughes and Frederic Harrison.[3]

A very serious question arises here as to whether legislation of a far more comprehensive character is not needed to place trades unions on a full legal footing: whether, in fact, a complete statute should not be enacted, analogous to the provisions of the Friendly Societies Acts and the Joint Stock Companies Acts, and the like, by means of which uniform rules would be framed for the formation, management and dissolution of these associations; and by which they should be enabled to sue and to be sued by their members, to recover from members their contributions or fines, and be made liable to members for the benefits assured. We are inclined to believe

[1] 32 & 33 Vict. c. 61.

[2] The Falsification of Accounts Act, 1875 (38 & 39 Vict. c. 24), and the Larceny Act, 1916 (6 & 7 Geo. V. c. 50), have since provided a better remedy than the 1871 Act.

[3] *Final Report of Royal Commission*, Vol. I, lix (1869).

that the time has not yet come, if it ever comes, for any such statute. . . . We are far from seeing any certainty that such an Act is even ultimately desirable. The Trades unions are essentially clubs and not trading companies, and we think that the degree of regulation possible in the case of the latter is not possible in the case of the former. All questions of crime apart, the objects at which they aim, the rights which they claim, and the liabilities which they incur, are for the most part, it seems to us, such as courts of law should neither enforce, nor modify, nor annul. They should rest entirely on consent. We think the right course is, that they should be left to that spontaneous activity which produced them, and that the State cannot with policy interfere to give them a permanent or systematic character. They differ, however, from clubs in the fact that from their quasi-mercantile character, and the sphere of their operations, they suffer severely from the want of bare legal recognition.

This passage brings out the real difficulty which remains to this day. Trade Unions are by their nature organizations having very mixed yet related objects. They are benevolent societies for their members, and at the same time mercantile bodies acting as labour cartels, "central selling agencies" for the labour of their members. They have business objects and propagandist objects; they belong to no simple type. Hence the difficulty of making them conform to any specific category of associations and the difficulty of framing a satisfactory legal status.

The Act of 1871 followed the course suggested by the Minority Report of the Royal Commission and devised a quasi-corporate status. Unions were given some but not all of the privileges and obligations of incorporated bodies. Section 3 of the Act declared that "The purposes of any trade union shall not, by reason merely that they are in restraint of trade, be unlawful so as to render void or voidable any agreement or trust." In other words, the agreements or trusts of a Trade Union could no longer be declared invalid and unenforceable merely because they were in restraint of trade; but certain agreements were declared to be unenforceable directly by the following section which declared:—

Nothing in this Act shall enable any Court to entertain any legal proceeding instituted with the object of directly enforcing or recovering damages for the breach of any of the following agreements, namely:—

(1) An agreement between members of a trade union, as such, concerning the conditions on which any members for the time being of such trade union shall or shall not sell their goods, transact business, employ or be employed.

(2) Any agreement for the payment by any person of any subscription or penalty to a trade union.

(3) Any agreement for the application of the funds of a trade union:—

(*a*) To provide benefits to members; or
(*b*) To furnish contributions to any employer or workmen not a member of such trade union, in consideration of such employer or workman acting in conformity with the rules or resolutions of such trade union; or
(*c*) To discharge any fine imposed upon any person by sentence of a court of justice; or

(4) Any agreement made between one trade union and another; or

(5) Any bond to secure the performance of any of the above-mentioned agreements.

But nothing in this section shall be deemed to constitute any of the above-mentioned agreements unlawful.

This section must now be read in conjunction with Section 2 of the Trade Disputes and Trade Unions Act, 1927, which provides that a member of a Trade Union refusing to take part or to continue to take part in an illegal strike (as defined in Section 1 of that Act) shall not be prevented by the above provisions of the 1871 Act from being able to claim benefits, etc.; the Courts are allowed to enforce payment in such cases. Otherwise the payment of Trade Union benefits, contributions, fines, etc.; collective agreements between Trade Unions and employers' associations; and rules and agreements inside a Trade Union, in regard to conditions of labour, are legally unenforceable, directly at all events, in the case of Unions that are unlawful at common law, and that therefore depend upon Section 3 of the 1871 Act for the legalization of their other agreements. If a Trade Union were a corporation, all its agreements, provided they were *intra vires*, would be enforceable, including those mentioned in Section 4 quoted above. If a Union is not unlawful at common law, all its agreements are enforceable provided they are within the rules, and are otherwise lawful, but they are enforceable only in the same way as for other unincorporated bodies not Trade Unions, i.e. by a representative action;[1] and this is the case even if the Union is registered.[2] If a Union is unlawful at common law, the enforceability of any of its agreements is due to the 1871 Act, and is subject to the limitations of Section 4, and the Union if registered can sue or be sued in its registered name, as if it were a corporation.

It is to be observed that there is nothing in the 1871 Act, or elsewhere, to prevent the Court from declaring a member of a Union to have been wrongfully expelled, from ordering his reinstatement, or from declaring the meaning of the Union's rules. But the Courts will not, in general, interfere with the internal affairs of an unincorporated body, whether a Trade Union or not.

In order to make it clear that the status of Trade Unions was regulated solely by the 1871 Act, Section 5 prohibited the registration of a Trade Union under the Companies Acts, the Friendly Societies Acts, and the Industrial and Provident Societies Act. The amending Act of 1876 provided that for certain purposes connected with insurance certain sections of the Friendly Societies Acts should apply to Trade Unions, but this did not affect the status of the Unions. The quasi-corporate

---

[1] But the possibilities of representative actions against unregistered Trade Unions and other unincorporated bodies are apparently very limited. *Hardie & Lane* v. *Chilton*, [1928] 1 K.B. 663; *Walker* v. *Sur*, [1914] 2 K.B. 930.

[2] Per Loreburn, L.C., and Lord Atkinson in *Russell* v. *Amal. Soc. of Carp. and Joiners*, [1912] A.C. 421.

status of Trade Unions was conferred by the 1871 Act by means of provisions for the registration of any Union having lawful purposes and coming within the statutory definition of a Trade Union. Such registration is entirely voluntary, and those Unions that are unregistered are more akin to ordinary unincorporated societies, though they are regulated to some extent by the Trade Union Acts. Thus, these Acts confer privileges and duties upon registered Unions that are not possessed by unregistered Unions, but they also give the latter privileges and duties that other unincorporated bodies do not have. The statutory distinctions between registered and un-registered Unions are chiefly in regard to the holding of land, summary remedies against fraud, duties of treasurers, disposal of sums payable at death, power to sue or be sued in the name of the Union, deposit of rules, etc., with the registrar, and exemption from income tax.

Registered Unions must vest their property in trustees, and this is usual in the case of unregistered Unions also, although it is not compulsory, and the trustees have not the legal status that they have where the Union is registered. The trustees of a registered Union may sue or be sued in regard to any property, right, or claim to property of the Union. The details of registration are not particularly relevant to this study, so there is no need to describe the remaining provisions of the 1871 Act, except in regard to the definition of a Trade Union. Until 1871 there was no statutory definition, although the term "Trade Union" was generally understood to mean a voluntary organization having the character both of a Friendly Society and of a trade club to regulate conditions of labour. Section 23 of the Act of 1871 defined a Trade Union as "such combination, whether temporary or permanent, for regulating the relations between workmen and masters, or between workmen and workmen or between masters and masters, or for imposing restrictive conditions on the conduct of any trade or business as would, if this Act had not been passed, have been deemed to have been an unlawful combination by reason of some one or more of its purposes being in restraint of trade." A proviso was added making it clear that this definition did not apply to business partnerships, contracts of employment, or certain business agreements.

This definition clearly excluded combinations lawful at common law. The Trade Union Act (1871) Amendment Act of 1876 accordingly repealed the above definition, except for the proviso, and enacted that a Trade Union was "any combination, whether temporary or permanent, for regulating the relations between workmen and masters, or between workmen and workmen or between masters and masters, or for imposing restrictive measures on the conduct of any trade or business, whether such combination would or would not, if the principal Act[1] had not been passed, have been deemed to have been an unlawful combination by reason of some one or more of its purposes being in restraint of trade." This remained the statutory definition until 1913. The proviso was retained, its purpose being to make it clear that the general law as to restraint of trade was not being changed; certain exceptions were being created in the case of Trade Unions, but that was all.

The net result of this tangled history is that the legislation of 1871 and 1876 gave Trade Unions some status, however haltingly defined. In the Acts of 1824 and 1825, which removed the previous statutory ban on workers' associations, no legal recognition whatever was given to these bodies. As far as the law was concerned they were merely unincorporated societies having purposes that the Courts could not recognize. The practical inconveniences of this position became more and more obvious as Unions grew in power and numbers, and in particular the scandal of there being no remedy against the embezzlement and theft of funds resulted in the passing of special Acts in 1868 and 1869. As a result of the inquiries of

[1] I.e. the 1871 Act.

the Royal Commission on Trade Unions, the Act of 1871 was passed, allowing Unions to register and so acquire legal personality and a quasi-corporate status. The effect of this Act and the amending Act of 1876 was to place Trade Unions in a new and distinct legal category, in which they have ever since remained.

In short, these Acts were understood to leave the position as follows:—

(i) Trade Unions lawful at common law could register, in which case they acquired legal personality and the right to sue or be sued in their own name. If they did not register, they remained unincorporated bodies that could only sue or be sued in a representative action. In either case their agreements were enforceable without exception, but in the case of agreements coming within Section 4 of the Act of 1871 they could only sue or be sued in a representative action.

(ii) Trade Unions unlawful at common law could register, in which case they acquired legal personality and the power to sue or be sued in their own name. If they did not register, they remained unincorporated bodies that could only sue or be sued in a representative action. In either case their agreements and trusts were only directly enforceable provided they did not come within the exceptions in Section 4 of the 1871 Act.

In Scotland, it should be observed, Trade Unions could sue or be sued in their own names, whether registered or unregistered.

Even these general statements of the law as it stood on the passing of the 1876 Act could not be made without some doubts and qualifications.[1] The lack of uniformity and the uncertainty of the position illustrate clearly enough the fact that the State had not thought out its attitude to Trade

[1] E.g. it is doubtful whether at that time unincorporated bodies could be sued in contract or in tort in a representative action. See p. 215.

Unionism. It had no clear idea as to the right relationship between Trade Unionism and the State, no underlying philosophy of the new industrial system and the functions of the important institutions within it. The Trade Union movement was equally devoid of such a philosophy.

CHAPTER XVIII

THE STATUS OF VOLUNTARY ASSOCIATIONS SINCE 1876

THE acquisition of some kind of legal status by Trade Unions under the Act of 1871 was bound sooner or later to raise the question of their collective powers and liabilities in regard to matters not specifically covered by that Act. The more the Unions were treated by the Courts as having full legal personality, the more would limitations applicable to corporations be imposed upon them. For this reason, the question already discussed of power to sue and be sued as a collective entity is no mere matter of procedure, but is an issue vitally affecting the substantive powers of Trade Unions, and even, in certain circumstances, their very existence. The liabilities of an individual in contract or in tort, however great and however strictly enforced, cannot jeopardize the power of the entire organization of which he is a member. If that organization is collectively liable, however, a successful action may deprive it of all its funds and therefore, perhaps, of its existence. Where an association is unincorporated it is regarded by the law as being nothing more than an aggregate of individuals. Where it has acquired some kind of legal personality, and can sue or be sued in its own name, the first step has been taken towards a corporate status that may carry with it very important consequences.

At the time the 1871 Act was passed there was apparently no thought in anyone's mind that the liabilities and limitations of corporations were in future to attach to Trade Unions. The Act expressly refrained from incorporating them, and made it impossible for them to incorporate under the Companies Act.[1]

[1] Sec. 5; but Trade Unions are allowed to become incorporated in certain States in the United States.

It withheld from them powers that corporations would normally have, and it was generally taken for granted that they were not to be regarded for other purposes as corporations. In the forty years that followed, however, there was a definite tendency on the part of the Courts to treat registered Trade Unions, at all events, as though they were corporations. It is sometimes suggested that this was part of a general movement towards greater realism in the development of the common law: that the tendency of the judges was to ask whether an association was *de facto* a corporation, whatever it might be *de jure*. There is a certain amount of truth in this, perhaps, but the development of the doctrine was apparently more a matter of procedure than of legal philosophy, owing its growth to the extension of the sphere of representative actions as a result of the abolition, by the Judicature Act of 1881, of the separation between the Common Law Courts and the Equity Courts.

Collective Liability

Collective liability in criminal cases has, with a few small exceptions, never been recognized by the Courts, and there has been no attempt to bring Unions under the criminal law; it is always individuals who are liable in cases involving criminal acts. Corporations are liable in certain cases where a pecuniary penalty may be inflicted,[1] but unincorporated associations apparently could not be made liable in any event. "The principle that in all criminal proceedings definite legal persons, whether natural or artificial, must be named as defendants is now too well settled to be shaken by any authority short of Parliament."[2]

Liability in tort and liability in contract have had a very

---

[1] E.g. for violation of pure food statutes (*Pearks, etc.* v. *Ward*, [1902] 2 K.B. 1); for violation of law regulating conditions of labour (*U.S.* v. *John Kelso Co.* (1898), 86 Fed. 304). For other cases see Smith, H. A., *Law of Associations*, chap. 5.

[2] Smith, *op. cit.*, 105.

different history. The liability of corporations in tort is decided by the law of agency. The liability of employers, whether natural persons or corporations, for the tortious acts of their agents is well established in English law (though many other legal systems do not recognize this principle), provided the agent concerned is acting within the scope of his employment. Corporations are commonly sued for all kinds of torts for which an individual could be sued. When we come to unincorporated bodies there is more difficulty. In the case of registered Trade Unions liability was affirmed by the Courts in the Taff Vale decision[1] but was definitely ruled out later, for both registered and unregistered Unions, by the Trade Disputes Act, 1906,[2] only to have this immunity removed, in the case of illegal strikes, by the Trade Disputes and Trade Unions Act, 1927.[3]

The history of this attempt to attach corporate liabilities to Trade Unions, in cases of tort, will be recounted in some detail. It seems doubtful whether other unincorporated bodies can be sued in tort by means of a representative action, as it will be practically impossible to prove authorization by all the members.[4]

Liability in contract is also very different as between corporate and unincorporated bodies. The chief development since 1876 has been in connection with contracts that were held to be *ultra vires* a Trade Union, and here we come to the subtle but very real distinction between associations created by the State and those arising independently of the State.

Corporations created under the old common law prerogative of the Crown may "enter into all those contracts which are lawful to a natural man, except a small number of strictly personal obligations, such as marriage, which are obviously impossible to aggregate bodies. If in a particular case any restrictions exist, they must be found, either expressly or by

---

[1] *Taff Vale Rly. Co.* v. *A.S.R.S.*, [1901] A.C. 426.
[2] 6 Edw. VII. c. 47.   [3] 17 & 18 Geo. V. c. 22.
[4] See discussion in Sophian, T. J., *Trade Union Law and Practice*, 307.

implication, in the enabling charter."[1] Corporations that owe their origin to an Act of Parliament, however (and the vast majority of corporate bodies fall into this class, e.g. joint stock companies), must not enter into contracts that are not expressly or by necessary implication contained in the Act[2] (or in the Memorandum of Association in the case of companies incorporated under the Companies Acts). The doctrine of *ultra vires* has been applied also to unincorporated bodies, but in these cases the rules of the association determine whether the action or contract is or is not *ultra vires*. There is no general enabling statute to set limits to the activities of such associations. The Articles of Association of a joint stock company may be altered by the shareholders, so changing the terms of the contract they have established between themselves, but the company must not in any event stray outside the limits set by the Memorandum of Association; this represents the framework prescribed by the State and can only be altered by permission of the Courts. The rules of an unincorporated society constitute a series of contracts between the individual members, and they can be altered, under whatever procedure is laid down by the rules themselves, without limitations or restrictions. This applied perhaps to an unregistered Trade Union also, but what about a registered Union? Was it to be regarded as occupying the position of a purely voluntary body or of an association that, like a corporation, worked under an enabling—and limiting—statute? On this issue has taken place another of the important legal and political struggles of the period since 1876, and this story will also be recounted in some detail.

Corporate Liability in Tort

At the time the Act of 1871 was passed there was seemingly no idea in anyone's mind that registered Trade Unions were

[1] Smith, H. A., *op. cit.*, 29.
[2] *Ashbury Rly. Carr. Co.* v. *Riche* (1875), 7 H.L. 653.

being given a corporate status except to the extent made obvious in that enactment. The liability of voluntary associations in tort was at that time quite undefined, and certainly no one thought of saddling Trade Unions, even registered Unions, with the same liabilities, in this respect, as corporations. To apply the ordinary law of agency to bodies with the peculiar mixture of functions and the comparatively loose organization of Trade Unions would in any case be a matter of the utmost difficulty, necessitating a complete recasting of Trade Union machinery and constitutions. In 1901, however, the Courts decided that the Amalgamated Society of Railway Servants, a registered Union, was liable for tortious acts committed during a dispute with the Taff Vale Railway Company by officials of the Union, acting within the scope of their employment.[1] This decision of the Court of first instance was reversed by the Appeal Court, but was restored by the House of Lords, and the Union had to pay heavy damages. The Law Lords held that the statutes which conferred certain privileges on registered Unions thereby implied the corresponding obligations. In fact, two rather different points of view were apparent among the judges who decided against the Union. Mr. Justice Farwell in the Court of first instance took the view that the fact of registration implied a certain legal status and the liability to be sued, and the Law Lords agreed with this reading of the Acts of 1871 and 1876 (though the Master of the Rolls took the opposite view in the Appeal Court).

The attitude thus taken up was briefly that by allowing registration a procedure had been created whereby an action which ought to be possible had been made possible, an entity had been created which could be named as defendant. According to this reading, an unregistered Union would not be suable in tort since it was not an entity having a legal existence. Several of the Law Lords went farther, however, and expressed the opinion that unregistered Unions would be suable also, not

[1] *Taff Vale Rly. Co.* v. *A.S.R.S.,* [1901] A.C. 426.

merely because a procedure had been provided by which they could be made defendants but on the more general ground that a body acting like a corporation must be held to incur the corresponding liabilities. Lord MacNaughten said, for instance,[1] "Has the legislature authorized the creation of numerous bodies of men capable of owning great wealth and of acting by agents, with absolutely no responsibility for the wrongs they may do to other persons by the use of that wealth and the employment of those agents? . . . If trade unions are not above the law, how are these bodies to be sued? I have no doubt whatever that a trade union, whether registered or unregistered, could be sued in a representative action. . . ." This view rests on a wider conception of the issue, since it brings under the same rule all bodies acting like corporations, whether they are in fact incorporated or not.[2] There is little doubt that the Parliament which passed the Act of 1871 had no such intention in mind, but deliberately stopped short of conferring full corporate privileges and liabilities.

The Royal Commission appointed as a result of the Trade Union agitation following the Taff Vale judgment gave a quite different interpretation of the previous immunity of the Unions,[3] linking it up with procedural difficulties alone. Until the Judicature Act of 1881 the Common Law Courts and the Equity Courts were still separate and distinct (as they are to this day in the United States). The device of the representative action was an invention of the Courts of Equity, going back to Lord Hardwicke's time in the eighteenth century, and was not recognized in the Common Law Courts, which firmly refused to find against defendants not named. Actions in tort were for the Common Law Courts, and representative actions in tort were therefore impossible. In 1881 the Common Law

[1] [1901] A.C. 426.
[2] The same view has been taken in the United States. *United Mine Workers* v. *Coronado Coal Co.* (1922), 259 U.S. 344.
[3] Report of Royal Commission on Trade Combinations, etc., 1906. Cd. 2825.

Courts and Chancery Courts were made divisions of the High
Court, and Rules of Court regarding parties to sue and be sued
thenceforth applied equally to both divisions. Thus, representative actions became possible in cases in either division.[1]
But the Appeal Court in *Temperton* v. *Russell*[2] decided that
the Order permitting representative actions did not apply to
a Trade Union because the parties must have or claim to have
a "beneficial proprietary right" in common, which they were
asserting or defending, and this was not the case with members
of a Trade Union. On the strength of this decision it was
thereafter believed that a Trade Union could not be sued in
a representative action in tort, and the Royal Commission on
Labour, 1894, accepted this view. In 1901 the decision in
Temperton v. *Russell* was overruled by the House of Lords in
Duke of Bedford v. *Ellis*,[3] not a Trade Union case, and thereafter
Order 16, Rule 9, was held to be universally applicable.

The Taff Vale case in the same year decided that a
registered Trade Union could be sued in tort, in its registered
name, and several of the Law Lords, as already mentioned,
held that any Union, registered or unregistered, could be sued
in tort in a representative action. The Royal Commission of
1906 (including Mr. Sidney Webb) were of opinion that the
principle of the Taff Vale decision ought to be adhered to
without alteration. They said:—[4]

Trade Unions, which originally were looked upon as illegal
combinations, have made out their claim to enfranchisement and
existence. But having done so they cannot put their claims higher
than to say that they are institutions which are beneficial to the
community as a whole. But so are many other institutions—banks,
railways, insurance companies, and so on. It may have been right
to provide, as has been done, that the Courts shall not have power
directly to enforce agreements between Trade Unions and their
members in the same manner as they can in the case of shareholders
and policy holders in the institutions above mentioned. But when

---

[1] Order 16, Rule 9, of the Supreme Court (1883).
[2] [1893] 1 Q.B. 715.   [3] [1901] A.C. 10.   [4] *Report*, p. 8.

Trade Unions come in contact by reason of their own actions with outsiders, and *ex hypothesi*, wrong those outsiders, there can be no more reason that they should be beyond the reach of the law than any other individual, partnership or institution. Such a claim has indeed in former times been made by the spiritual as against the civil authority, and has been consistently disallowed. What was denied to religion ought not in our judgment to be conceded to Trade Unionism.

The significance of this statement from the wider point of view with which this work is concerned will be obvious.

The Royal Commission recommended the "facultative separation of the proper benefit funds of Trade Unions, such separation, if effected, to carry immunity from the funds being taken in execution," and that means should be provided "whereby the central authorities of a Union may protect themselves against the unauthorized and immediately disavowed acts of branch agents." Logically enough, they further advised that means should be provided whereby Trade Unions could either become incorporated or at any rate be given the power to make enforceable agreements of the kinds coming within the range for which direct enforcement was made impossible by Section 4 of the 1871 Act.

In the event, the recommendations of the Royal Commission were not followed, and the Trade Disputes Act of 1906[1] gave the Trade Unions what they wanted—the statutory affirmation of the position believed by everyone to exist prior to the Taff Vale judgment. Section 4(1) of the 1906 Act declared:—

An action against a trade union, whether of workmen or masters, or against any members or officials thereof on behalf of themselves and all other members of the trade union in respect of any tortious act alleged to have been committed by or on behalf of the trade union, shall not be entertained by any court.

The second part of the section ran as follows:—

Nothing in this section shall affect the liability of the trustees of a trade union to be sued in the events provided for by the Trades

[1] 6 Edw. VII. c. 47.

Union Act, 1871, section nine, except in respect of any tortious act committed by or on behalf of the Union in contemplation or in furtherance of a trade dispute.

The exact meaning of this latter subsection is obscure,[1] but some authorities[2] hold that the trustees of a registered Union can still be sued for damages in respect of tortious acts committed by the Union's agents, provided such acts are not in contemplation or furtherance of a trade dispute, in which case immunity is complete. Since the liabilities of trustees of an unregistered Union are not defined by statute, they cannot be sued under this subsection, and registered Unions are thus placed in a less advantageous position in this respect. The immunity from actions in tort, either by means of representative actions or in any other way, that was conferred on Trade Unions by this section, was bitterly attacked by some jurists and by many opponents of Trade Unionism. Dicey, for example, said:[3] "This enactment therefore confers upon a trade union a freedom from civil liability for the commission of even the most heinous wrong by the union or its servants, and in short confers upon every trade union a privilege and protection not possessed by any other person or body of persons, whether corporate or unincorporate, throughout the United Kingdom." Sir E. Carson, in the discussion on the clause as the measure was passing through Parliament, said that such a proposal was without precedent in the history of English law. The Royal Commission, he continued, had declared that this policy was opposed to the very idea of law, order, and justice.[4]

The provision thus criticized has remained substantially unimpaired to the present day, and there has been little

[1] Per Lord MacNaghten and Lord Moulton in *Vacher* v. *London Compositors*, [1913] A.C. 107.

[2] Per Lord Haldane and Lord Atkinson in Vacher's case.

[3] Dicey, A. V., *Law and Opinion*, 2nd ed., Intro. xlv.

[4] *Parl. Deb.*, August 3, 1906, 1729 ff.

complaint of its being used irresponsibly.[1] The only limitation since has been that imposed by the Trade Disputes and Trade Unions Act, 1927,[2] Section 1(4) of which enacts that "The provisions of the Trade Disputes Act, 1906, shall not . . . apply to any act done in contemplation or furtherance of a strike or lock-out which is by this Act declared to be illegal. . . ." This means that in the case of an illegal strike or lock-out (as defined by the 1927 Act) a Trade Union will not be able to claim immunity under the 1906 Act from an action in respect of torts alleged to have been committed by or on behalf of the Union. As far as a registered Union is concerned the principle of the Taff Vale judgment will presumably apply, and the Union funds will be liable. How will an unregistered Union be affected? The 1927 Act does not establish any liability; it merely removes the immunity conferred by the 1906 Act, and an unregistered Union will apparently come under the decisions in *Mercantile Marine Service Assn.* v. *Toms*[3] and *Hardie & Lane* v. *Chilton*[4] and will not be suable in a representative action. Since it cannot be sued in its own name, an unregistered Union apparently retains immunity from actions in tort even where Section 1(4) of the 1927 Act removes the protection of the 1906 Act. The odd position results that in this respect also it is a positive disadvantage for a Trade Union to become registered.

Trade Unions and Contracts

With certain exceptions set out in Section 4 of the 1871 Act, contracts and trusts entered into by Trade Unions unlawful at common law were validated and made enforceable by Section 3 of that Act, and Section 8 provided for the appoint-

---

[1] A Bill similar to the 1906 Act was proposed by Massachusetts in 1912 but the Supreme Court of the State held in advance that it would be unconstitutional. 98 N.E. 337.

[2] 17 & 18 Geo. V. c. 22.

[3] [1916] 2 K.B. 243.   [4] [1927] 43 T.L.R. 709.

ment of trustees, in the case of a registered Union, who should be suable in any action concerning the property or claims to property of the Union. A registered Union may sue or be sued in its own name or through its trustees in such cases, but an unregistered Union cannot be sued in its own name, and its trustees (if it has any) have not the legal standing of the trustees of a registered Union. Thus the only possible way of suing an unregistered Union, on a contract, would be in a representative action, but recent cases[1] appear to have decided that this avenue also is barred against actions for damages, so that it would seem that an unregistered Union cannot now be sued for damages in contract at all.

Issues of another kind are raised if the "internal" contracts of an association—the contracts made by the members among themselves—are considered. When persons make lawful agreements among themselves, and the rules of an association are no more than a series of such agreements, any of those persons may take action in case of breach of agreement. In the case of Trade Unions certain "internal" agreements are made unenforceable by Section 4 of the 1871 Act, but otherwise any contracts thus made between the members are enforceable.[2] On the other hand, agreements and activities not expressly or impliedly authorized by the rules (or by resolution passed in accordance with procedure laid down in the rules and having equivalent authority) may infringe upon a member's rights and be legally forbidden. For instance, if the rules of a Union do not allow of the funds being used to give financial help to another Union, any member may object to funds being so used and may obtain an injunction to prevent such action being taken. Again, a member who is expelled otherwise than in accordance with the rules may ask the Courts to restrain the

[1] *Hardie and Lane* v. *Chilton,* [1927] 43 T.L.R. 709; *Walker* v. *Sur,* [1914] 2 K.B. 930.

[2] But a member of a voluntary unincorporated association cannot obtain damages against the association for such a breach of contract.

Union from acting upon the expulsion.[1] These considerations apply to all associations. Thus, the committee of the Oxford and Cambridge Club proposed to raise the subscription, although the rules made no provision for this to be done. Despite the fact that the change was sanctioned by a general meeting of the club, one of the members succeeded in obtaining an injunction restraining the committee from expelling him for refusal to pay the increased subscription.[2]

In the case of a company, similarly, the Articles of Association for the time being in force constitute a series of contracts between the shareholders. An association such as a company which is incorporated is, however, subject as a whole to limitations and restrictions as to the agreements it may make and the activities it may pursue. The Courts take the view that the State, in granting incorporation, has created a body for certain purposes, and for those purposes only; it has not created an independent entity with a free hand to do anything and everything. The purposes for which the corporation is created are set out in the Charter or Act or (for joint stock companies) in the Memorandum of Association. The corporate body may not stray outside the limits thus laid down, and this limitation is not at all a matter of contract between the members or shareholders but is imposed upon the entire body by the State. Thus, a company formed to build rolling stock may not contract to build a railway.[3] In practice the Memorandum of Association of a joint stock company may be drafted so as to cover as wide a variety of objects as the promoters please; so much so that North, J., said of one case that the Memorandum was "so wide that it might be said to warrant the company in giving up banking business and embarking in business with the object of establishing a line of balloons between the earth and the moon."[4]

---

[1] E.g. *Braithwaite* v. *Amal. Soc. of Carpenters*, [1922] 2 A.C. 440.
[2] *Harrington* v. *Sendall*, [1903] 1 Ch. 92.
[3] *Ashbury Railway Carriage Co.* v. *Riché* (1875), L.R. 7 H.L. 653.
[4] Re *Crown Bank* (1890), 44 Ch.D. 641.

A corporate body is restricted by its enabling Act, then, and any action outside the limits laid down will be forbidden as *ultra vires*. This doctrine only applies to unincorporated bodies in the sense that an agreement or act may be *ultra vires* the rules; in other words, an agreement or act not authorized expressly or by implication by the rules, or in some other way recognized by the rules as binding upon the association, will be *ultra vires* simply because it is not part of a contract between the individual members.[1] An unincorporated association does not owe its existence to the State, and does not derive its powers from an enabling Act, and there is thus no restriction on its power, by agreement of its members, to make any contract or do any act otherwise lawful.

What was the position of a registered Union, with its quasi-corporate status? Was it subject to the doctrine of *ultra vires* as applied to corporations, or was it as free as a completely unincorporated body? The Courts decided in the Osborne case[2] that the limitations imposed upon corporate bodies were applicable to registered Trade Unions and that the Trade Union Acts were to be regarded as defining and delimiting the purposes of a Trade Union. The 1871 Act for the first time gave a legal definition of a Trade Union, Section 23 declaring that "The term 'trade union' means such combination, whether temporary or permanent, for regulating the relations between workmen and masters, or between workmen and workmen, or between masters and masters, or for imposing restrictive conditions on the conduct of any trade or business *as would, if this Act had not been passed,* have been deemed to have been an unlawful combination by reason of some one or more of its purposes being in restraint of trade." The latter part of this definition would exclude Unions lawful at common law, and therefore this undesirable restriction was removed by the 1876 Act, Section 16 of which repeated the above definition

[1] This applies also to a corporation, of course.
[2] *A.S.R.S.* v. *Osborne*, [1910] A.C. 87.

amended to read "whether such combination would or would not, if the principal Act had not been passed" instead of the words italicized.

The Osborne judgment regarded this definition as being equivalent to the Memorandum of Association of a joint stock company in the sense that it was a limiting definition. It was not merely a definition for the purpose of describing what was meant by a Trade Union; it set out, according to the Courts, the things Trade Unions might do, and by implication it forbade them to do anything outside the defined objects. Some of the judges implied that this consideration applied only to a registered Union. Lord MacNaghten said:[1] "This principle is not confined to corporations created by special Acts of Parliament. It applies, I think, with equal force in every case where a society formed for purposes recognized and defined by an Act of Parliament places itself under the Act, and by so doing obtains some statutory immunity or privilege." On the other hand, Lord Halsbury held that the judgment would apply equally to an unregistered Union. The Osborne case did not decide this issue, but in a case in the same year Vice-Chancellor Leigh Clare, in the Lancaster Chancery Court, applied the *ultra vires* principle to an unregistered Union, while in the following year Lord Skerrington expressed the view that the doctrine did not apply to an unregistered Union.[2] Like the similar division of opinion in the Taff Vale case, this issue really depends upon one's views as to the real nature of a voluntary association. Is it, whether unincorporated or quasi-corporate, a mechanical creation, a convenient legal category, or is it a living flexible body? Those Law Lords who held that an unincorporated association must be held liable for the torts of its agents may have ignored the practical difficulties, but they did view such a body as being something that could exist

[1] [1910] A.C. at p. 94.
[2] *Wilson* v. *Scottish Typographical Assn.*, [1911] 1 S.L.T. 253. Prof. Geldart held Lord Skerrington's view (see 25 H.L.R. 600).

and act as an entity. If this view is accepted, however, it is a step backward, not forward, to say that such a body must be bound and restricted by the application of the *ultra vires* doctrine as laid down in the Osborne judgment. Lord Shaw expressed this in the words,[1] "I have some hesitation in so construing language of statutory recognition as a definition imposing such hard-and-fast restrictive limits as would cramp the development and energies and destroy the natural movements of the living organism."

Professor Geldart has urged that while the Taff Vale judgment was in accordance with the growing recognition by the Courts of the independent origin and vitality of organized groups in the State, the Osborne judgment was a denial of that principle. "A trade union," he said, "is neither one of the organs of the State nor is it a body whose aims are limited to the promotion of the pecuniary and individual interests of its members. . . . In these circumstances we shall see something inappropriate in a policy which would narrowly define for the future what shall and what shall not be the lawful purposes that a trade union may pursue."[2] The Osborne judgment was, in fact, a reversal of principles accepted not merely by the Unions and the public but by the Courts themselves, for in 1907 it had been held that the statutory definition of a Trade Union was not exhaustive and did not prevent a Union from pursuing other objects, provided they were lawful. Moreover, the precise power questioned and held *ultra vires* in the Osborne case, namely, the provision of a fund to provide Parliamentary representation, was held in the earlier case to be within the scope of a Trade Union provided it was authorized by the rules.[3]

As a result, the Trade Union Act, 1913,[4] was passed,

---

[1] [1910] A.C. at pp. 107–8.
[2] Geldart, W. M., *The Osborne Judgment and After* (1913), 21.
[3] *Steele* v. *S. Wales Miners' Fedn.*, [1907] 1 K.B. 361.
[4] 2 & 3 Geo. V. c. 30.

reversing to a considerable extent, though not completely, the principle laid down in the Osborne judgment. As regards the specific question of political action full freedom was not given, but Unions were empowered under certain conditions to expend funds on the furtherance of candidatures, the holding of political meetings, the distribution of political literature, the maintenance of Members of Parliament, and other specified political objects, there being no restriction on the expenditure of funds on political objects not mentioned. The conditions were that the furtherance of the specified political objects must be approved as an object of the Union by a ballot vote of the membership taken in accordance with the Act; that rules, to be approved by the Registrar, must provide for payments to be made for these objects out of a separate "political fund," from payment to which any member of the Union could claim exemption; and that no member claiming exemption must be placed in any way at a disadvantage (except in relation to the control of the political fund) as compared with other members, nor must contribution to the political fund be made a condition of admission to the Union. The provision as to members claiming exemption is termed "contracting-out," and the Trade Disputes and Trade Unions Act, 1927,[1] changed this procedure to "contracting-in"; i.e. since the 1927 Act was passed members of Unions having political funds must sign a statement of their willingness to contribute, if they are so willing, and the onus is no longer on those who object to claim exemption.

Although this question of political action has aroused much controversy, the other provisions of the 1913 Act are really more important, and thes: have remained unaffected by the 1927 Act. The attitude taken by the Courts in the Osborne case meant that not merely political action but all other activities not included in the statutory definition of the objects of a Trade Union were *ultra vires*, including the publishing of a newspaper, for example. Section 1 of the 1913 Act declared

[1] 17 & 18 Geo. V. c. 22.

P

that a Trade Union might have other objects than the statutory objects and that, subject to the special conditions attaching to political activities mentioned above, the funds of a Trade Union might be spent on "any lawful objects or purposes for the time being authorized under its constitution." This freed Trade Unions completely from the application of the *ultra vires* doctrine as it applies to corporations, the only exception being that relating to political action, where special conditions obtain. At the same time the statutory definition of a Trade Union was revised, and since 1913 the term "Trade Union" has meant, legally, "any combination, whether temporary or permanent, the principal objects of which are under its constitution statutory objects."[1] Statutory objects are defined as[2] "the regulation of the relations between workmen and masters, or between workmen and workmen, or between masters and masters, or the imposing of restrictive conditions on the conduct of any trade or business, and also the provision of benefits to members." Since 1913, in fact, a Union may expend the greater part of its funds and devote the major part of its activity to the furtherance of other than statutory objects, provided its principal objects as set out in its rules are statutory objects.

The Acts of 1906 and 1913 placed Trade Unions in a position of greater freedom from the jurisdiction of the Courts, and while imposing restrictions in regard to political activities left the Unions in a very independent position, which recent judicial decisions have extended rather than contracted. The Act of 1927 did not affect the status of Unions except in connection with illegal strikes. These developments, it is clear, have been without plan. They have not conformed to any positive theory of the place of Trade Unions in the modern State. They have been of a negative character.

There have been some positive advances of a fragmentary kind, however, embodied in legislation affecting specific

[1] Sec. 2(1).   [2] Sec. 2(2).

industries or new functions of the State. Legislative provisions for Trade Union representation on executive or administrative boards set up under statute are, at least, an indication of such a positive attitude. A member of the committee that administers the statutory Miners' Welfare Fund must be appointed "after consultation with the Miners' Federation of Great Britain,"[1] and similarly two members of the National Committee of Investigation and one member of each District Committee of Investigation under the Coal Mines Act, 1930,[2] must be "appointed to represent workers employed in or about such coal mines," such bodies being first consulted as appear to the Board of Trade "to represent that interest." The Coal Mines National Industrial Board established by the latter Act to settle wages disputes, etc., must have six members appointed after consultation with the Miners' Federation of Great Britain and one after consultation with the General Council of the Trades Union Congress.[3] Twelve members of the general panel for appointment to the Railway Rates Tribunal must be appointed after consultation with such bodies as are considered "most representative of the interests of labour and of passengers upon the railways,"[4] while the Railway National Wages Board must include six representatives of railway employees, two being chosen by each of the three railway Trade Unions, and a further member must be nominated by the General Council of the Trades Union Congress.[5]

Certain members of the Port of London Authority must be appointed after consultation with "such organizations representative of labour" as are thought "best qualified to advise" upon the matter.[6] An "association of employed persons" may be brought into the administration of the State Unemployment

[1] Mining Industry Act, 1920, 10 & 11 Geo. V. c. 50, sec. 20.
[2] 20 & 21 Geo. V. c. 34, sec. 5.   [3] *Ibid.*, sec. 15.
[4] Railways Act, 1921, 11 & 12 Geo. V. c. 55, sec. 24.
[5] *Ibid.*, sec. 64.
[6] Port of London Act, 1908, 8 Edw. VII. c. 68, sec. 1.

Insurance system.[1] There are other provisions of a similar
kind which show, in a casual and piecemeal fashion, to be sure,
some progress towards a clearer conception of Trade Unions
as public institutions having positive functions within the State.
This tendency has gone much farther in actual practice than
is recognized in law, as will be evident from the survey of
modern Trade Union activities given in an earlier chapter.[2]
In some countries where Unions are really less powerful than
they are in Great Britain, legal acceptance of their character
as public institutions has been much more pronounced. They
have the right in Germany, Poland, and Brazil, for instance,
to defend the interests of their trade as a whole, and in France,
Italy, and Russia they have the sole right to do so; in these
cases they are accepted as being representative of their respective
industries and so as institutions having to some extent at least
a public character. A faint approach to this conception in
Great Britain may perhaps be seen in a recent case in which
a duty to a profession was held to justify an Actors' Trade
Union in procuring a breach of contract.[3] Even in the United
States the Trade Union label is protected by statute in some
States;[4] but in general, although the American Courts have
tended to treat Trade Unions as corporations, whether incorporated or not,[5] the public character and standing of Unions
has been denied by the Supreme Court.[6]

During the past fifty years of rapid change and development
in industrial organization, and in the power of Trade Unionism,
there has been no concurrent progress in either statute law or
case law, as affecting the Unions, which is at all adequate to
the position they now occupy. Parliament has freed them from
restrictions imposed by the Courts, but has not created any
positive system in which they can function constructively.

[1] Unemployment Insurance Act, 1920, 10 & 11 Geo. V. c. 30, sec. 17.
[2] See p. 135.   [3] *Brimelow* v. *Casson*, [1924] 1 Ch. 302.
[4] E.g. New York, Illinois, Missouri.
[5] Coronado case (1922), 259 U.S. 344.
[6] *Coppage* v. *Kansas* (1915), 236 U.S. 1.

IV

THE THEORY OF GROUPS
IN RELATION TO THE STATE

CHAPTER XIX

THE APPROACH TO THE PROBLEM

THE conflicts and problems described in earlier chapters constitute such a grave challenge to the stability of modern communities as to necessitate a re-examination of the bases of political organization, so far as concerns the position of groups like Trade Unions in relation to the State. In such an investigation much depends on the angle from which the approach is made. The classical theories of politics took as their starting-point the formulation of the conditions necessary to the realization of the "good life"; or, rather, they first had to give some kind of definition of the "good life," and from that proceed to work out the type of political mechanism that would encourage the growth of the necessary conditions. Their State was therefore an ideal, not an actual, State. Every definition, being conceived in relation to ideals, was largely of an abstract character. The theories themselves were not merely out of touch with reality, but were frequently pushed to such extremes of metaphysical subtlety as to suggest a logical exercise rather than an attempt to discover helpful principles of social organization. Further, there was a natural tendency to regard the ideal State as actually existent in the State of to-day. The movement of reaction against the classical method would, in its extreme form, banish the ethical factor from political theory and make politics a positive science. The expert would say to the statesman, "Tell me what kind of end you wish to achieve and I will tell you what kind of political structure you need to build to obtain the desired result with the utmost efficiency and economy." Political science would become "social engineering," the designing of machinery (and its construction) to give certain specified results.[1] This is a very

[1] See Catlin, G. E. G., *The Science and Method of Politics* (1927) for this view. Also Florence, P. S., *The Statistical Method in Economics* (1929).

attractive idea, for it seems to hold out the prospect of establishing the vague and fluctuating doctrines of political theory on the sure and substantial foundations of a science, in which data are measurable and events predictable. It enables us to relegate the ethical and therefore indeterminate elements to a separate sphere called political philosophy, a changing unresting sea of speculation in which the idealists may disport themselves while their more practical colleagues remain on the solid earth of ascertained facts.

In truth, the task is not so simple, for the social engineer's materials are not steel and stone but the bodies and minds of human beings, about whom we as yet know very little. The very "arrangement" of the materials often changes the entire problem and produces a set of new ones, owing to the reactions and interactions thus set up. The "materials" are alive and insist on arranging themselves to quite a considerable extent; in fact, the ends cannot possibly be divorced from the materials, where human beings are concerned, for they *are* the ends. At least, that is the essence of the democratic philosophy. On any other hypothesis Sir H. Campbell-Bannerman's saying, "Self-government is better than good government," would be grotesquely untrue. So we are plunged immediately into the very heart of controversy over final ends. Nevertheless, the more modern method is fundamentally sound, even though the classical theories realized the impossibility of any complete separation between ends and means, for it places the emphasis on the existing facts of political and social life rather than on concepts which are unrelated to real conditions. We cannot merely investigate "facts" and expect them to lead us somewhere of their own accord. There are no such things as "facts in general"; argument, like art, is a process of selection, and we have to select with reference to some broad aim. But we can and should, on the other hand, formulate our aims in relation to our own experience of the world, and not create them in the void. Our knowledge of human beings and of the world of nature should, and indeed must, if our reasoning is to be fruitful, determine and control the ends we pursue. This is only another way of saying that every objective must be related in some way to the actual situation it is intended to supersede.

Such a view leads to two further considerations in method. In the first place, we shall attach great importance to the institutional pattern that has evolved for the expression of social forces and desires. It is largely because of, as well as through, institutions that the continuity underlying social change shows itself. In the second place, we shall tend to judge what an institution *is* by what it *does*. We live in a society which is not only highly complex but which is essentially dynamic in character. "Whirl is king, having driven out Zeus," said Pythagoras, but no community of ancient times knew the kaleidoscopic changes which are a commonplace to-day. Institutions remain the same in name, but their nature, as expressed in what they do, is constantly changing. To attach importance to labels inevitably results in confusion, because we thereby tend to think of the institutions themselves in terms that are already obsolete. When we analyse them we find that the only reality they possess is the way in which they act; abstract that and nothing is left, certainly nothing that is significant to our purpose. Thus, taking this behaviourist view, we shall not regard the State as an ideal, "a fellowship of men aiming at the enrichment of the common life."[1] The conception of such fellowship may indeed be a potent factor in the building up of social relations, but from our point of view the State *is* what the State *does*. We should therefore agree with Professor Laski that "a theory of the State . . . is essentially a theory of the governmental act,"[2] and again "a working theory of the State must in fact be conceived in administrative terms."[3] The same authority tells us later that

[1] Laski, H. J., *A Grammar of Politics*, 37.
[2] *Ibid.*, 28.   [3] *Ibid.*, 35.

"we must differentiate sharply between State and government. To define the function of the State is not to define the powers of government; it is to define only the purpose it is the end of government to secure."[1] To be sure, State and Government are not synonymous terms, any more than in a limited liability company the "company" is the board of directors. The State is an association, and the Government may be regarded as its agent. We are thus justified in defining the State in terms of Governmental action. "The State is, for the purposes of practical administration, the government," says Professor Laski,[2] and, we may add, for the purposes of political theory the only difference is that we may regard the State as the "principal," a somewhat intangible one, to be sure; the Government, consisting of individual men and women, being the instrument and agent. We need not look beyond what Government, in the widest sense, does to find out what the State at any given time is. In so far as the Government, in actual practice, reconciles and adjusts conflicting claims in the community we shall say that the State is the mechanism which functions as the supreme co-ordinating authority. In so far as the Government controls and ensures the operation of transport services, electricity supply, and such matters, we shall say with Duguit that the State is a public service corporation.[3]

We shall apply the same tests to other institutions, and notably to Trade Unions, and while this attitude is at variance with the classical method of political theory it is at least realistic in that it focuses attention on what is actually happening in the world with which we are dealing, and it accords with the modern tendency of jurisprudence to attach more weight to behaviour than to formal categories. Viewed in this general way, what is the central problem in political theory that we have to face in this study? Conflicts of a grave, sometimes

[1] Laski, H. J., *A Grammar of Politics*, 70   [2] *Ibid.*, 131.
[3] Duguit, L., *Law in the Modern State* (Trans. by F. and H. Laski) (1919).

violent, character are found on an increasing scale in modern industrial societies. Organized groups of workers—Trade Unions—stop work, and thereby paralyse both industry and the public services, in defiance of the State's prohibition of such action, a prohibition usually backed up by the forces of coercion the State is able to exercise through the judiciary and police, and even in some cases with the aid of the military power. This action of the Trade Unions is construed as a challenge to the position and authority of the State, and therefore as a blow dealt at the very foundations of society. Why is a challenge to the supreme status and authority of the State especially heinous? Why, for instance, is the action of the State not spoken of as a challenge to the position and authority of the Trade Unions? Because, we are told, the State is sovereign, and sovereignty has been concisely defined as "the legal competence to issue orders without a need to refer to a higher authority. The orders so issued constitute law, and are binding upon all who come within their jurisdiction."[1] If, then, the policy and actions of any individual citizen or organization come into conflict with the policy of the State as laid down in the laws of the land, the will of the State must prevail, for its orders are supreme and unchallengeable. This is so, according to classical theory, as of right, and because society cannot be organized on any other basis. The State not only *is* obeyed because it can enforce obedience, but it ought to be obeyed because it is the highest embodiment of political wisdom.

We shall have to examine this thesis, and assess its validity, for if it is correct the attitude and actions of the organized workers, in the conflicts previously described, must be characterized as profoundly mistaken if not indeed criminal; we shall have to condemn them as subversive of the very foundations of society and productive of the most harmful

[1] Laski, H. J., "Law and the State," *Economica*, November 1929, 267.

consequences to mankind, if the sovereignty of the State is such an inviolable principle and a political reality which must at all costs be maintained. On this view a group, such as a Trade Union, can have no valid claims as against the State, and the problem of resolving the discord that has arisen becomes merely a question of the technique of relegating the unruly member to its rightful place of subordination within the State. This immediately raises the issue of actual power. Can such a technique be devised, even if it ought theoretically to be possible? There have been many instances in which the State has successfully asserted its supremacy, but there have been others—the South Wales Miners' strike in 1915, the French Postal strike in 1908, and the Norwegian general strike in 1916, for instance—where the attempt has failed and "sovereignty" has in actual fact broken down. Such breakdowns force us to re-examine the basis of the entire doctrine of State sovereignty and the foundations of the State itself. That has been the preoccupation of political theory for the past half century, and it is naturally impossible, within the limits of this work, to do more than touch briefly on the results of the inquiry as far as they affect the problem under discussion.

The State, as custodian of final authority in the idealist theory, and proving so sufficiently often in practice, has been fiercely attacked from many angles. Communism has held, since the time of Marx, that the State is merely the instrument of class domination, and that, following the Revolution, the Dictatorship of the Proletariat will, when it has accomplished its purpose, give place to a classless society from which the State has finally disappeared. But that is clearly to use the term "State" in a very different sense from that employed by non-Communist political theory.

At the other extreme, Anarchism has preached the doctrine of a society without any authority external to the individual, and therefore of a society without government. That is what Nietzsche meant when he said, "The State! Whatever the

State saith is a lie; whatever it hath is a theft; all is counterfeit in it, the gnawing, sanguinary, insatiate monster. It even bites with stolen teeth. Its very bowels are counterfeit."[1]

"The State," said Shaw, "will sell you up, blow you up, knock you down, bludgeon, shoot, stab, hang—in short, abolish you, if you lift a hand against it."[2] The dream of a golden age of perfect individual freedom, without coercion or authority being necessary, has indeed haunted the minds of men since time immemorial. But that is not the origin of the modern attack on the doctrine of State sovereignty, except in the sense that certain aspects of that attack have been inspired by the desire to enlarge the sphere of individual liberty and to stimulate and widen the scope of creative activity for the individual citizen. This has been the motive more especially in the case of the English critics of idealism. The attack resolved itself, however, into a challenge, not to the State as against the individual, but to the State as against other associations and groups in society. "The sphere in which autonomy may be and should be permitted to what English political theory has termed *voluntary associations*, that is to say, the relationship in which they must stand to the state," is, we are told by one writer, "the problem with which all modern political theory is faced."[3] That, perhaps, is to narrow the issue somewhat, but it will serve as a convenient definition of the particular problem raised by the Trade Union challenge.

[1] Nietsche, F., *Thus Spake Zarathustra*.
[2] Bernard Shaw, *Essay on Anarchism*.
[3] Elliott, W. Y., *The Pragmatic Revolt in Politics* (1928), 423.

CHAPTER XX

PLURALISM

IT is worth remembering that the State itself, as an actual fact rather than an ideal, is not of particularly ancient lineage. The Greek "city-state" was clearly something entirely different from the territorially vast and functionally complex industrial State of to-day. The difference is not merely that of size and complexity; it is a difference in quality as well as quantity, for the city-state, by reason of its relative simplicity and small size, could be organized on a very simple pattern compared with the modern community. There was, so to speak, no room for more than the one important grouping of citizens. Relations between individuals were direct, interests concentrated, authority undifferentiated. As nations developed, and even more as empires grew, the situation completely changed. Closeness of contact between parts was impossible, interests were dispersed, and authority was divided. In the Middle Ages the notion of sovereignty was unknown. There was diversity of authority and diversity even of positive law. In the religious sphere especially, in an age when religion as much as any civil power ruled the lives of men, there was the spiritual empire of the Pope in Western Europe. Canon law, as laid down by the Church, was as real and as living as the secular law. It had its own courts, procedure, and practitioners, just as the secular authorities in each region had theirs, and no secular lawyer would have disputed the validity of the ecclesiastical judgments in their own sphere. Then there was a separate code of commercial law which, after the eleventh century, was applied to mercantile relations in many countries, and enforced by courts such as those of the Hanseatic League, whatever the local law might be. The civil law itself was not unified over England until the passing of the feudal age. The threefold division into civil, commercial, and religious law lasted until the thirteenth century or later, and during this period there was no such thing as sovereignty in the realm of law. Sovereignty was equally unknown in the political sphere. In the feudal era it was quite possible for a "sovereign" to be taken prisoner by a vassal, who could vow homage of a purely formal sort while exacting a substantial ransom! The idea of sovereignty was first formulated by the Church, Pope Gregory VII in the eleventh century claiming a *plenitudo potestatis*, an authority as complete as that of a Roman emperor, but over a far wider realm. The term sovereignty was not used until much later, but the essential idea emerged in the victory of the Church over the feudal lords of Western Europe. Even so, it was a supernational and not a national sovereignty that was developed. Not until the seventeenth century did the modern doctrine of sovereignty appear, with the writings of Bodin and Hobbes, to be expanded and elaborated later by a long line of political theorists. "*Non est potestas super terram quae comparetur ei*"; the words, blazoned forth like a challenge over the head of the crowned figure in the frontispiece to Hobbes's *Leviathan,* give us the modern conception of sovereign power, *super terram* being understood as the territorial limits of the State. Not only the modern doctrine, but the essential feature of its clash with some, at any rate, of the modern opposition movements, can be seen in Hobbes. In his *Dialogue of the Common Laws,* he says succinctly that it is not wisdom but authority that makes a law.[1] Invert this, and we have the core of Professor Laski's pluralist revolt against the classical doctrine. It is by the wisdom of its content that the validity of a law must be tested, says the pluralist of this school, and the individual citizen must judge of that wisdom. In behaviourist terms, law is what can get itself accepted as law; and what gets itself accepted is what commends itself to the persons it affects. In other words, the sovereignty of the State, as classically

[1] Gooch, G. P., *Political Thought from Bacon to Halifax* (1915), 53.

conceived, is utterly denied. The State is not merely *not*, in actual fact, the sovereign power, in the sense understood by Hobbes and his successors, but it ought not to be.

It is clear that if political power is rightfully pluralistic, divided, and not unitary, not concentrated in the State, our judgment of Trade Unions in relation to the State must be vitally affected, and our attitude towards the conflicts we are considering must be very different from that of the supporters of the "orthodox" doctrine. It is not possible to expound in detail the views of either the monists or the pluralists, and still less is it possible to trace the course of the long controversy that has raged over the opposing views. It will be sufficient here to summarize what seems to be the present state of political thought on the subject. But first it is necessary to point out that the many attacks that have in recent years been launched against State sovereignty have had no common basis or origin.

Historically, the pluralistic doctrines may be said to have originated with Beseler's attack on the "corporation theory" of Savigny and his contemporaries, about the middle of the nineteenth century.[1] This was not primarily a revolt against the sovereign State. It was part of the revival of Germanism, with its emphasis on native institutions and its rejection of the domination of Roman law. The "reception" of Roman law in Germany had been so complete and the consequent disappearance of German jurisprudence so marked that the nationalist movement, stressing the revival of ideas and institutions of native growth, was able to instance the failure of the alien doctrine to accord with typically German beliefs. The teaching of Roman law in regard to corporations was embodied in the concession theory, according to which the corporation was a *persona ficta* whose legal personality owed its existence to the fiat of the State. Apart from such bodies created by the State, no groups within the State were recognized.

[1] Beseler, G., *Volksrecht und Juristenrecht* (1843), 158–94.

Beseler and his successors, especially Gierke,[1] who gave the newer view its full development, held that this theory made no provision for the "fellowships" (*genossenschaften*) which had developed spontaneously in Germany, as elsewhere, since very early times. The *Genossenschaftstheorie* urged that these associations were real group-persons and no mere fictions of the law; they were living organizations with their own wills and their own laws of growth and activity. Such a doctrine, popular with all associations that felt the domination of the State, was an admirable weapon against the alien system of Roman law. The development of a similar theory was not quite so necessary in England, since Roman law was not "received" here to any great extent, and the Court of Chancery had perfected the device of the "trust," which enabled a good deal of autonomous group activity to be carried on. So we find that to this day Trade Unions, for example, have never been incorporated bodies in England but have almost always administered their property through trustees.[2]

Nevertheless, the *Genossenschaftstheorie* was applied to our own problems by English legal and political theorists, and with remarkable results, for Gierke's ideas were developed out of all recognition and on the new doctrine was based the most powerful of all the attacks on State sovereignty. Maitland, whose profound insight and learning mark an epoch in the history of English legal and political thought, took Gierke's ideas and made a number of ingenious applications of them to English problems.[3] He also referred to the State as being simply one among a number of associations, and one, moreover,

---

[1] Gierke, O., *Das deutsche Genossenschaftsrecht* (1868–1913).

[2] Cf. "A trade union holds property by trustees; but not being incorporated, there is no one legal person or entity in whom the beneficial interest in the property of a trade union is vested. The beneficiaries are its members, collectively and severally." *Yorkshire Miners Assn.* v. *Howden*, [1905] A.C. 256.

[3] Maitland, F. W., *Collected Papers* (1911), Vol. III, and Introduction to Gierke's *Political Theories of the Middle Age* (1900).

with no right to pre-eminence. Here, we may say, began the modern pluralist movement in this country. Since that time Dr. Figgis has applied the doctrine to a defence of the group rights of the Church,[1] and Professor Laski and Mr. Cole to the vindication of Trade Union rights. Professor Laski especially has greatly elaborated and modernized the theory, and applied it more particularly in his recent work to the relations between the individual citizen and the State. Referring to bodies like Trade Unions and the Churches he says, "These associations are in their sphere not less sovereign than the State itself; with of course the implication that their sovereignty is similarly limited by the refusal or willingness of the individual member to accept their decisions."[2] The ultimate unit is neither the State nor the group, but the individual human being, a conclusion of some importance in the changing character of pluralism. A similar idea is expressed in his assertion that "to exhaust the associations to which a man belongs is not to exhaust the man himself."[3] Always the emphasis returns to the individual human being and his personal standard of judgment, even when one group interest is being vindicated against another. "I shall be with my Church and against the State, with my trade union and against the State, if the impact of the State upon my experience seems inadequate compared to the impact of the Church or the trade union."[4] In short, with the central idea of the *Genossenschaftstheorie* as his starting-point, Professor Laski proceeds to demolish State sovereignty and its associated doctrines in order to vindicate, first, group rights against the State, and then—a matter of even greater importance—the individual's rights against both State and other groups. "The ultimate isolation of the individual personality is the basis from which any adequate theory of politics

[1] For a recent instance of a Church standing for group independence see p. 20 *supra*.
[2] Laski, H. J., *A Grammar of Politics*, 60.
[3] *Ibid.*, 67.   [4] *Ibid.*, 251.

must start," he says in a recent work,[1] and this is in a sense
the key-note to his pluralistic scheme.[2] His entire approach is
ethical in the sense that he starts with a strong conviction of
the value of human personality and of the fundamental
importance of individual freedom, both of which the monistic
theory seems to stifle and kill. State sovereignty, with its
paraphernalia of "general will," geographical representation,
and the rest, and its idealist philosophy, neither corresponds
to the actual facts of life, it is argued, nor offers any solution
which safeguards the individual citizen's personality and
freedom. Authority must be pluralistic, not unitary, if it is to
avoid being tyranny. Power must be divided and a degree of
self-government on functional lines established. "The structure
of social organization must be federal if it is to be adequate.
Its pattern involves not myself and the State, or my groups
and the State, but all these and their interrelationships."[3]
Only so will any place be found for the creative activity and
personal freedom of the individual man or woman. From this
point of view the individual citizen has a right, even a duty,
to scrutinize every command of the State and of every other
group, and to ask himself whether it ought, in the given
circumstances, to be obeyed, as conforming to his own sense
of what is right. He is entitled to disobey if the command
violates his deepest convictions. This does not mean that every
time he disagrees with the substance of an order he should
rebel, for there are very many matters on which conformity is
the lesser evil, and disobedience should always be a last
resource. But it should be a possible resource, to be seized if
the attempt is made to force upon him a course of action
which outrages his own moral code. It is, therefore, a doctrine
of "contingent anarchy" that Professor Laski preaches.

[1] Laski, H. J., *Liberty in the Modern State* (1930), 28.
[2] In violent opposition, therefore, to the philosophy underlying both
Fascism and Russian Communism (see Chapter xxxi *infra*).
[3] Laski, H. J., *A Grammar of Politics*, 262.

If this attitude is accepted, the member of a Trade Union may be acting rightly, may even be fulfilling his clear duty, in siding with his Union against the State in a conflict of the kind described in earlier chapters. For he is, on this theory, bound to examine the substance of the dispute, to decide for himself which party is right in the given situation, and to determine his active allegiance accordingly. His allegiance is where justice is, and not where authority is, and he himself must be the judge. Whatever the difficulties of accepting this doctrine may be, it will be found even harder to return to the pure idealist position, for the attacks made by a host of critics from different points of view have certainly made the theories of Hobbes and Austin untenable.

Mr. Cole, like other pluralists of the same school, has stressed the functional aspect of human activity.[1] In relation to his daily work a man is primarily a producer, and the interests of the producer weigh most heavily in his judgment of, let us say, economic policies. In relation to his religious beliefs, if any, he is a churchman or a nonconformist. As a citizen he may be a Liberal or a Conservative or a Socialist, and as a householder the consumer's point of view will constantly appeal to him. So one might continue in illustration of the fact that human personality is many-sided and is functionally pluralistic. From this, Mr. Cole urges that no single association, even one so all-inclusive in its claims as the State, can adequately represent a human being. To secure adequate representation for all his functional interests there must be a number of associations to which he owes allegiance and through which he seeks to express the whole of his many-sided personality. Thus, the doctrine of group autonomy and group rights gains validity from the facts of human nature and needs as well as from the history and activities of voluntary associations. Groups are not merely entitled to exist and to act because they have arisen spontaneously and independently of the State; they are

[1] Cole, G. D. H., *Social Theory* (1920).

necessary to the fulfilment of the human need for many-sided representation. In his early writings Mr. Cole regarded the State as the group organization representing the consumers' interest, and consequently the status and authority of the State were held to be equal, but no more than equal, to those of other groups like Churches and Trade Unions. His position changed somewhat later, the State becoming essentially a final authority for co-ordinating other groups and settling inter-group disputes. Even so, Mr. Cole would deny that this means a return to a belief in State sovereignty. The later Guild Socialism certainly stressed the pluralist principle of functional representation as strongly as ever, but it is clear that a final authority was postulated ("National Commune," or whatever its name might be,)[1] having the duty of reconciling conflicting claims and composing differences between national Guilds. The question whether this position is really pluralistic or monistic will be considered at a later stage.

Duguit's attack on sovereignty rests on entirely different considerations from any of the foregoing theories.[2] He starts from the need to define the basis of law. Law, he asserts, is based on human solidarity, on the fundamental fact of common needs and complementary needs in any human society. This principle of solidarity is far more basic than the State, being a universal postulate of social life, a primary fact which is antecedent to any political, economic, or other association. Instead of the State creating law, Duguit holds that law, being based on the fundamental principle of solidarity, is binding upon the State. The State, as the instrument of law, has to find out by trial and error how to translate this solidarity into legislation and administration, and the measure of its success will be the extent to which it can satisfy the general body of citizens. There is no question of State sovereignty in such a theory. Duguit's analysis being realistic, he denies both the

[1] See Cole, G. D. H., *Guild Socialism Restated* (1920).
[2] Duguit, L., *Études de droit public* (1903), etc.

fact of State sovereignty and the idealist theory of State personality. The State is, for all practical purposes, the Government, and the Government and its officials are not the mouthpiece of a "corporate person issuing its commands. They are simply the managers of the nation's business."[1] That business is not solely negative, it is not merely the prevention and punishment of crime and civil wrongs; it is positive in the main, and consists above all in ensuring the continued operation of the public services. What is a public service? "Any activity," says Duguit, "that has to be governmentally regulated and controlled because it is indispensable to the realization and development of social solidarity is a public service so long as it cannot be assured save by governmental intervention."[2] Thus, the modern State is really a business undertaking for securing to citizens the essentials of material civilization, and the concept of sovereignty is quite out of place in this connection. Organization is the significant feature of State functioning, and not the mere exercise of authority. It follows from this that wherever solidarity is expressed in rules, law is created. The State is therefore not the sole law-making body. Other associations serving the public interest and engaged in assuring to the general body of citizens the primary requisites of civilized life are in their spheres the instruments of law just as clearly as is the State. Hence, Duguit's theory is also pluralistic, and in so far as any co-ordinating authority may be necessary he appears to rely on the Courts as the guardians of that primary social law which he deems to be fundamental. It must be pointed out, however, that Duguit does not believe in the sovereignty of law. He asserts the supremacy of the concept of solidarity, it is true, but the concrete application of this almost metaphysical abstraction is to be worked out progressively, in the light of experience, and

[1] Duguit, L., *Law in the Modern State* (Trans. by F. and H. Laski), 51.   [2] *Ibid.*, 48.

the results are to be viewed objectively, the criterion being their effect upon the life of the community.

Duguit did not work out in great detail the pluralist aspect of his theory. Professor Laski links him with Leroy[1] in the claim for technical autonomy for each public utility service, and says that "he seems also, though with some hesitation, to regard the trade unions as destined one day to form an integral part of a state federalized not by regions but by functions."[2] But Duguit's insistence that "The idea of public service lies at the very base of the theory of the modern State"[3] leads him to restrict somewhat narrowly the rights of Trade Unions, at any rate in the public utility services. He does not admit the right of workers in such services to go on strike, and he is concerned less to defend their "rights" than to assert the subordination of all groups to the principle of solidarity.

Mr. Dewey's theory of politics has much in common with Duguit's, though the similarity is rather in the method of approach and the general philosophical basis than in the detailed conclusions reached. Duguit was first and foremost a jurist, and the legal bias is evident throughout his work. Mr. Dewey is primarily a philosopher who is chiefly concerned to destroy the idealist doctrine and its implications in politics and elsewhere.[4] It is often said that he has tried to place Pragmatism, which is usually taken to be the inspiration and basis of political pluralism, on a thoroughly scientific foundation. William James was essentially a Romantic, and his elaboration of pragmatism was anything but logical. Mr. Dewey's attitude is realistic, objective, positivist, like Duguit's. He strongly emphasizes the view that human activities, ideas, and beliefs, and supposedly free human wills, are determined in reality by the material

[1] Leroy, M., *Les Transformations de la puissance publique* (1907).
[2] Duguit, L., *Law in the Modern State*, Translators' Intro., xxiv.
[3] Duguit, L., *op. cit.*, xliv.
[4] Dewey, J., *Human Nature and Conduct* (1922); *German Philosophy and Politics* (1915).

environment. Morals are merely social habits of thought and behaviour, and it is therefore impossible for politics to take as its starting-point an ethical objective. There is at any given time some ethical objective, but this is a product of existing circumstances and it must be taken as a fact along with other relevant facts. From this point of view, political machinery is to be judged simply in relation to its efficiency in achieving the momentary objective. The idealist conception of the State as a sovereign power with a moral purpose disappears, as do such abstractions as the "general will" and the like.

The State as a specific piece of machinery is a fact, and its significance depends merely upon what it actually does and is. Its power and authority likewise must be considered in relation to actual facts; there is no "ought" about it. So other associations may wield power in their own spheres. Mr. Dewey is thus a pluralist in that he recognizes the fact of pluralism, and the fact is all that matters to him. Ideals, theories, policies, institutions, all are ultimately determined by, though also they interact with, the material factors and forces that operate unceasingly, and all are data to the political scientist, whose task is to evaluate the efficiency of the existing political machinery in achieving immediate objectives and to devise new, or adapt the existing, methods where greater efficiency is desired. In short, the task of political science is really one of co-ordinating or harmonizing the actual forces and factors existing at any given time in a given society, the aim of the theorist being to eliminate waste and confusion and not to move towards some new moral order. The State is therefore an organization having no particular sanctity, and no authority beyond what its members choose to recognize. So far from creating law, in virtue of its own authority, the State is subject to law in the performance of its work. Thus, Mr. Dewey's view of law is similar to Duguit's. For both, law is superior to the State, though even to law the adjective "sovereign" cannot be applied.

Internationalists like Mr. Norman Angell, and the school
of international lawyers associated with the Austrian jurist,
Kelsen,[1] have similarly attacked the doctrine of the sovereignty
of the national State, though from a different angle. A
world order is held to be unattainable without the universal
acceptance of a detailed code of international law. Such
a code—and its organ, the World Court—is already coming
into existence. But its acceptance by national States is an
admission that those States are not sovereign, since they
are subject to the wider law of nations. Moreover, they
are not "sovereign" even in their dealings with their own
nationals, since it is no longer true that international law is
concerned only with States and not with individuals. Jellinek
and his school have camouflaged this fact of the submission of
States to international law by the fiction of "auto-limitation."
The doctrine of "auto-limitation" of States has been riddled
with criticism by the internationalists.[2] What, then, is the basis
of international law and its authority? Verdross argues that it
is the universal acceptance of a code of elementary principles
(*Pacta sunt servanda*, for example) that gives international law
its real authority. Such a code of "natural rights" is not based
on abstract morality, however. It is accepted as the result of
hard experience in the first attempts to build up civilization.
As MacIver in the more limited sphere finds the "will for the
State" to be the controlling factor,[3] so the internationalist sees
the "will for civilization" as the motive force behind the
development of international law and a world community.
This view, while powerfully reinforcing the pluralistic attack
on State sovereignty and the equally characteristic emphasis
on the pragmatic solution of the problem, still leaves undeter-

[1] Kelsen, H., *Das Problem der Souveränität und die Theorie des
Volkerrechts* (1920).
[2] For such criticism see the brilliant paper by Verdross, A., "Le
Fondement du Droit International," *Académie de Droit International,
Recueil des Cours*, 1927, Vol. I, p. 251.
[3] MacIver, R. M., *The Modern State* (1926).

mined the ultimate source of international authority. The principle that law is unitary is now taken as a fundamental axiom by some pluralists, including even so thoroughgoing an opponent of political monism as Professor Laski, but this appears to hand over the ultimate power to the Courts, or at any rate to the World Court. For who else is to interpret those basic principles that are supposed to be the very essence of civilization? However, this point will be more fully discussed in later pages. For the moment it is sufficient to note that the Austrians, along with Professor Laski and others in England, are still working out the implications of the theory outlined above.

These, then, may be said to be the leading ideas of those who have assailed the sovereignty of the State and applications of the idealist philosophy to politics. The merest outlines have been drawn, as it is obviously impossible to describe these theories in detail in a work of this kind.[1] It will be necessary, however, to discuss at some length the meaning of pluralism, its place in contemporary political thought, and its bearing on the problem we have set out to investigate.

[1] For a full exposition and criticism see Hsiao, K. C., *Political Pluralism* (1927); Elliott, W. Y., *The Pragmatic Revolt in Politics* (1928). And see Ward, P., *Sovereignty* (1928); Rockow, L., *Contemporary Political Thought in England* (1925).

CHAPTER XXI

THE ECLIPSE OF SOVEREIGNTY

WHAT is the net result of the long struggle between monism and pluralism? Can it be said that either has succeeded in establishing itself in an impregnable position? Frankly it is impossible to say that either theory has emerged completely victorious or that any really satisfactory theory of politics has yet emerged. But it is beyond doubt that the extreme claims of the idealist school have had to be given up in face of the pluralist attack. The supporters of State sovereignty are on the defensive, and their defence very largely consists of the plea that they have never advanced the views attributed to them by their opponents. There are still diehards, to be sure, and one may guess that if Dr. Bosanquet had still been alive he would not have acknowledged defeat, but if one turns to contemporary criticism of the pluralist position one finds frequent assertions that the monistic attitude has been misrepresented.[1] It is admitted that some writers have vulgarized the doctrines of the classical idealists and applied them to politics in quite unwarranted ways, but Hobbes and Austin, and even Hegel himself, have been quoted to show that they did not hold those extreme theories of State omnipotence that have been pilloried by the pluralists. Thus, Mr. Hsiao says that Duguit seeks to "prove that law is more than the decrees of government or parliament. . . . But this truth, as we saw, is also admitted, or at least undisputed, by the monistic jurists, especially by writers like Bodin and Bentham."[2] Again, "Hegel is in favour of a system of functional or class representation,"[3] and Hobbes, who "raises the leviathan to the sanctity of a mortal god on earth," never

---

[1] See, for example, Hsiao, *op. cit.*
[2] Hsiao, *op. cit.*, 28.   [3] *Ibid.*, 80.

forgets "that there is, over and above it, an immortal and more powerful spiritual God to whom the claims of the former must finally be subordinated."[1] Bodin again is cited by Mr. Hsiao to show that the typical monists did not in fact hold absolutist theories of State sovereignty.[2]

But this line of defence is somewhat disingenuous. It can hardly be maintained that Hobbes's reference to an "immortal and more powerful spiritual God" is more than the formal concession to current belief. The ruler is required by God to rule well, but if he does not his punishment is to be left to God and not to human agency. Hobbes, says Dr. Gooch, "would have welcomed Gibbon's historic sneer that all religions were to the believer equally true, to the philosopher equally false, to the magistrate equally useful."[3] It is easy to find quotations of the kind cited by Mr. Hsiao, but it cannot be denied that the tendency of political monism has been to magnify the power of rulers and justify absolutism. The pluralists have not, in this respect, been tilting at windmills.

In any case, one can say with confidence that few if any contemporary monists would put forward extreme claims for the authority of the State. It seems clear that this more cautious attitude is due to the pluralist criticisms, but whether this is so or not it would now be difficult to find any defence of State omnipotence or political absolutism in any form. It must be observed, of course, that formal democracy is not incompatible with extreme claims for State sovereignty. Rousseau's ingenious use of the "general will" concept enables democracy and sovereignty to be reconciled with ease, though it must be said that the "general will" also has succumbed to the pluralist attack, despite some valiant efforts to defend it.[4]

Socialist movements have in the past been convinced

---

[1] Hsiao, *op. cit.*, 128.   [2] *Ibid.*, 217.
[3] Gooch, G. P., *Political Thought from Bacon to Halifax* (1915), 46.
[4] E.g. Hsiao, *op. cit.*, 146 ff.

supporters of the idea of sovereignty. The collectivist State is the kind of leviathan that Hobbes is usually supposed to have advocated. Marxism, owing its philosophical inspiration to Hegel, might be expected to hold this position, and it is indeed thoroughly monistic in character, even though it defines the State as an organ of Capitalism which will disappear after the dictatorship of the proletariat has done its work. The evolutionary Socialism of the Collectivist school, typified by Mr. Ramsay MacDonald and the early Fabians, would seem to be equally monistic, however. Hence, in England, the revolt of the Guild Socialists, inspired by the anti-State Syndicalist doctrine. The result of this influence has been that many of the leading Fabians are now in the pluralist camp, and even Mr. and Mrs. Webb have had to concede a good deal to the newer point of view, for in their *Constitution for a Socialist Commonwealth* they recognize the wisdom of functional decentralization.[1]

Professed democrats like T. H. Green and Dr. Bosanquet, who were not Socialists, of course, have not found it difficult to give a monistic interpretation of democratic principles. Yet there seems to be a fundamental connection between democracy and individual liberty, and between individual liberty and pluralism. What is the explanation of the apparent "neutrality" of democracy towards the rival schools of political thought? Evidently the precise meaning given to the term "liberty" varies. To pluralists like Professor Laski "liberty" means what it means to the ordinary man—freedom from restraint. To the idealist it has a different meaning. It is a complicated metaphysical concept the practical sense of which was well understood by Henry Ford when he told his customers that they were free to choose any colour they liked for their cars provided they chose black! Democracy, on this view, means that the people are free to go whatever way they desire provided they act through a body of persons who will decide

[1] Webb, S. and B., *Constitution for a Socialist Commonwealth* (1920).

what it is the people *really* want as distinct from what they only *think* they want!

So, the existing democratic system, being cast in the idealistic mould, is sometimes no more than a device for persuading the people that they are governing themselves. The application of psychology to the improvement of the arts of publicity thus tends to make modern politics a study in the dynamics of deception, but being on the grand scale the process remains almost invisible to those it chiefly affects. Certainly the mechanism of the modern democratic State is of a type that does not allow of the degree of freedom for the individual personality that Professor Laski and his school deem essential, or the scope and autonomy for associations that Maitland and Figgis held necessary, or the recognition of actual social and economic facts that seems all-important to Dewey and Duguit. Although it is not possible, the pluralists would say, to assure these desirable aims under an undemocratic regime, they are not necessarily assured in a democracy; the basis of democracy may be monistic or pluralistic, but only the latter can give the kind of system in which freedom can thrive and flexibility can be found for an unceasing process of experiment and change. It is not necessary to destroy the political system as it exists to-day in order to pluralize democracy. It is quite possible to reorganize the present democratic method and mechanism, and Professor Laski for one has shown how it can be done.[1] But it should also be noted (though this sounds like a contradiction in terms) that an autocratic regime may be constructed in a pluralist form, as in the case of Italy to-day.[2] It is by no accident that pluralists like Duguit and Dewey have at times seemed to display some sympathy with Italian Fascism,[3] just as it is by no accident that Mussolini, himself an ex-Syndicalist (and to that extent a pluralist), has sponsored the Corporative State. In practice, State sovereignty has no

[1] Laski, H. J., *A Grammar of Politics*.
[2] See Chapter xxvi.   [3] See Elliott, *op. cit.*

better example in the world to-day than Italy, and no more determined exponent than Mussolini, but *in form* the Corporative State is pluralistic—with a monistic mechanism superimposed, almost as a separate part of the Constitution! One can no longer, apparently, find in Western political thought any theoretical justification of the thoroughgoing State sovereignty that was implied in the teachings of Hobbes and Austin. It was the march of economic and political events that killed it and the pluralist theories were the expression of the new conditions. The "general will," too, that odd abstraction of the metaphysicians, has dissolved into the nothingness from which it was conjured. The conception of the State as a real person, a super-person, has disappeared with the triumph of the realistic method in political thought. And with it has gone the equally unreal personification of associations. Gierke and Maitland, with others of the early pluralists, set up against the State-person the association-person, not as a fictitious personality, useful as a legal symbol merely, but as a real person, real in some sense known only to the elect. It was good tactics to turn the metaphysical weapon of the monists on themselves, but let it be freely admitted that "the conception of a body of members as a real being which can be truly said to have a personality"[1] is no longer tenable if we adopt an objective method of thought. It is quite a different matter to say that "if twenty old ladies in the workhouse club together to provide themselves with a special pot of tea, and agree that one among them shall be the treasurer of their painfully hoarded pennies, as a common fund, they do in fact create a social entity."[2] Pluralism can rightly build a theory on the existence of groups as social entities without needing to insist on a "real personality." Maitland held that the personality of associations "is no fiction, no symbol, no piece of the State's machinery, no collective name for individuals" but that such a

---

[1] Geldart, W. M., *The Osborne Judgment and After*, 19.
[2] Webb, S. and B., *History of Trade Unionism*, 611.

group is "a living organism and a real person, with body and members and a will of its own." Professor Ernest Barker comments very wisely on Maitland's conception in relation to the entire doctrine it was devised to support: "It is possible to have doubts about part of this doctrine, and yet to accept and to urge its main tenet. To talk of the real personality of anything, other than the individual human being, is to indulge in dubious and perhaps nebulous speech. When a permanent group of ninety-nine members is in session in its place of meeting, engaged in willing the policy of the group, it is permissible to doubt whether a hundredth person supervenes. The solution of the doubt would involve the determination of metaphysical questions beyond the scope of this argument. But we are entitled to assume that permanently organized groups are at any rate juristic personalities. . . . Even if we reduce the group to the category of a juristic person we may still hold to Maitland's main tenet, and plead that such personality grows and is not made."[1] In this case, Professor Barker argues, we have to agree that the theory of the State is vitally affected. "Every State, we feel, is something of a federal society."[2] On this conception, groups are at once limited in certain ways and freed in others, says Professor Barker. They are limited in that whether or not there is any legal recognition of them they have to be treated as corporate bodies and held responsible for their actions. They are freed in that, even if they are only *de facto* associations, they must not be treated as though they have no legal existence, and they must not be rigidly confined within the bounds set by a statute, but must be allowed to grow and develop freely. But Professor Barker does not go all the way with the pluralists. "Our doctrine," he says, "will not exempt such associations from the control of the State."[3] As the meaning of this word "control" will be found to be of great importance in the discussion of this, the crucial

---

[1] Barker, E., *Political Thought from Spencer to To-day* (1915), 178.
[2] *Ibid.*, 181.   [3] *Ibid.*, 178 ff.

point in the problem of the relations between State and group, it is advisable to set out Professor Barker's argument in his own words. "The State, as a general and embracing scheme of life, must," he says,[1] "necessarily adjust the relations of associations to itself, to other associations and to their own members—to itself, in order to maintain the integrity of its own scheme; to other associations, in order to preserve the equality of associations before the law; and to their own members, in order to preserve the individual from the possible tyranny of the group." Here the pluralist will pertinently ask, "Quis custodiet?" However, these principles are further elaborated: "The State will not tolerate such modes of action of recognized associations as fundamentally contradict its own purposes. . . . It will not readily tolerate the possession by one association of a privileged and exceptional position which other associations do not enjoy. . . . The State will demand from an association that it shall have a definite basis of action, and that such a basis shall be unitary, in the sense of not combining different kinds of action. . . . If we apply these principles to Trade Unions, we may see what they involve. In the first place the State will have to decide whether the use of the funds of Trade Unions to support pledged members in Parliament is compatible with the public policy of England, or whether the purposes of Parliamentary representation are contravened by the exaction of political pledges. In the second place the State will have to decide whether the freedom from certain kinds of legal action claimed by Trade Unions and conceded by the Trade Disputes Act of 1906, is compatible with the principle of equality of associations. Finally, the State will have to decide whether a Trade Union which combines political action, and a levy for political action, with economic action and an economic levy, is not combining different kinds of action, and failing to maintain a unitary basis; and whether, by such procedure, it may not be coercing unduly those of its

[1] Barker, E., *Political Thought from Spencer to To-day* (1915), 178 ff.

R

members who approve of the one kind of action and disapprove of the other. These considerations may lead us to see that we must not push too far our claims on behalf of group-persons."

To go back a little, Professor Barker holds that it is the function of the State to adjust the relations of associations (*a*) to itself, (*b*) to each other, and (*c*) to their own members. That is what he means by the State "controlling" associations, and it is essentially a monistic interpretation. Yet Professor Barker apparently holds no brief for the idealist conception of the State as a moral personality. "The State," he says else-where,[1] "has no direct moral function. Its business is simply to guarantee rights of persons." But what rights? Legal rights? If so, he places law above the State, and the State's function of adjusting relations of and with associations is a co-ordinating function under the authority of a superior law. The State, he says above, will not tolerate, in an association, modes of action which fundamentally contradict the State's purpose, which is to guarantee the rights of persons. But who determines those rights? Not the State, for that would give the State a direct moral purpose. Not Government, for that would make the State merely the agent and executive arm of Government. Not the Courts, for this would make the Courts the origin of law and the superiors of both law and the State, a position incompatible with Professor Barker's conception of the State as "a general and embracing scheme of life." Yet if law itself is to be regarded as supreme, after the pluralistic fashion of Duguit (if such a principle can be called pluralistic), not only does this leave unexplained the origin of law and the source of its authority (a problem discussed later), but incidentally it deposes the State from its sovereign position and makes it something less than sovereign while something more than any other association. Is this a tenable theory? Whether it is

[1] Barker, E., "Democracy and Social Justice," *Contemporary Review*, March 1930, 303.

Professor Barker's position or not,[1] it is a doctrine of some consequence in contemporary discussion. First we have the monistic position, the sovereign State. Then the pluralistic doctrine of group rights, the denial of State sovereignty, and the reduction of the State to the rank of an association on a level with other associations. But, argues the monist, some co-ordinating authority is needed among all the associations that are exercising their group wills. The pluralists in the main agree that a co-ordinating body is necessary. Mr. Cole provides a co-ordinating mechanism for resolving disputes between groups and calls it a Guild Congress, or a National Commune. M. Duguit, and perhaps Professor Laski, as well as internationalists of the Kelsen school, are disposed to say that law is to be the co-ordinating force. Mr. Dewey would say the State actually *is* the co-ordinating body and that is sufficient. But all would agree that in any case no sovereignty attaches to mechanism of this kind, whether National Commune, or State, or law and the Courts. Co-ordination is merely a function, an important one, but one which is not equivalent to sovereignty. The monists, on the other hand, are disposed to triumph over the admission that some co-ordinating force must be recognized. They do not care what it is called; the fact that it is admitted is, they think, a surrender of the pluralist position in its most essential feature. Based on this view Mr. Hsiao roundly claims Mr. Cole and even Professor Laski as monists.[2] Having shown that Hegel, Hobbes, and Bodin were really good pluralists he proceeds on this new argument to prove that the leading exponents of pluralism are really sound monists at heart! This leaves one somewhat dubious as to the precise state of controversy between the two views, but perhaps Mr. Hsiao is really indulging in the Hegelian sport of effecting a Higher Synthesis! However,

[1] Professor Barker sometimes seems to lean towards this view, and at other times to revert to a more idealistic doctrine.
[2] Hsiao, C. K., *op. cit.*

the question of co-ordination is clearly one of considerable importance. Assuming with the pluralists that associations and groups have an origin and a validity independent of the State's fiat, and that they should be free to develop along their own lines and to grow in accordance with the laws of their own nature, and assuming also that the notion of State sovereignty, in the sense commonly attributed to Hobbes and Austin, must be given up, it is yet clear that if there is to be any form at all in society, if anarchy is not to be perpetual, in short if civilization is to be achieved, some means must be found for settling disputes between groups and for co-ordinating their activities. Does this necessarily mean that there is to be a controlling authority, which must be obeyed by the groups without regard to the merits of any case at issue? One may reply by saying that "control" may be positive and continuous, or negative and intermittent. We use the same word to denote both possibilities, but in fact there are the two different conceptions. This difference may perhaps be illustrated by reference to the typical form of joint stock company management in Germany and other countries. There is a Board of Management,[1] as we should say, which exercises day-to-day control over the company's affairs, makes decisions on points that arise, takes the initiative in evolving policy, and so on. But there is also a Supervisory Board[2] (usually though wrongly translated into English as "Control Board") which keeps a general supervision over the Management Board, in the interests of the shareholders. It does not exercise positive directive functions but rather keeps a general oversight, having the right to inspect the books, investigate the financial position and generally to report to the shareholders on the conduct of affairs. We might make an analogous distinction in political structure and suggest that a co-ordinating body need not exercise positive directive powers over groups. It should not, and need not, be part of the functions of such a body to prescribe the modes of activity of groups, to

[1] German *Vorstand.*   [2] German *Aufsichtsrat.*

lay down rules for associations, to limit their scope or in any way order, or even advise them, how best to carry on their own work. Such matters should be quite outside the power of a co-ordinating mechanism, which, in fact, would only function when conflicts arose. This would seem to place the co-ordinating body in the position of a Court, which normally functions only in the settlement of disputes, in reconciling differences or making decisions where reconciliation is found impossible.

Can a Court ever be said to exercise sovereignty? There are many who will answer in the affirmative. It is often held, for instance, that in the United States sovereignty resides, if anywhere, in the Supreme Court. But the pluralist will quote with approval J. C. Gray's dictum that "the real rulers of a society are undiscoverable" and will say that true as this is in any State, it is particularly apposite in the case of a federal constitution. Certain specific acts of sovereignty may seem to be the prerogative of the President or Congress, others—concerning only the internal affairs of one of the states—within the power of a state Government, while some will say that the Constitution itself is sovereign in many fields. But a Constitution cannot be said to exercise sovereignty, though its authority may be said to be paramount when it is applied and interpreted by the Supreme Court. Let us ask the plain question—are there any matters in which Congress can legislate and not be overridden? It is possible to hold that there are. The United States Supreme Court can only invalidate legislation, which has been properly passed, if in its judgment such legislation is contrary to the Constitution. It may be said that no one knows or can know the limits of judicial interpretation of the Constitution, but that is only rhetorically true. Certainly a very high authority has said, "With us it is not enough to know what wisdom and experience suggest. We are met with the further question: Can we do it under our constitutional system? This is true of every important concern of cities, states and

Nation, of business, trade unions and the professions. Most of the problems of modern society . . . are sooner or later legal problems for solutions by our courts, and ultimately by the Supreme Court."[1] But, even so, certain fields are now marked out as free for the exercise of unlimited authority, according to the interpretations given by the Supreme Court to the "due process" clause and to the meaning of "police power," for example. That such delimitation is the work of the Supreme Court does not seem to be a restriction of sovereignty within those fields; a geographical restriction of sovereignty is never regarded as a destruction of such sovereignty, and there is no *a priori* reason for regarding a functional division of sovereignty in any other light. It may be said that the Supreme Court is not bound by its own previous decisions,[2] and that since it can thus move the limits of any such functional divisions at its will, it must be regarded as having sovereign status. But again, machinery is provided in the Constitution whereby such decisions of the Supreme Court may be overthrown, and who is sovereign then? If there were no such provision, however, can we say that the Supreme Court would exercise more than an "intermittent sovereignty," which, surely, is not sovereignty at all in the old sense of the term?

X is endowed with comprehensive powers and normally acts with complete freedom. Y cannot normally interfere with X's actions. In case a certain class of conflict arises, and only when that position is reached, Y can override X. Does sovereignty, in any reasonable sense of the term, reside in Y? An affirmative reply is hardly possible, and it even becomes absurd when the only machinery that can enforce Y's decision is at the command of X! In a situation of this kind we can only say that sovereignty does not exist, in the older sense, but that

[1] Frankfurter, F., and Landis, J. M., *The Business of the Supreme Court*, v.

[2] E.g. the Slaughter House cases.

X and Y have divided authority. A division of powers may make sovereignty a fiction, and so may a territorial division of power in certain types of federation. A functional division of authority is equally possible and may, equally, make the concept of sovereignty, in the Austinian sense, quite untenable.

CHAPTER XXII

THE RENASCENCE OF NATURAL LAW

THE idea of an "internal" and an "external" sovereignty has been invoked in the case of international law to reconcile the notion of national integrity with that of a binding international law.[1] The problem here is, as indicated in an earlier chapter, to see how a State can be sovereign and yet recognize the binding force of international law. If the State has to obey no higher authority, what are we to make of its submission to the awards of a World Court? Attempts to represent this submission to international law as a fiction are quite unconvincing, but on the other hand those theorists who would recognize the sovereignty of an international organ—a World Parliament at Geneva, for example—are landed in the same difficulties as their fellow monists. There is, in fact, no world sovereignty in this sense, and he is a rash theorist who would prophesy that there ever will be. There is certainly no kind of reason to suppose that what people have refused to submit to in national affairs they will tolerate in the international sphere. The position of those who arrive at a belief in a unitary law brings us back to the problem of a co-ordinating body, for law has to be interpreted by the Courts, which is to say law has to be made by the Courts.

Is a system of world law applied by the World Court a system which recognizes sovereignty? The international lawyer who wishes to adhere to some kind of monistic doctrine would say, with Westlake, that we must differentiate between internal and external sovereignty; that a State *is* sovereign in its own sphere, but that in the international sphere, *and in that sphere only*, sovereignty inheres in some other body (World Parliament or World Court). On the line of reasoning already indicated

[1] E.g. Westlake, J., *International Law* (1904–7).

in regard to co-ordinating bodies, the pluralist would hold that this is a last vain attempt to bolster up sovereignty, and that in fact a sovereignty which is limited or divided in this way is not sovereignty at all. We may, however, apply the distinction between internal and external authority to the general problem. It seems quite reasonable to speak of a body having sole authority within its own sphere, whether that sphere be territorial or functional, even though in matters where it comes into contact with other bodies—where, in fact, its sphere intersects other spheres—authority is transferred to some other organization. If such a division is territorial, by nations, the national State may be the sole authority in the internal affairs of the nation, while an international body has the power of decision in international disputes. A division on functional lines would mean that an organization was autonomous within its own functional field, no other authority, even the State, having the right to interfere, while in cases of disputes between functional bodies some other organization would be entitled to adjudicate and take the decision. The power of the adjudicating body would be limited in each case to its own special field of application and could not extend to internal matters. It would therefore not be sovereign since its authority would be thus limited and defined. But in actual practice who would (a) fix the lines of demarcation between internal and external affairs, (b) decide when the inter-group authority should be called in, and (c) enforce the final decision when given? Also (d) on what basis is the final decision to be reached? These are the crucial questions. The reply seems to be as follows, confining ourselves to functional groups since it is in these we are especially interested. No dividing line need be drawn. Any formal demarcation would be futile, because continuous interpretation would be necessary. A group coming into existence as the result of a demarcation laid down by law or otherwise would not be an autonomous group, except to the extent allowed by the law or charter so defining it, and in this case the ordinary

Courts would interpret the charter or law in question. A group arising spontaneously would not, in the nature of the case, have a set of limiting rules or a charter marking off its field of work in detailed terms. Its emphasis is rather on the performance of a positive function. No outside intervention is needed unless and until it comes into conflict with another group and the dispute cannot be settled without such intervention. Any group, then, has the right to appeal to the co-ordinating authority when it feels that its own rights are menaced by the action of another group. So far no great difficulty seems to arise. Now come the questions that really lie at the heart of the controversy: On what kind of basis are decisions of the co-ordinating body made, and how are they to be enforced? Here we may draw valuable analogies from international law and also from British industrial relations. How does the World Court enforce its decisions? The answer is that it does not. The sanctions behind its decisions are entirely moral sanctions; awards are observed because the nations have agreed to observe them. A strict observance of the awards of the World Court depends on the public opinion of the world and on that only. If the maxim *Pacta sunt servanda* is no longer honoured, one of the bases of civilization has gone. We are able to say that it is honoured, in the modern world, to a sufficient degree to warrant us in regarding a World Court with no physical sanctions as a quite workable proposition, and events have justified this attitude.

Nor is this true in the international realm alone. What power of enforcement have the numerous arbitration and conciliation boards in industrial disputes? None at all, yet, with few exceptions, their awards are duly honoured. In practically every case the awards of the Industrial Court have been observed in the various classes of industrial disputes in which it has functioned. Here, also, there is only a moral sanction, the force of public opinion and the feeling deeply implanted in the minds of the conflicting parties that civilized life and civilized industry are impossible if unpleasant decisions are flouted. No disputes could well be more bitter than many of these industrial conflicts; in these cases it is not a matter of settling academic differences but of deciding issues of vital importance to the respective parties.

But even if such adjudication fails occasionally, and open conflicts sometimes happen, this should not be held to imply a breakdown of the system. Only when conflict becomes so continuous that it really threatens the foundation of society and the maintenance of civilized life can a pathological condition be said to exist. In fact, a state of "contingent anarchy" is only a form of that vigilance which is the price of liberty and of sound administration. We need not worry unduly if there is no absolute guarantee of complete order, for there is and can be no such guarantee if there are physical sanctions. Compulsory arbitration in industrial disputes has led to no greater absence of conflict than has our voluntary system with its moral sanctions.

The question of the principle on which decisions are made must likewise be answered in pragmatic terms. What basis does the World Court adopt? In part positive rules, but in part it must, according to the modern view, rely upon this new conception of natural law, which means in effect those principles of settlement that commend themselves to the generality of people and which they will accept. "The Renascence of natural law," says one authority,[1] "has found its way from legal philosophy and from municipal law into the domain of international law, where the influence of the new ideas was facilitated by the depressing consciousness, strengthened by bitter experience, of the practical inadequacy of positivist international law. Of course, it is not the old law of nature; it is rather the modern 'natural law with changing content,' the 'sense of right,' the 'social solidarity,' the 'engineering' law in

[1] Lauterpacht, H., "Westlake and International Law," *Economica*, November 1925, 315.

terms of promoting the ends of international society." These terms, quoted in order to express different conceptions of the same principle, recall Duguit (social solidarity) and Kelsen (natural law) among other opponents of sovereignty, and are an illustration of the real difference in attitude between typical monists and typical pluralists. Duguit has not, perhaps, carried his own conceptions to their logical conclusion. He tends to make mystical principles of what can, in fact, be simply described in pragmatic terms. This pragmatic, or, perhaps more correctly speaking, this behaviourist, view is most clearly expressed by Professor Laski and Mr. Dewey. Leading monists bewail the obtuseness of pluralists for failing to see that the whole idealist conception is that of the "pure instance." "A true theory of sovereignty," says a distinguished idealist,[1] "must fit all times and all forms of the state." The pluralist appreciates that this is the monist's approach but he rejects it. A *true* theory of the State, he would say, must fit *this* time and this existing form of society and it cannot possibly fit any other time or any other form. It is because he feels that no theory of sovereignty fits this present time and these existing conditions that he rejects the entire conception as a basis for a theory of the State. A theory that fits all times fits no time. The "pure instance" is an abstraction.

Now, the newer conception of "natural law" has nothing abstract or metaphysical about it. It takes the fact that people desire to maintain a civilized society; otherwise there is no such thing as a theory of "politics." From this initial reality springs an entire complex of forces and institutions whose content at any time is strictly conditioned by the experience of the community and the state of social organization already achieved. The process of translating into institutional terms the "will to civilization" is largely a process of trial and error. This is so not merely because our knowledge of social forces and their

[1] McIlwain, C. H., "Sovereignty Again," *Economica*, November 1926, 267.

application is only fragmentary, but also because society itself is dynamic, moving in ways which though related are not, to us at any rate, predictable. Consequently, what is called progress is the continuous series of partial adaptations of social institutions to a changing world, adaptations which are made empirically, for the most part, and which, incidentally, are often made too late to meet the conditions for which they were devised. At any given time these adaptations may be rationalized into a code of principles and this forms what we have called "natural law." It is a code of principles, not laid down, not worked out by pure reason operating on a basis of introspection, not formulated in the light of a desired future state of society, but a code which has been *inferred* from the existing facts of social organization and social forces. It is in large measure a social heritage, too, for while the situation at any given moment is new, and is different from the situation at any preceding moment, it has not come into existence mysteriously, out of the void, but is a product of all preceding situations and is linked causally with them. Therefore, the process of adaptation already referred to is one which includes the rejection of certain ideas and institutions that have outworn their usefulness, the modification of others to fit the new situation, and the retention of others again which seem to be of a more enduring—perhaps permanent—character. These last may be said to constitute our code of "natural law." Their origin and validity arise purely out of experience. The code is essentially pragmatic. But at the same time it may be regarded as more permanently grounded than the possibly ephemeral principles that have emerged from a transitory situation. In short, we may say (to use mathematical language) that the dynamical state of society at any moment may be expressed by an equation, the right-hand side of which consists of two distinct parts, the first representing the operation of forces conditioned by pre-existing institutions and the second representing the new terms introduced to fit new circumstances. The first part, our body of "natural law" in the sense already defined, may be regarded as more or less permanent. The second part may not appear in any future equation, but certain elements in it may some time have to be transferred to the first part.

Since no authority formulates the code of "natural law," so determined by the test of experience, there must in the last resort be freedom of private judgment. Conscience, in social matters, is no more than a summing-up of these more deeply rooted, more permanent principles, assimilated consciously or unconsciously as part of the social heritage. Both the State and the Group are more often than not concerned with the more ephemeral features in the social structure, since their immediate tasks consist of adaptations to new situations and solutions for temporary problems. The business of society has somehow to be kept going, and that is their function. To hold aloft the torch of civilization is not their only task. That is the mission of individuals who in the last resort will assert the claims of "natural law," of the basic principles that have been proved by experience to be essential to civilization, even against the urgent commands of authorities preoccupied by the expediencies of the moment.[1]

How, in the light of the foregoing analysis, is it imagined that the Pluralist State will actually work? How, it should rather be asked, are the State and the international community working to-day and how are they tending to develop? For it is claimed that the principles and forces already indicated are the principles and forces actually in operation in the modern world, even though disguised by outworn labels and hampered by relics of a bygone age dominated by the concept of sovereignty. This, to be sure, is a statement of direction, of tendencies, more than of accomplished facts. But it is direction that is important in this matter. It may be that the logical conclusion will never be reached in its extreme form, and whether it is or not is of little significance, for nothing is more

[1] Cf. Benda, Julien, *La Trahison des Clercs* (1927).

futile than to set up a static objective. Movement is a fact, and the direction of that movement is a fact at every moment of time, not a goal to be attained in the future. In the field of political philosophy, as in other journeyings, it is better to travel hopefully than to arrive.

What are the forces that actively determine the direction in which we travel? The ultimate fact of human experience, as Professor Laski well says,[1] is the "uniqueness of individuality, that sense that each of us is ultimately different from his fellows. . . . The ultimate isolation of the individual personality is the basis from which any adequate theory of politics must start." This most deeply rooted fact of personal experience means that human beings unceasingly try to adapt their environment and institutions in such a way as to maximize individual freedom. Social organization is also an accepted fact, implied equally in the terms "politics" and "civilization." Broadly speaking, it is the function of social organization to secure the environment in which the personal freedom of every citizen can have the maximum scope, and of that the individual human beings themselves can alone, on our hypothesis, be the judges. They do, in fact, insist on being the ultimate judges. If and when ordinary persons cease to concern themselves with their own individual liberties, and openly or tacitly accept unlimited restraint, a new situation will have arisen; then, indeed, political theory will have to be re-written and political institutions remade. As it is, the complicated mechanisms that the political world has evolved are the result of mankind's attempts to subordinate social organization to personal freedom.

The expression of personality through voluntary groups and associations is one of the ways in which men and women have sought to utilize social organization in the service of their own creative activities. The history of the unceasing attempt to achieve liberty has been the history, not of the destruction of social organization, but of its division, its splitting up into

[1] *Liberty in the Modern State*, 25, 28.

a multitude of associations, each being more efficient than an undifferentiated authority in the creation of the conditions of freedom, and each being less likely to obtain overweening power over the lives of its individual members. The territorial associations called States become co-ordinating and adjudicating bodies for the multitude of internal organizations concerned with the functions of citizenship, with functions, that is to say, connected with common territorial interests. But equally the World Court, and the League of Nations and its organs, become adjudicating and co-ordinating bodies as between States. Thus, there is a territorial scheme ranging from local councils through counties, provinces, and the like, through States, possibly even through groups of States (*blocs*, unions, *ententes*), to the final stage of the World Community itself. Equally important, however, are the concurrent federalisms of vocational bodies, religious bodies, and so forth. In so far as these have territorial interests and afford possibilities of territorial conflicts they are part of the complex of associations which the State co-ordinates. But they have no national boundaries; their limits are functional, not territorial, and they will have both national and international functional co-ordinating bodies of their own. In practice the structure will be even more complicated than this, as we shall show later, but these are the main lines of the group organization that tends to be adopted throughout the world. The organs of the World Community (in so far as any exist) are therefore multiple and not unitary, being separated along vocational, religious, cultural, territorial, and other lines. To use a familiar metaphor, association is "vertical" territorially and "horizontal" in other respects. The one type is as real as the other and neither has any theoretical pre-eminence. For the process of co-ordination and adjudication each tends to have its own code of law which is unitary in a geographical sense. That is to say, international law is the unitary law of States (territorial organization) and as such overrides local law where necessary. But the "international law" of vocational, religious, or other associations, no less real for not being called "law," is something quite different with its own validity and maybe its own sanctions. There is no hint of a unitary law in the extreme sense of a body of law covering not only the whole world but all aspects of human activity, any more than there was in the Middle Ages when the Canon Law, the Commercial Code, and local law existed side by side, each acknowledged in its own sphere. Internationally, as nationally, there is no formula for co-ordinating these groups of different kinds, for their "laws" are different in kind. No unitary law can be imagined to "co-ordinate" or judge between individual allegiances. Each group stands or falls by the degree to which its own policy commends itself to the members of the group. The decision will lie where the individual human beings finally wish.

This argument naturally simplifies, and abstracts from, reality, but for the purpose of exposition this is unavoidable. In the last resort the individual personality is the test and touchstone of it all, and every device and mechanism has to be judged according to its reactions on individual persons. Only in so far as groupings and associations and their accompanying mechanisms satisfy the urge towards individual freedom and creative activity will they finally endure.

S

CHAPTER XXIII

TRADE UNIONS IN POLITICAL THEORY

THE discussion in the preceding chapters has been concerned with the general theory of the State in relation to groups, but Trade Unions as such have received special attention in some of the recent developments of political thought. It will, therefore, be desirable to consider briefly some of the current views regarding Trade Unions and their place and functions in the modern industrial State. This is a matter of the more importance since in two modern constitutions, those of Russia and Italy, these organizations assume a new role and form an integral part of the mechanism of the new society in each country. In surveying these developments we shall be concerned not so much with actual practice in the countries concerned, nor even with the formal relationships and mechanisms created by the Constitutions and subsequent legislation, but rather with the ideas underlying these new experiments. To some extent those ideas have been consciously thought out, but in large part they must be inferred from speeches, decrees, laws, and regulations.

Although controversy regarding the powers and functions of groups has not been confined to the discussion of any particular type, certain categories of association have naturally received more attention than others. The struggles of earlier centuries, between secular Governments and the Church, only reflected the conflict in men's minds and activities between two powers that stood for something very real in the society of the period. Other associations were also real and in the aggregate were an important factor in the national life, but the influence of religion was still so strong and pervasive that the Church at first, and for long, was an authority dominating even the civil power. The religious State has gone and the industrial

State is with us. Hence it is now industrial groups that challenge established government and claim a reality and authority, in their own sphere at least, that would make the political State but a shadow of its former self. If economic forces more and more dominate the lives and thoughts of men they will also mould the organization of the State, and the growth of autonomous economic institutions and associations is one evidence that this is happening.

There is no necessary conflict here with the concept of sovereignty. A sovereign State can be "religious" or industrial; that is to say, its mechanism can be captured by religious or industrial interests. In Marxian theory the State has, in fact, been captured by the capitalist class and is merely an instrument of their domination. The present Russian State is a sovereign State which is also an instrument of class domination, but in this case it is the working class that has captured the machine. The hierarchy of State institutions, then, may represent the predominance of economic interests in a unitary State, and in such a case the tendency will be for the place and functions of Trade Unions to be determined by the degree of power possessed by the working class. If Capitalist interests are overwhelmingly powerful Trade Unions may be suppressed altogether or at any rate unrecognized, while the State mechanism itself embodies Capitalist organization. If the workers' interests are all-powerful, Capitalist organizations may similarly be suppressed or not recognized, and Trade Unions may become organs of the State, or may even dominate it. Where there is active conflict between classes, the economic organizations may exist outside or partly outside the State mechanism and exert varying degrees of power.

On the other hand the State may openly assume a functional form, with sovereignty divided, in which case Trade Unions may become, not subordinate, but co-ordinate organs of a pluralistic State. All these possible forms have figured in theories of politics, especially in Socialistic theories. Except for

Socialistic writers, and sometimes among them, too, theorists of the "unitary State" have attached no special importance to Trade Unions. Modern pluralistic theories, however, whether Socialistic or not, have given the Unions functions and position corresponding to their actual power in the industrial society of to-day.

Of the unitary theories, the older type of Collectivism or State Socialism, and Marxian Socialism (of which Russian Communism is the most detailed example), may be taken as having something definite to say on the place of Trade Unionism within the sovereign State. Of pluralistic theories, Syndicalism and its variants provide examples in which Trade Unionism is the very basis of the State, but unfortunately the political theory of Syndicalism has never been worked out very fully. The ideas of Laski and Cole differ from each other and from Syndicalism, but they have obvious affinities with the latter doctrine, and Trade Unions figure largely in both.

Finally, there are attempts to reconcile unitary and pluralistic ideas; such are the theories underlying the Corporative State in Italy, under the present regime, and apparently in Nazi Germany. The former owes its origin largely to Syndicalism and has an important place for Trade Unionism, even though in practice the division of sovereignty is a mere sham.[1] The principles underlying the 1919 German Constitution, and to some extent the new Constitution of Czechoslovakia, indicate a faint attempt to "pluralize" some aspects of political and economic government. It will be convenient to divide all these theories and experiments into two categories, those owing the whole or part of their inspiration to Syndicalism, and therefore elevating Trade Unionism to a position of great importance or even supremacy, and those deriving from Marx and based

[1] See also Elliott, W. Y., *The Pragmatic Revolt in Politics*; but his "co-organic" theory will not be considered here as it has no peculiarly Trade Union interest.

on political monism. Before Sorel transformed its theoretical basis, Syndicalism itself owed a good deal to the ideas of the Anarchist-Communists. Division of sovereignty, economic federalism, functional decentralization—whatever terms are used, the conception is as familiar to the student of Syndicalism in France or Spain, of Guild Socialism in England, of Corporative theory in Italy, as to the reader of Proudhon and Bakunin. The "free commune" of the Anarchists reappears in later Syndicalist and allied theories; in the conception of the Bourses du Travail held by Pelloutier, the real founder of Syndicalism; in the schemes of Guillaume de Greef,[1] that early Syndicalist, as Mrs. Douglas rightly terms him; and even in the "communes" of Cole's later versions of Guild Socialism.

The fact that Syndicalism and Marxian Socialism differ fundamentally in their political philosophy has often been pointed out, and indeed the early history of the Socialist International, with its clash of view and ultimate split between Marxists and Bakuninists, reminds us that the two wings of what is often held to be one movement spring from radically different sources. They agree in their economic analysis, for both are Socialistic in the sense that they are anti-Capitalistic and accept the class-struggle as their central feature. Nevertheless, although the overthrow of Capitalism is the primary aim of both movements, and therefore they have tended sometimes to organize together, and even to borrow occasionally from each other's practical programmes of action, they have different philosophical origins and—important for our purpose —different political theories (in so far as they can be said to have political theories at all).

Marx and his school were powerfully influenced by Hegel, and their whole habit of thought, politically, is monistic. The Marxians have remained almost untouched by the development of pluralist thought. Syndicalism, on the other hand, is

[1] Douglas, Dorothy W., *Guillaume de Greef; an early Syndicalist* (1925).

commonly supposed to derive its philosophical basis from Bergson. Actually this is only true of Sorel and his school, in the later history of the movement. The early Syndicalism of Pelloutier (which is more important for our present purpose, since Sorel confined himself to a theory of the method of overthrowing Capitalism and contributed nothing to the theory of a Syndicalist society), goes back to Proudhon and Godwin, and their Anarchist forerunners.[1] To regard Marx and Proudhon as the prophets of Collectivist Socialism and Syndicalist Socialism respectively would be accurate enough, but it would not be altogether fair to make this distinction. A true picture would have to be more complicated than this, for Marxism itself has taken divergent paths leading, on the one hand, to revolutionary Socialism (or Communism) and on the other to Revisionism. The former alone is entitled to call itself thoroughly Marxian, for Revisionism, despite its profession of a Marxian economic basis, is fundamentally different, not merely in its theory of tactics, but in its whole outlook. In its general philosophy, in fact, Revisionism has a great deal in common with the older British Socialism of the Collectivist school as expounded by J. R. MacDonald. It is evolutionary, whereas the complete Marxian is necessarily revolutionary, and the class struggle, the central feature of Marxism, is, if not denied, at any rate considerably toned down by the Revisionists.

On the other hand, the Syndicalist stream of thought also split into divergent currents. The Syndicalism of Pelloutier, with its basis of the local *syndicat* and the local *bourse*, was transformed even in France, and much more in America, into the doctrine of national *syndicats*, with the further addition, in the United States, of the One Big Union idea. At the same time Guild Socialism, which developed in England, adapted

[1] Kropotkin traces Anarchism back to Aristippus and the Cynics, Zeno and the Stoics, and Lao-tse! Kropotkin, P., *Modern Science and Anarchism* (1912).

Syndicalism to a system of national Unions, elaborated its social theory, and added provision for non-producer interests which the Syndicalists neglected. Of these schools of thought, French and American Syndicalism were revolutionary in the Marxian sense and accepted Marx's economic analysis, while Guild Socialism was also, though not very convincingly, revolutionary, though Marx's economic theories were not a necessary feature, and both the Marxian tactics of revolution and the Syndicalist tactics of the general strike were rejected.

When all these theories are analysed it will be seen that the difficulty of comparison lies in the fact that each one of them is (a) a theory of the economic basis of Socialism, (b) a theory of the tactics of transition to Socialism, (c) a theory of the Socialist community. Communists, Revisionists, and Syndicalists agreed on the economic basis, but British collectivists and many Guild Socialists did not accept it. On the tactics of transition the Communists differed from all the others; Revisionists and British Collectivists took much the same view; Syndicalists had their own ideas, and Guild Socialists never really had a clear policy. In their political theory all except Guild Socialists were decidedly sketchy, but Communists, Revisionists, and British Collectivists were supporters of undivided sovereignty, while Syndicalists and Guild Socialists were pluralistic.

Now, the relation of Trade Unions to the State in these theories was conditioned by all the above differences in basis, economic and political. To the Communists, the strict Marxians, Trade Unions were merely a by-product of the Capitalist system, class organizations, important as a means, one of the predestined means, of overthrowing Capitalism. "Permanent combinations have been formed," said Marx, "Trade Unions which serve as a rampart for the workers in their struggle with the Capitalists."[1] Otherwise the Unions did not enter the picture. Marx's notion of the proletarian State during

[1] *The Poverty of Philosophy* (trans. H. Quelch), 187.

the period of the dictatorship, following the revolution, was based on the experience of the Paris Commune of 1871. It was a "thoroughly expansive political form," said Marx,[1] and again, "It was the political form, at last discovered, under which to work out the economic emancipation of Labour." The Commune, in Marx's words, "was formed of the municipal councillors, chosen by universal suffrage in various wards of the town, responsible and revocable at short terms. The majority of its members were naturally working men, or acknowledged representatives if the working class. The Commune was to be a working, not a Parliamentary body, executive and legislative at the same time. . . . Like the rest of public servants, magistrates and judges were to be elective, responsible and revocable."[2] The Communes, purely local bodies, as in Paris, were to elect district assemblies of delegates, and these in turn were to send delegates to the National Delegation, each delegate to be bound by the mandate of his constituents and to be subject to recall.[3] In its pyramidal structure and indirect election, as well as in its proletarian constituencies on a geographical basis, this scheme foreshadowed the Soviet constitution actually adopted in Russia after the 1917 November Revolution,[4] but in this case the democratic features were deleted; in addition to the "dictatorship of the proletariat" in the Marxian sense there was the dictatorship of the Communist Party within the proletariat, a departure from pure Marxism justified by the Russian Communists on grounds of practical necessity.

In the system expounded by Marx, then, the Trade Unions did not figure save as ramparts of the proletariat in the attack on Capitalism. We shall see later how they fared in the establishment and functioning of the unitary proletarian State in Russia.

[1] *The Civil War in France* (trans. E. B. Bax), 48.
[2] *Ibid.*, 43–4.   [3] *Ibid.*, 44–6.
[4] For this and other aspects of Communist political theory see Chang, S. H. M., *The Marxian Theory of the State* (1931).

What of the State (or rather the community, for according to Engels the proletarian State itself is ultimately to disappear), after the period of the proletarian dictatorship? Here, Marx was extremely vague and sketchy. In fact, he was not primarily a political theorist and he was apparently not very interested in this aspect of the question, which in any case must have seemed remote.

Most Marxists refuse to particularize, claiming it as a virtue that they will not draw up a Utopia to be realized in the future. Such things, they say, must be left to work themselves out when the time comes, since we cannot foresee all the circumstances. This is doubtless a sound view if it means a refusal to go into great detail, but at the same time it is necessary, if one claims to be scientific, to have some idea of the way in which society might be organized and might function. Marx said: "In place of the old bourgeois society, with its classes and class antagonisms, we shall have an association in which the free development of each is the condition for the free development of all."[1] Later he became a trifle more helpful and stated that in the Stateless Communistic society the division of labour would disappear, wealth would be ample in quantity for all, antagonism between manual and intellectual labour would have disappeared, and the rule would be, "from everyone according to his faculties, to everyone according to his needs."[2] This, however, can hardly be termed a working model of Communist society, or even a blue-print for a model. More detail has been given by Lenin, who was especially interested in the political theory of Communism, even before the Revolution. From Lenin's exposition,[3] which elaborates, but adds little that is new to, Marx's description, it is clear that the Stateless society contemplated would be without government; it would, in fact, be the Utopian society

---

[1] *Communist Manifesto.*
[2] *Criticism of the Gotha Programme* (1875).
[3] Lenin, N., *The State and Revolution* (1917), ch. IV.

of the Anarchists. Men would work voluntarily according to their abilities,[1] wealth would be abundant, there would be no need for police, prisons, laws, etc.[2] Why this slide into Utopia on the part of thoroughgoing realists? The suspicion is inevitable that it is preached rather as a "vital lie," in the language of Sorel, than as something which will really come to pass. How long will it take for the proletarian State, the dictatorship, to wither away, leaving the Stateless Utopia to flourish? Two or three generations, say Bukharin and Preobraschensky, but Lenin, more cautious, says, "We do not and cannot know,"[3] and he adds significantly, "As long as the 'highest phase' of Communism has not arrived, the Socialists demand the *strictest* control *by Society and by the State* of the quantity of labour and the quantity of consumption."[4] "It has never entered the head of any Socialist," he says, " 'to promise' that the highest phase of Communism will actually arrive."[5] The proletarian dictatorship will remain, the State will remain, until all are ready and fitted for anarchy. Marxians and Anarchists were in agreement in looking to the abolition of the State as a final aim, said Marx,[6] but the Anarchists thought they could jump to this position immediately, whereas Marxians urged that the proletarian dictatorship and the use of the State so created were essential to the attainment of this aim. The Marxian view, so much more realistic and intelligent, inevitably pushes the "final aim" into the Utopian and never-realized future.

The Syndicalists, unlike the Anarchists, whose basis they in some degree took over, also realized the importance of tactics of transition. Their doctrine has indeed become identified in the public mind with the theory of the General Strike, the philosophy of direct action, of mass emotion as opposed to

[1] Lenin, N., *The State and Revolution* (1917), ch. iv.

[2] Bukharin, N., and Preobraschensky, E., *ABC of Communism* (1924).

[3] *The State and Revolution*, ch. IV.   [4] *Ibid.*

[5] *Ibid.*   [6] *Ibid.*

rationality. There were two distinct phases of Syndicalism in France, however, the earlier being the more interesting from the point of view of this chapter.[1] The ideas of Pelloutier were nearer the Anarchist tradition of Proudhon and Bakunin. The basis was local—the local Trade Union, the local Bourse du Travail, and then the free association of the Bourses in a federation. The Bourse was to be not merely a local federation of Trade Unions (a Trades Council, as this would have been called in Britain) but, in addition, the local centre of civic life, a kind of municipality with an industrial basis, the "commune" of Anarchist-Communism; in short, the Commune of Paris in 1871, Marx's model for the proletarian State. The federation of Bourses, like the All-Union Congress of Soviets in the U.S.S.R., would have the task of reconciling local needs and differences. The local basis was the keynote of the early Syndicalism and association or federation over a wider area was to be voluntary. There was to be no sovereign State, either of an industrial or any other kind. Each local unit was to be autonomous, but all were to associate voluntarily to settle differences and arrange for the satisfaction of each other's needs. This local foundation was, of course, a natural consequence of French Trade Union and industrial structure at the time. There were very few national aggregations either of Labour or Capital. At the close of the nineteenth century industry and Trade Unionism were developing on national lines, hence the conflict from 1895 to 1902 between the two rival forms of organization, local and national. The new constitution of the Confédération Général du Travail in 1902 provided for two sections constituted respectively of federations of Bourses and National Unions or federations of Unions, but this was the beginning of the end of "localism." The evolution of industry necessitated the development of national Trade Unions and the Bourses soon degenerated into Trades

[1] For the history of French Syndicalism see Levine, L., *The Labor Movement in France* (1912, under title *Syndicalism in France*).

Councils, local federations of Trade Union branches, with a quite subordinate position and relatively unimportant functions. The early Syndicalism, then, was cast in a pluralistic mould without, however, having any definite conception of pluralism in the modern sense. It was, in fact, a form of federalism and not a functional pluralism.

The later doctrine, as elaborated by Sorel,[1] and others, in France, Italy, and Spain, was preoccupied with the general strike, with the overthrow of Capitalism, with a philosophy of tactics based on Mirabeau's saying, "Ce peuple dont la seule immobilité serait formidable," but proceeding beyond passive resistance to mass violence. These Syndicalists rejected with scorn all speculation regarding the organization of society after the revolution, though at the same time they constantly talked of the new industrial commonwealth.[2] Their one positive idea was control of industry by the workers, but how this control was to be exercised, how different units were to be co-ordinated, how "non-producing" interests were to be provided for, even how industrial capital was to be owned—on these and other vital points they were either silent or else hopelessly confused. Centralization in the Trade Union sphere was a cardinal feature of the later syndicalism which, as Cole says, "denied the sovereignty of the State only to enthrone the General Confederation of Labour in its stead."[3] Similarly in the United States, where the later version of Syndicalism was taken over by a small section of organized labour, there was a somewhat vague idea that the national industrial Unions that were postulated should be federated in One Big Union or in a Trade Union centre, possessing so much authority as to be the sovereign State once more in industrial disguise. On similar lines was the Syndicalism of *The Miners' Next Step*, the South Wales Miners' famous programme of the disturbed

[1] Sorel, G., *Reflexions sur la Violence* (1908).
[2] See Cole, G. D. H., *Self Government in Industry*, Appendix A.
[3] *Op. cit.*, 85.

years immediately preceding the war. The proposal was to establish the "co-ordination of all industries on a central production board who, with a statistical department to ascertain the needs of the people, will issue its demands on the different branches of industry, leaving to the men to determine under what conditions and how the work should be done."

But in general, the later Syndicalist writers refused to think of the future; that was to be left to the *élan vital* which would carry through a successful general strike and find in the inspiration of the moment a suitable form for the new society. In so far as they had any ideas at all on the subject they were perhaps only restrained by their anarchist origin and early history from aiming definitely at a sovereign State based on associations of producers (the Trade Unions) federated in a central body, the wider implications of government and civic organization being ignored.

The points of similarity and of difference between Syndicalism, in both phases, and Marxian Communism will be apparent. Superficially the similarities are more striking than the differences. Sorel and the later Syndicalists, especially, were thoroughly Marxian in their economic and historical analysis and their acceptance of the class-struggle as the central feature of their creed, as well as in their emphasis on revolutionary tactics of transition. Again, the Anarchist tendencies of the vague Marxian conception of the ultimate Stateless society, as well as of Pelloutier's social theory, have been pointed out. But the philosophical basis and general outlook of Marxism are different from those of Syndicalism. Even the later Syndicalists, who were much less influenced by Anarchism than their predecessors, did not, following Marx, go back to Hegel or Feuerbach but professed to base their doctrines on Bergson and William James. Sorel and his school, in fact, belonged to a movement covering a much wider field than any industrial or economic doctrine. They were part of the twentieth-century anti-intellectualist movement which represented a revolt against Rationalism, against the domination of intellect, against the application to human phenomena of nineteenth-century methods of natural science, and which exalted instinct, "intuition" and action.[1] In comparison with the new and subtle metaphysics of Bergson, and the rich content of Durkheim's sociology, the metaphysics of Hegel, and the sociology of Spencer seemed naïve and out of date. The role of these factors in a propagandist social movement can easily be exaggerated, but they undoubtedly affected the theories current at the time. As philosophic systems both Bergsonism and Pragmatism were short-lived, but the broad stream of thought of which they were part flows to-day with more force than ever. Syndicalism, in this aspect, belongs as emphatically to the modern age as Marx's doctrine did to the age of Darwin and Spencer. The Syndicalists would have hailed with joy the introduction of the "principle of indeterminacy" into politics and economics as well as into physics.

The emphasis laid by Syndicalism on Trade Unions and their functions, both in bringing about the revolution and in forming the basis of the new society, was not altogether unconnected with these philosophical influences. The Unions stood for the spontaneous, free association of workers, a movement based on a mass impulse or emotion, owing nothing to the careful plans of "intellectuals" or the theoretical schemes of statesmen. The strength of the Unions was precisely in their will to action, arising out of their most primitive needs. The State was something formal and alien, the Unions were entirely the creation of the workers and the natural vehicle of their power.

It is therefore not surprising that Trade Unionism was a detail in the Marxian framework, but the very corner-stone of Syndicalism.

[1] See Elliott, W. Y., *The Pragmatic Revolt in Politics*; Scott, J. W., *Syndicalism and Philosophical Realism* (1919).

CHAPTER XXIV

TRADE UNIONS AND SCHEMES OF ECONOMIC DECENTRALIZATION

BETWEEN the extremes of the sovereign State and the sovereign producers' group, a number of theories have sought a *via media* which would allow of considerable autonomy to organized economic interests while preserving a central cohesive and co-ordinating authority. Such solutions have been worked out both for a Capitalistic and for a Socialistic regime, though in no case with sufficient practical detail to be thoroughly satisfactory. At the same time, all these theories are closer to reality than was Syndicalism, with its impossibly vague ideas about the organization of society, and all are more satisfactory from the democratic point of view than the theories of the omnipotent State.

Whether Capitalistic or Socialistic these schemes usually involve a devolution of authority to economic interests, if the approach is from the angle of State sovereignty, of a federalism of economic interests if the approach is pluralistic. In practice there may be little difference between the two types of proposals, but economic federalism usually involves occupational representation in the election of a central authority. Occupational representation, however, is not necessarily incompatible with a unitary State. It merely emphasises economic rather than geographical interests. Bismarck many years ago proposed to adopt this basis for the Second Chamber in Germany, but he would not thereby have devised a pluralistic constitution. To take a more recent example, Soviet Russia has adopted a unitary system based partly on occupational representation working through a hierarchy of elected bodies. Devolution of power, in a unitary State, may give quite a large degree of autonomy to certain subordinate organs representing economic interests, but in the long run this is only a variant of the concession theory, and the central Government remains not merely the co-ordinating mechanism, but, if it desires, the organ capable of overriding all particular interests even in matters they themselves deem "internal." On the other hand, federalism either reserves certain powers to the constituent bodies and makes them supreme in the field thus delimited, or else it defines the powers of the central Government and leaves the constituents with unquestioned authority in all that remains. Even in the latter event, the federal Government's rights, though limited, are very real and, within the field assigned, are not subject to an overriding veto of the constituents; thus, there is a genuine division of powers. That such federalism is practicable in the economic sphere has been the contention of many pluralists.

De Greef has already been mentioned, but he is worth more extended notice, not so much for the intrinsic importance of his ideas as for his historic interest. Deriving his philosophy largely from Proudhon and Durkheim, he elaborated the notion of functional federalism in a way that strongly recalls the much later work of the Guild Socialists in England, the Labour sections of the Weimar Constitution in Germany, in 1919, and even the development of the Corporative State in Fascist Italy. It is unnecessary to detail the proposals advanced by De Greef, historically interesting though they are, for his successors are more important to our present purpose.[1] "Each of his two-sided[2] single-occupational councils," we are told, "from the local unit up to the national, was to fill affirmative economic functions. Its role was not merely advisory but legislative and executive. It was itself the administering agency of the Government which it helped to form. Now what did this mean for the Labour branch of that agency? It meant its organization for the first time into an active and responsible

[1] For a detailed study see Douglas, D. W., *Guillaume de Greef* (1925).
[2] I.e. representing employers and Trade Unions.

bargaining agency. The same official machinery that selected the composite occupational grouping of Parliament was to select the collective bargaining groups within each trade all along the way. Labour was, under Government sanction, to be formed into a coherent body, articulated at its own natural divisions, and harnessed in independent working relationship to its more experienced partner in industry, for the binding decision of many matters of common moment."[1] With his framework of Works Councils, District Councils, and National Councils, each consisting of employers' and workers' representatives, De Greef reminds us of the much later Whitley Reports, but his councils were to have legislative and executive powers, they were to be part of the occupational-plus-geographical State, not merely industrial advisory bodies. The similarity to the economic councils provided for in the German Constitution of 1919 and the Works Councils Act of 1920 will be even more apparent, and the national Corporations foreshadowed in the Fascist reorganization of the State will seem to be but the more modern development of some of De Greef's nineteenth-century ideas.

Guild Socialism, too, accorded in some of its main principles with these views. Though its philosophical basis and social theory were much more fully worked out, by Cole and others, it may be doubted whether De Greef's industrial scheme was not more realistic; it was a practical policy he tried to expound, and not a Utopia. The political theory of Guild Socialism has already been referred to,[2] but we may add here that, apart from their pluralistic outlook in regard to sovereignty, the doctrines of Cole, Hobson, Penty, and the rest had particular reference to the reorganization and government of productive industry.[3] In the initial stages, indeed, the concept of society as a whole was shadowy if not entirely absent. Penty and the earliest

[1] Douglas, *op. cit.*, 349.   [2] See p. 244.
[3] Cole, G. D. H., *Self Government in Industry; Guild Socialism Restated*, etc.

T

Guildsmen held views reminiscent of the Anarchists and early Syndicalists, and the local rather than national organization of "Guilds" was for long a matter of sharp controversy. Cole and the National Guilds League were always aware that the modern development of industry on large-scale lines made such ideas as those of Penty obsolete, but in trying to combine the virtues of both Collectivism and Syndicalism while avoiding their weaknesses, they wavered between the essentially different concepts of the State underlying those two movements. Beginning with a completely pluralistic scheme, Cole finally revised his doctrine on lines which left some doubt whether the sovereign State had not in fact been re-enthroned.

Throughout all these changes Trade Unionism remained one of the vital factors in the new plan for industry and for society as a whole. Whether influenced from time to time by Syndicalism or Collectivism, Anarchism or Monism, Guild Socialism was firmly based on the recognition of organized Labour as an integral part of the mechanism by which society must function. Never viewed as the sovereign power in disguise, it was always regarded as an active, equal partner, responsible for legislation and execution and not merely for advice. The demand for "workers' control," the slogan popularized and incessantly preached by the Guildsmen, very deeply influenced the development of Trade Union and Socialist philosophy in the years 1910–20. As has been said, the precise role of the Unions in the projected reorganization of industrial Government was never worked out very convincingly. Throughout the many changes in Guild Socialist thought, the concept of the National Guild as the body responsible for the operation and control of an industry was maintained. Ownership was to be vested in the community, but for management and internal policy the Guild was to have sole competence. Being composed of all the workers in the industry, from "managers" and technicians down to office cleaners, all being represented through their appropriate vocational associations, each Guild would be a democratic body and industrial autocracy would no longer be possible. Where the spheres of different Guilds intersected, the Congress of Guilds would have the deciding voice. Where the spheres of Guilds and consumers overlapped, some joint organization of Guild Congress and political Parliament would decide. Inside a Guild, the workers would have certain powers of electing managers and foremen, or of rejecting appointees.

It was just at these points of difficulty—the clashing of Guild with Guild, or Guilds with society at large, and the appointment of technical and commercial experts and managers—that the theory was weakest and most uncertain. The concrete problems that arise in running complicated industries in a world of international competition were at first ignored and were never satisfactorily faced. Finally, Cole's exposition became cluttered up with such a bewildering series of committees and sub-committees, councils and boards, all apparently devised in order to act as checks upon each other, that the existing industrial structure began to look comparatively simple, and Guild Socialism began to look like a Civil Servant's nightmare. The chief fault of the gifted author of the theory was that he tried to build on a logical basis instead of a psychological basis.

Instead of following the development of Trade Unions along what they themselves seemed to think their natural path of progress, the Guild theorist blandly transformed them, amalgamated them, divided them, juggled with them in a manner that decidedly ignored the facts of the Trade Union and industrial world. The idea of democratic control of industry undoubtedly took firm root in the minds of Trade Unionists, but the realities of it were never faced. Autonomy and self-determination sound well, but what happens when, either with industries or with nations, policies and actions have effects which ripple outwards until they vitally touch industries and nations at the other end of the earth? We have the choice between unending competition and conflict or the creation of a superior authority to decide. Guild Socialism finally chose the latter, with great reluctance, and so dropped the cruder ideas of democracy that had been associated with it. Nevertheless, a solid contribution had been made to social theory and to the programme of Trade Unionism. Though the development of the constructive functions of Trade Unions was not a new idea, the Guildsmen stressed it so much that subsequent thought and even events were profoundly affected in this direction.

The Whitley Reports[1] themselves were obviously influenced by the current propaganda for industrial democracy, and even though Whitleyism was designed to have only advisory powers within Capitalist industry, its insistence on the constructive functions of Whitley Councils consisting of equal numbers of representatives of organized employers and organized workers was in itself a notable step forward. It would have meant a good many steps, of course, if "joint control" and constructive functions had been accepted in practice, and not merely in the pages of the Whitley Committee's Reports. The Unions would then have become more important and powerful elements in the structure of industry and, though doubtless this was not in the mind of the Whitley Committee, the way to some kind of economic decentralization would have become much easier.

Both the inadequacy of Whitleyism and the weaknesses of the primitive democracy of Guild Socialism were seen by the Webbs, who propounded their own scheme of what might be called functional Collectivism.[2] If Guild Socialism came midway between Syndicalism and Collectivism, the Webbs' plan came between Collectivism and Guild Socialism! The chief innovation was the creation of two Parliaments, the House of Lords being abolished and no Second Chamber in the ordinary

---

[1] See Seymour, J. B., *The Whitley Councils Movement.*
[2] Webb, S. and B., *Constitution for the Socialist Commonwealth of Great Britain.*

sense of the term being put in its place. One of the Parliaments would be "political," dealing with such matters as foreign affairs, defence, internal order, etc., and the other would be "social," dealing with all economic questions as well as social services such as education and public health. Both Parliaments would be elected on a geographical, not vocational, basis, and would have legislative and not merely advisory powers. Finance would, subject to certain limitations, be in the hands of the Social Parliament, and disputes would be settled by a joint session of the two chambers, or by the Courts if the interpretation of the fundamental statute was in question. In the control of industry itself, primitive democracy with its election of managers by the workers, and so on, would be rigorously excluded.[1] Standing Committees of the Social Parliament would supervise high policy for each socialized industry, with permanent and separate control departments to watch costs, research, etc., while for current administration there would be National Boards appointed by the Social Parliament on the advice of the appropriate standing committee. Each Board would consist of representatives of the technical staff and management, the Trade Unions concerned, and consumers generally, the last named being in a minority.

These proposals deserved more consideration, at the time they were put forward, than they received, for they were framed on more realistic lines than many propagandist schemes, and they had the great merit of taking into account economic institutions as they actually were, with all the human prejudices and feelings attached to them. The Webbs' plan now seems as "dated" as Guild Socialism itself. It appears to over-simplify the problem. We have, with further experience, become sceptical of neat solutions and dubious about the idea of dividing Parliament in this way. Nevertheless, there is still a lot to be learned from the penetrating discussion of the whole question that precedes the outline of the Constitution.

[1] *Op. cit.*, 158 ff.

Later writers have been more cautious in their actual proposals. Laski, for instance, whose political theory has already been discussed,[1] does not specify in detail the structure of industrial Government in a pluralist society, though, like the earlier schemes, his proposals make the Trade Unions an essential factor in the functioning of the economic system. While a network of advisory organs is suggested to bring expert knowledge into effective use, while keeping a democratic system free from the tyranny of bureaucratic or autocratic control, the application of this idea to industry is only indicateed in general terms. The establishment of a so-called "Industrial Parliament" representative of industry as a whole is condemned.[2]

Very different from these Socialistic plans is the scheme proposed by a group of "advanced" Conservative M.P.s, whose conception of the relation between industry and the State is bounded by their desire for a smoothly working Capitalism.[3] There is little or no idea of economic decentralization, and Trade Unions are scarcely mentioned except for vague suggestions that they should be able, after the provision of better machinery for the settlement of wages and conditions, to take on more constructive functions. Labour participation in industrial Government is hinted at, but it is apparently hoped to satisfy the workers' aspirations through co-partnership, employee stock ownership, and similar expedients.

In a later scheme[4] MacMillan has advanced a stage further, and it is now proposed to establish a representative National Council for each industry with the ultimate object of enabling the industry to "evolve towards the highest possible unity of" policy and the necessary degree of centralization of control. These Councils would be recognized by the Government as

[1] See p. 242.   [2] *A Grammar of Politics.* See also p. 377.
[3] Boothby, R., Loder, J. de V., MacMillan, H., Stanley, O. *Industry and the State* (1927).
[4] MacMillan, H., *The State and Industry in 1932.*

the "authority with which it would deal on all matters affecting the interests which they represented," and provision would be made "for the association of Labour with the discussions of these Councils in all matters affecting the welfare of the workers with a view to avoiding Strikes or Lockouts." Recognition of workers' organizations is hardly mentioned at all, but the opinion is expressed that "we have reached a stage when functional representation is essential."[1] These proposals are only included here because they are among the very few, relevant to the purpose of this book, that have emanated from Capitalistic quarters.

Of much greater importance among non-Socialist schemes is that propounded in some detail in the Report of the Liberal Industrial Inquiry.[2] "Industry should be assisted," say the distinguished economists and industrialists who sign the Report,[3] "towards a system of self-government and co-operation." The dominating idea, however, is that of State supremacy. The State "exists to maintain peace, justice and liberty for all its citizens, and this obligation does not cease in the sphere of industry."[4] The tendency towards industrial decentralization is noted, and indeed welcomed. "There has also been a steady movement of opinion towards the view that the voluntary organization of industries for self-regulation offered the true line of advance." In making suggestions for applying this conception the Liberal Committee seem to have in mind only, or at any rate chiefly, the avoidance of industrial disputes and the improvement of industrial relations generally. There is little indication of any real approach to industrial self-government. The status and power of the workers should be increased, it is evidently thought, by an extension of profit-sharing,[5] employee stock ownership,[6] and similar devices, rather than by any scheme of "workers' control," which is roundly con-

[1] *Loc. cit.*, 15. [2] *Britain's Industrial Future* (1928), ch. 16–19.
[3] *Ibid.*, 140. [4] *Ibid.*, 166.
[5] *Ibid.*, 198–204. [6] *Ibid.*, 249 ff.

demned as impracticable and undesirable.[1] "We are often told that in the Socialist State, or at any rate in the Guild Socialist State, 'workers' control' will be so complete that managers and foremen will be elected by the men who have to work under them. This would ensure complete failure. . . . Consultation with a body of workers will improve and strengthen" the management of a business; "Anything that can be accurately described as 'workers' control' will destroy it." The appointment of workers to the Board of Directors is dismissed as useless, except perhaps where profit-sharing is in force, or where there is a Supervisory Board, on the German model, which might well have representatives of the workpeople sitting upon it.[2] Works Councils are approved, and it is suggested that they should be made compulsory, as in Germany, while employers should also be compelled to circulate regularly to their workers or Works Councils full information regarding profits, costs, prices, and so on.

As regards general industrial organization, the Liberal Committee contemplates the continuance of Capitalism in a unitary State, and merely proposes the creation of a permanent Council of Industry, consisting of nine employers' representatives, nine Trade Union representatives, and six other members appointed by the "Minister of Industry." This Council would work in close touch with the Ministry and should be given certain advisory powers, as well as the function of keeping industry under continuous review. When industry is more fully organized, a large National Industrial Council, representative of the whole of industry, might be established.

The problem of serious clash between Trade Unions and the State, as a result of the stoppage of essential services, is the subject of special recommendations. "It is not possible," say the Committee, "even in these industries, to abrogate the ultimate right to strike or lock out, since this is the foundation of negotiating power. No absolute guarantee against interrup-

[1] *Britain's Industrial Future* (1928), 227–8.   [2] *Ibid.*, 228–9.

tion is therefore possible."[1] It is suggested that apart from the more complete development of negotiating machinery, compulsory delay of a stoppage while investigation is made (as under the Canadian Industrial Disputes Investigation Act), should be enforced. Other possibilities mentioned are the placing of workers in essential services on an establishment basis (with pensions and other privileges as in the Civil Service); lengthy contracts of employment with penalties for breach of contract similar to those provided in the Conspiracy and Protection of Property Act, 1875;[2] the deposit of substantial sums by employers and Trade Unions, to be forfeited in the event of a stoppage; and removal of Trade Unions from the immunities conferred by the Trade Disputes Act, 1906,[3] in cases where the negotiating machinery had not been fully utilized.

Throughout the Report of the Liberal Industrial Inquiry—and this is the most considerable survey made in recent years by non-Socialist investigators—the emphasis is on the coercive powers of the State over industry, aided, but not supplanted, by joint mechanisms inside industry for consultation between Trade Unions and employers, and for advice by industry to the Government. Except on minor matters, there is no real movement towards industrial self-government, and no strong feeling that Trade Unions may have other functions than negotiation on wages and conditions.

We may turn now to consider briefly the contributions made to the solution of the problem by Soviet Russia and Fascist Italy.

[1] *Britain's Industrial Future* (1928), 215.   [2] See p. 183.
[3] See p. 185.

CHAPTER XXV

TRADE UNIONS AS AGENTS OF GOVERNMENT

THE relationship between Trade Unionism and the State has assumed a special importance in the post-war period in two countries that have followed very different roads in the attempt to reach social solidarity and industrial harmony.

It is naturally not possible even to outline in this short space the experience of Trade Unionism in post-Revolutionary Russia and Italy, and it is assumed that the reader is familiar with the recent history of these countries. All that is attempted here is to isolate the most significant features of their development, so far as they affect the problem under discussion, and to compare the contemporary tendencies in the two countries. Although at very different stages of economic evolution, Russia and Italy have this in common, that they have been in the past predominantly agricultural but have set themselves, after carrying through political revolutions, to create a modern industrial structure. It is with their methods of dealing with Trade Unionism in the new structure that we are concerned.

The State in the U.S.S.R. is federal in constitution, though there is no real division of powers. Political and administrative devolution exists, but the U.S.S.R. is essentially a unitary State.

This is in strict accord with Marxist political theory as amplified by Lenin, as is the adoption of indirect election to higher bodies in the hierarchy of authorities, and the subservience of the judiciary to the mixed legislative and executive body.[1] The model of the Paris Commune as expounded by Marx[2] is followed, as Lenin and Trotsky are careful to point out,[3] in designing the mechanism for the proletarian dictator-

---

[1] See p. 280. [2] Marx, K., *Civil War in France*.
[3] Lenin, N., and Trotsky, L., *The Proletarian Revolution in Russia*.

ship. There is a big difference, however, in that the U.S.S.R. has a dictatorship of the Communist Party rather than a dictatorship of the proletariat. This is defended on the ground of necessity in the face of counter-revolutionary attacks.

Also the city Soviets are supposed to be elected on an occupational basis, not geographical, as in the Paris Commune, and urban workers have larger representation than peasants in the various Congresses.

In the main, then, Communist theory in U.S.S.R. has followed Marxist theory, and practice has differed mainly in the realities of the dictatorship, which is not "proletarian democracy" with Communist Party leadership, as claimed by Lenin and Stalin.[1] The position of Trade Unionism is precisely what would be expected in such a system.

The right to combine in Unions is given only to workers and peasants, and these Unions are legally recognized as representative of all workpeople.

In the first phase of the Revolution, the Unions entered enthusiastically into the organization and management of industry. One of the first decrees (November 14, 1917) dealt with workers' control and provided that "control shall be exercised by the workers in each undertaking as a whole through the medium of their duly elected representatives . . . working in conjunction with the delegates appointed by the salaried employees and technical staff."[2] A "commission for workers' control" was attached to the factory committee in each business, there was a Trade Union Committee for each branch of industry, and finally an All-Russian Council for Workers' Control was set up.

In factories and workshops up and down the country the workers assumed power and practically took possession. The result was not unlike that found at a later date in Italy. Pro-

[1] Lenin, N., *The Proletarian Revolution* (1918); Stalin, J., *Leninism* (1928).
[2] I.L.O., *Trade Unions in Soviet Russia* (1927).

duction fell, distribution was chaotic where it existed at all, and a complete breakdown seemed imminent.

Early in 1918 the experiment came to an end by the decree of March 3rd, which enacted that the management of concerns abandoned by their owners was, with few exceptions, to be placed in the hands of Boards representing workers, technical staff, and the Supreme Economic Council, in equal numbers. In June 1918 the decree of nationalization was issued, under which all concerns were taken over by the State and leased free of charge to the former owners who would be subject to checks exercised by workers' control commissions. As a result of the disputes that followed, the Trade Unions and technical staffs were given the right to nominate, between them, a majority of the members of executive boards of undertakings.

From this time the policy was steadily pursued of squeezing the Unions out of their position of power in industry, and limiting them to the defence of workers' standards as in a Capitalist State. Towards the end of 1919, Trade Union leaders were suggesting that the economic organization as a whole should be placed under their control, with management of industries by the Unions concerned, but this was rejected by the Communist leaders.

Lenin, at the third Congress of Economic Councils, said: "Experience proves, on all sides, that the more perfect the organization of a State becomes, the more restricted is the collective principle. Practical work depends on the responsibility of one person . . . it is evident trade unions must take part in economic administration, as this is the foundation of our programme, but it is sufficient for them to put forward candidates."

The system of individual management was finally established in 1921 with the introduction of the N.E.P. Unions could still put forward candidates, but the selection was entirely in the hands of the special economic organizations set up, and the

Unions, as such, had no further functions in connection with industrial control. In a joint circular issued by the Supreme Economic Council and the All-Russian Central Council of Trade Unions, in 1923, it was declared "inadmissible that the trade unions should interfere in any way with the management of the undertakings," but they were given advisory functions in connection with the choice of managers, economic programmes, foreign business relations, and so on.

In 1926, an authoritative declaration[1] stated that "In the U.S.S.R. a sharp distinction is made between the function of managing industry and the function of organizing and defending the interests of the workers and employers in industry. The former function is in the hands of the National Economic authorities of the Trust and industry managements, and the latter function is in the hands of the workers' organizations and the trade unions." Later, the Unions were made to take a still more subordinate part in the industrial mechanism. An order of the Central Committee of the Communist Party in 1929 laid it down that "the trade union organizations, while defending the economic and cultural interests of the workers, must collaborate energetically is increasing their output . . . they must not in any case interfere in the management or place obstacles in the way."

Workers were, by an order of the Labour Commissariat, May 21, 1931,[2] forbidden to take part during working hours in the activities of Soviets, Trade Unions, co-operatives, etc., or in any other duties not directly concerned with production.

Thus, the Unions were deprived of their position of equality with all other organs of the State and became a subsidiary part of the State machinery. If Trotsky had had his way, in

---

[1] Melnitchansky in *International Press Correspondence*, October 7, 1926.

[2] *Industrial and Labour Information* (I.L.O.), June 22, 1931, 442.

the controversy with Lenin, the "militarization" of Labour and the regimentation of Trade Unions would have been even more complete, but Lenin's realistic temper caused the rejection of this view, and the adoption of a system which preserved the separate existence and functions of the Unions, while at the same time denying them independence and real power. That Trade Unionism should be *independent* of the State, even in furtherance of the interests of the members of the Unions, has been accounted a heresy of the worst kind. The Unions themselves accepted unquestioningly the domination of the State and even of the Communist Party. Tomsky, then the leader of the Trade Union central organization, said in 1925, "The All-Russian Central Council of Trade Unions works under the direct control of the Central Committee of the Party, under its sleepless observation."

At the first International Congress of Revolutionary Trade Unions[1] it was laid down that "The idea of the independence of the Trade Union movement must be energetically and resolutely rejected" and Losovsky summarized the Communist-Trade Unionist conception in the following words:[2] "This movement . . . is above all Communist . . . it differs from anarcho-syndicalism in that it is not opposed to the State in the abstract metaphysical meaning of the word. The only State to which Russian Trade Unionism is opposed is the bourgeois State. . . . It is not the form but rather the composition of the State that interests it."

Thus in the U.S.S.R., after a short preliminary period during which Trade Unionism tried to be an independent force, actively exercising powers in the control of economic life and the management of industrial concerns, the theory triumphed that under Communism Trade Unions cannot be independent; they must be a subordinate part of the State machine, under the direct control of the political power, and must

[1] *Resolutions and Statutes*, 29.
[2] *The Universal Trade Union Movement*, 24-5.

not interfere in any way with the management of industry, though they may within limits[1] defend the standards of their members.

Naturally, signs are not wanting that active spirits in the Trade Union movement, who have not been absorbed into Governmental posts, resent the attitude of the Communist Party. But opposition is neither strong nor sustained, partly because of repressive measures against any activities regarded as counter-revolutionary, and partly because Russia had no long tradition of independent and virile Trade Union organizations.

Superficially, it might seem that Soviet Russia has solved the problem of Trade Union conflicts with the State by establishing a powerful dictatorship, which gives the Unions a place, albeit a subordinate one, in the mechanism of government, and keeps them there partly by propaganda and partly by sheer force.

The question arises, however, whether a movement arising spontaneously among workers, for the purpose of furthering their interests as workers, is likely to remain permanently under the control of a political machine. It will probably be conceded that dictatorship can never expect to be immortal. Is it supposed that the urban workers of Russia will all, and always, be such convinced Communists that they will remain willing to surrender their own organizations to the State? Perhaps the answer depends upon the success of the Soviet State in giving the workers an ever-rising standard of living, in the widest sense of the term. On the other hand it may well be that in any event producers of a commodity will always have a point of view, different from that of other producers or of the State machine, regarding the means by which they earn their living,

[1] On this see Childs, S. L., and Crottet, A. A., "Wages Policy in Soviet Russia," *Economic History*, January 1932, 443, and "Trade Unions in the Soviet State," by the same authors in *Economic History*, January 1933, 617.

their share of the product, and so on. The maintenance of
strict discipline and the concentration of all energy on increased
production are now the main tasks of the Unions in Soviet
Russia but a state of national emergency does not last for ever.
Episodes like that of the Metal Workers' Union complaining
of the meanness of the Government in keeping to time rates
in order to save money[1] were frequent in the early days of the
Revolution, and will doubtless often recur. However great
national solidarity may be, groups do and will have their own
interests and points of view.

Similar questions arise on surveying the very dissimilar
development of Fascism in Italy. If the Russian State is based
on Marxism, the Fascist State as clearly owes a great debt to
Syndicalism. From the practical point of view dictatorship is
dictatorship, and the façade of the Corporative State may be
even more insubstantial than that of "proletarian democracy"
in Russia. Workers' organizations are no more free in Italy
than they are in the U.S.S.R.; they are as strictly controlled
by the Fascist machine in the one case as by the Communist
machine in the other. Bottai, Minister of Corporations,
put this very clearly from the Fascist angle, pointing out
that the Trade Union was a political instrument of ·the
authorities and consequently a Fascist political organ. The
Trade Union official, he said, was essentially a politician who,
through his technical and administrative work, could and did
influence the political opinions of the masses.[2] This sentiment
might equally well have been expressed, *mutatis mutandis*,
by Stalin. Fioretti, President of the Fascist Confederation of
Industrial Trade Unions, likewise told the National Congress
of Trade Union National Federations and Provincial Associations that Fascist Trade Unionism was based on the political

---

[1] At the Second Trades Union Congress, January 1919, Childs
and Crottet, *loc. cit.*

[2] *Industrial and Labour Information* (I.L.O.), September 14, 1931,
346.

system with which it was connected and outside which it would become barren and would change its character.[1] There is a striking parallel between this and the Resolution of the 1st Congress of the Revolutionary Trade Unions, in Russia, already cited.[2] How then can Fascism be said to derive in part from Syndicalism, which always regarded the State as the arch-enemy, and which had a pragmatic, pluralistic basis? It may be pointed out, first, that many of the Fascist chiefs were ex-Syndicalists, followers of Sorel. F. Corridoni, E. Rossoni, M. Bianchi, S. Panunzio, A. O. Olivetti, and many others had been active Syndicalists, and Mussolini himself, it is worth remembering, warmly approved of the workers' seizure of the factories in the first stages of that remarkable experiment in 1920.[3] There was, in fact, a strong Syndicalist tradition in the Italian Trade Union movement, and the "forced marriage"[4] of Fascist nationalism with Syndicalism was not merely a union of two parties each needing the other for political reasons; it was also a union of theories, both of which had considerable vitality, and some of the essential characteristics of both were retained in the new doctrine. The peculiar features of the "new Syndicalism" were, at first at any rate, its intense nationalism and its virtual rejection of the class struggle.

The pluralistic structure of Syndicalism was transformed into a larger unitary scheme as a result of the predominance of idealists among the constitution makers. Croce and Gentile, commonly supposed to be the chief authors of the new constitution, were extreme idealists in philosophic outlook, yet both had written in support of Syndicalism, and Croce was a close friend of Sorel. S. Panunzio in 1910 had written in praise of Duguit's political theory which he termed "integral Syndicalism." As has been pointed out[5] the concept of solidarity was

[1] I.L.I., November 17, 1930, 260.   [2] See p. 302.
[3] Schneider, H. W., Making the Fascist State (1928), 61.
[4] Ibid., 147.   [5] See p. 245.

given by Duguit a unifying and compelling role in the working of functional organization, and this feature strongly commended itself to those Syndicalists who wished to retain the basis of vocational associations while subordinating class emancipation to nationalist ideals. From this it was an easy transition to the Corporationist theory.

It would be out of place to describe here the evolution of "Corporationism" from these diverse philosophical bases,[1] but before dealing with the Corporative State as it now exists, on paper at all events, something should be said about the attempt to introduce "Anarcho-Syndicalism" in 1920, for this experiment and the discussions it provoked show how deeply rooted in the Italian mind is the idea of functional organization.

Arising out of a wage dispute leading to a lock-out in the metal industry, the workers seized and occupied the factories, intending to conduct them on Syndicalist lines. No political revolution was aimed at, and though the Socialist Party wished to convert the movement into a genuine revolutionary struggle, the Confederation of Labour was resolutely opposed to this and insisted on keeping the fight within Trade Union limits. The aim of the Confederation was "to get the employers to recognize the principle of Trade Union control in enterprises; this would eventually lead to collective administration and to socialism."[2]

The principle of joint control was actually accepted by the employers' organization, the Confederation of Industry, and a decree was issued setting up a Joint Commission to draft a Bill to carry this into effect. The Trade Union members of the Commission and the employers' representatives were utterly unable to agree and they presented rival proposals.

---

[1] An admirable account is given in Schneider, *op. cit.*, ch. iv. See also Olivetti, "The Reform of Parliament and the Question of National Representation" in *Survey of Fascism* (1928).

[2] *The Dispute in the Metal Industry in Italy* (I.L.O.), September 14, 1920.

Very briefly[1] the workers' side proposed to institute pure Trade Union control of undertakings, the elected representatives of the workers being entitled to sit with the Boards of Directors and the Trade Unions having the right to appoint members to the Boards. Each branch of industry was to have a Higher Commission of Control consisting of Trade Union representatives and having powers to regulate the entrance of new firms to the industry and to report on general policy. The engagement and dismissal of staff was to be strictly regulated.

The employers, for their part, interpreted control as meaning the right to full information, and they proposed the establishment of Joint Control Commissions, representing Trade Unions, employers, and the State, for the various industries. These bodies would regulate wages, hours, and labour conditions; the collection of statistics, industrial information, etc.; and would consider matters of general policy. In addition to the National Commission of Control for each industry as a whole there would be district commissions, and also a general Council of Industry for the co-ordination of National Commissions and for the discussion of industrial policy as a whole. Committees inside industrial undertakings would, in co-operation with the management, consider welfare, apprenticeship, efficiency, methods of wage payment, distribution of hours, and so on. The engagement and dismissal of workers were to be regulated in consultation with the Trade Unions. The Bill introduced by the Government followed neither plan precisely, but in its main objective it leaned more to the employers' idea of control. Control Commissions were to consist entirely of workers (including technical and supervisory staff) and the Commission for each industry was to select workers, for each undertaking, who would be entitled to receive full information regarding costs, processes, wages, profits, etc. No actual control over or

[1] Full details in *The Bill to Establish Workers' Control in Italy* (I.L.O.), February 28, 1921.

share in management was suggested outside this limited scope, but provisions were inserted for regulating the engagement and dismissal of workers through joint machinery. The workers, on the whole, were prepared to accept this position[1] and to recognize the need for freedom of action for the technical management. In the event, the Bill was not proceeded with, as the political situation became more and more disturbed throughout 1921 until finally the Fascist coup put an end to the existing regime. The triumph of Mussolini on a programme of extreme nationalism did not mean the destruction of Syndicalist thought. On the contrary, both "national Syndicalists" and Socialist Trade Unionists remained active inside the workers' movement and though the latter were finally suppressed, the Syndicalist stream of thought was never interrupted. One of the most extraordinary events of the period, D'Annunzio's Fiume adventure, was an evidence of this, for the proposed Constitution for Fiume owed its inspiration entirely to the doctrines of functional decentralization that had now become an accepted feature of Italian[2] Trade Unionism, whether Socialist, Syndicalist, or nationalist. The Corporative structure itself was no part of Fascism originally. Mussolini had no political theory[3] and the whole idea of functional organization was due entirely to the Trade Union element and its theorists. The structure and powers of the syndicates were adopted as a result of the pressure of the national Syndicalists, headed by Rossoni, and the Corporations would probably not have come into existence at all had it not been for Rossoni's defeat over his pet project of mixed syndicates, and Mussolini's need to conciliate him by the creation of some kind of "integrated" organization.

[1] See report of speech by Turati (Socialist Party) in *The Bill to Establish Workers' Control in Italy* (I.L.O.), February 28, 1921, 24.

[2] See Olivetti, *loc. cit.*, 124.

[3] The Fascists originally advocated economic councils of experts. This view was expounded by M. Rocca at the foundation of the Fascist Party in 1921.

As finally embodied in the Acts of 1926 to 1930, the scheme for the Corporative State is based on functional representation and organization. The Senate itself is non-elective and consists of persons appointed nominally for their learning, abilities, and public service. The Chamber[1] consists of 400 members, appointed in a novel way; the national confederation and syndicates (described below) nominate 800 candidates, of whom 320 are nominated by the confederations (employers), 320 by the Syndicates (workers), and 160 by the national federation of artists and professional workers. A further 100 are nominated by various bodies carrying on educational, welfare, and other national work. Out of the 900 candidates so proposed, the Fascist Grand Council (which is thus recognized by law) selects 400 (or it may include in the list members who have not been included in the 900), and then the final list is put before the electorate to be voted on as a whole. If there is not a majority for the list, new "elections" with competitive lists must be held. The Law of Corporations, 1926, antedated this electoral reform and provided that for every category of industry and commerce there should be one legally recognized association of employers and one legally recognized association of workers. Other associations are permitted, but have no legal status, and all workers and employers must pay dues to the appropriate association whether they are members or not. Also, by the provisions of the Labour Charter, it is only collective agreements between legally recognized associations that have legal force. The directors and staffs of these associations must provide guarantees of "capacity, morality, and a firm national faith." The workers' syndicates and the employers' associations in any industry are, in theory, grouped together to form a Corporation, which is a State organ for the supervision of associations, the maintenance of labour exchanges, the compila-

[1] Late in 1933 Mussolini announced sweeping new reforms, including the abolition of the Chamber and its supersession by the National Council of Corporations. *The Times*, November 15, 1933.

tion of statistics, the co-ordination of welfare work and conciliation in Labour disputes. The Minister of Corporations exercises general supervision over these bodies. Strikes and lock-outs are forbidden and if a Corporation fails to settle a dispute, the matter goes to one of the ordinary Appeal Courts, aided for the occasion by expert assessors. The associations of employers are grouped into national confederations corresponding to the major divisions of industry and commerce, and workers' associations are similarly grouped. There are thirteen confederations of employers and federations of syndicates, twelve representing the employers' and workers' sides, respectively, in agriculture, industry, banking, commerce, transport by sea and air, and transport by land and waterways; the thirteenth being the federation of professional workers' associations. Co-operative societies are separately organized in the E.N.C. (National Co-operative Institute) which is a kind of Corporation on its own account. All the employers' confederations are further organized in the Union of Employers' Confederations, while the National Confederation of Fascist Trade Unions includes all the workers' federations (except the Sea and Air Transport Federation, which insists on remaining autonomous) and also the professional workers' federation.

An Act of 1930 somewhat changed the structure as far as Corporations are concerned. There was formerly a National Council of Corporations attached to the Minister in an advisory capacity. This has been re-established as a State organ at the apex of the Corporative system. Its president is the head of the Government, the Minister of Corporations acting only as his deputy. There are seven sections in the Council, corresponding to the occupational groups already mentioned, and employers and workers are equally represented in each. The General Assembly of the Council consists of representatives of all the occupational interests, social institutions, and so on, as well as economic experts. The Central Corporative Committee of the

Council, which is the effective Executive, consists of the presidents of the thirteen national confederations and federations of the E.N.C., of the National Institute for Social Assistance, and the General Secretary of the Council, in addition to the Secretary of the Fascist Party, the Under Secretary for Corporations and three Ministers *ex officio*. The Council has both consultative and legislative functions, the former including the right to be consulted on matters affecting the trade associations and Corporations, the Labour Charter, and new legislation affecting production and labour. Legislatively, the Council makes rules for co-ordinating relief, employment exchanges, and so on, and regulates economic relations between trade associations, when requested by them to do so. Rules drawn up and agreements ratified by the Council are obligatory on associations and individual undertakings.

It is freely said that the National Council of Corporations will perform the functions originally assigned to the Corporations themselves and that these bodies (which in fact have not been set up) will be unnecessary.[1] It is impossible to say how the system will develop, for at present its form is determined in many respects by the needs of Fascism as a political dictatorship.

The ideas behind it all are more or less fixed, however, and it is these ideas which are of interest from the point of view of this study. The Secretary of Cinef[2] summarized the general aim of the Corporative system as being "the organization of the productive forces of the country within the orbit of the State, so that private interests may be more easily made to coincide with the interests of the community: to put an end to class warfare, to promote co-operation between the various factors of production; to substitute the justice of the State for wasteful strikes and lock-outs as the means by which industrial disputes

[1] As already stated, the National Council of Corporations may supersede the Chamber of Deputies itself, under the reforms of 1933–34.
[2] Centre International d'Études sur le Fascisme.

may be settled; to make productive labour and a sense of responsibility to the nation as a whole the basis of citizenship."[1] Bottai, Minister of Corporations, puts it more comprehensively when he says the Corporative organization means the "establishment of national economic unity by means of the solidarity of economic forces and the necessary sacrifice of divergent and contingent interests, whether of individuals or of groups," and he goes on to say that there is no obstacle in this to international economic co-operation.[2]

"The Corporative State amalgamates companies," we are told elsewhere, "fixes prices, wages and hours of labour, determines the number of men that ought to be employed by this or that master, and if necessary takes upon itself the direct management of the factories (Article 9 of the Labour Charter). Both economically and politically the State is everything; it absorbs everything; it does everything. It works through the Syndicates formed, organized and disciplined by itself."[3] Mussolini himself put this aspect of the system in his notorious phrase, "All for the State, nothing against the State, nothing outside the State."

Is Corporationism, then, the apotheosis of State sovereignty? Such a conclusion is natural enough, yet its accuracy may be doubted, in the light of recent events. It must never be forgotten that the functional structure was no part of the early "pure" Fascism, but has been steadily forced upon the Fascist politicians, and even upon the idealist school of Gentile, by Syndicalist pressure. "The politics of the dictatorship," said an acute observer[4] in 1927, "of 'down with Parliament,' of the new aristocracy, of Mussolinianism, and kindred products of the

[1] Barnes, J. S., "The Reform of the State in Italy" in *Survey of Fascism* (1928), 89.

[2] *Industrial and Labour Information* (I.L.O.), July 13, 1931, 34.

[3] *The Corporative State in Fascist Italy* (Documents published by Friends of Italian Freedom), 1929, 5.

[4] Schneider, H. W., "Italy's New Syndicalist Constitution," *Pol. Sc. Q.*, June 1927, 161.

March on Rome, are gradually giving ground to 'the economic organization of producers,' the legal and juridical recognition of syndicates, the organization of national corporations, and finally the talk about 'organic representation' and a syndicalist parliament." Some Fascist writers, he went on, "go so far as to say that Fascism was merely a necessary means for introducing national syndicalism." In practice, as well as on paper, the workers' syndicates and the employers' confederations have recently shown that they have minds of their own. Nor do decisions always favour the one interest or the other. Whatever may have been the rule in the early years of the dictatorship it is no longer true to say that "the employers' interests are identified with national interests."[1] Hence, "the masters are murmuring, and some of them go so far as to whisper that Signor Mussolini is introducing into Italy State Socialism . . . they bewail the loss of the much calumniated Liberal State, and would be happy to return to it—but there is the Militia."[2] "Many complain that the Government and the Fascist Party are partial to the employees."[3] Not that the workers are satisfied either, of course, for they have no freedom in their syndicates and they criticize some features of the regime as boldly as they dare.[4] We may trace, not only in the development and powers of the economic organizations, but in recent legislation and in wage decisions of the Courts, the growing influence of the syndicates of workpeople and federations of employers, especially upon the Government and the Fascist Party. We may safely infer two things, in fact: First, that the State is not sufficiently "sovereign" to have carried out its avowed aim of establishing national economic unity and of eliminating class warfare; and second, that there has been a continuous infiltration of the power of economic organizations into the "pure"

[1] Modigliani, G. E., "Compulsory Trade Unionism," *Labour Magazine*, June 1927.
[2] *The Corporative State in Fascist Italy* (Documents published by Friends of Italian Freedom), 1929, 6.
[3] *The Times*, September 17, 1931.   [4] *Ibid.*

political dictatorship. It is not necessary to exaggerate the extent of these changes in Fascist practice; if there are even signs of such developments, the fact is significant.

The new Corporative institutions may have been established in deference to a strong pre-existing current of Italian opinion, without any intention that they should be effective, but, like all institutions, they tend to become effective because of their own vitality. In using such an expression no metaphysical interpretation is suggested. It is simply that when institutions evolve or are created, a number of persons are brought together who acquire vested interests and a professional outlook which tend to give their work an effectiveness and independence that may not have been contemplated at the outset. That Corporative institutions, whether called by this name or not,[1] could exist in a political democracy need not be doubted; how they would work under such conditions is a matter of speculation, but without question their present association with Fascism greatly modifies their operation. It will be more fruitful to consider the application of "Corporative" ideas in a democratic State than to dwell too long on their actual working under a dictatorship.

The differences in theory between the place and functions of vocational associations in Italy and Russia will be as obvious as the similarities in practice. In both countries the dictatorship has taken precautions to ensure the complete subservience of these associations to the State and to establish their control by the party in power; and in both there have been signs of refusal to accept such a position, though this is more evident at present in Italy, with its long tradition of organization, than in Russia. As a matter of political theory there is the amusing paradox that the Communist revolution, which set out to destroy

---

[1] "In France, the word 'corporatism' arouses mistrust. We should prefer to use the word 'syndicalism' or 'professional federalism' as M. Paul-Boncour calls it." Professor C. Bouglé, in *The State and Economic Life*, 99.

the State as being an organ of Capitalism, in the main adopted
the institutional pattern of the ordinary Capitalist, democratic
State; while the Fascist revolution, which set out to defend and
glorify the State, adopted an institutional pattern inspired in
the main by an anti-State movement, Syndicalism!

THE FUTURE OF TRADE UNIONS
AND THE STATE

CHAPTER XXVI

THE PASSING OF SCARCITY

IN the preceding chapters an attempt has been made to state the central problem of the relations between Trade Unionism and the State, and to analyse each phase of the conflict that makes the problem one of increasing urgency in nearly every industrial community.

The facts of the recurrent clash, the continued challenge, between the industrial State and the power of organized Labour were first described. The nature of Trade Unionism was then discussed, and its group characteristics and functions were shown in the process of development. The actual legal relationships between Trade Unions and the State in Britain were next traced from their origins in the Middle Ages, and it was shown that the present state of those legal relationships is neither clearly defined nor, indeed, clearly conceived by any of the parties concerned. Leading types of State theory were finally outlined, and in particular the bearing of pluralist speculations on the problem under consideration was emphasized. Practical attempts, in two new European constitutions, to eliminate or reconcile the conflict were analysed.

It is not the aim of this concluding section to construct an ideal solution of the problem that has been shown to be so intractable and yet so urgent. To do so would be easy but not very useful. Rather is it hoped to assess the probable tendencies that will, in the next stage of political and industrial evolution, influence the power and functions of the State and of Trade Unions, and so to indicate possible ways in which the present menacing conflict may be resolved, as it must be if the entire structure of modern economic society, whether Capitalistic or Socialistic, is not to perish.

It is implicit in the foregoing chapters that social institutions and their relationships are in the main shaped and changed by the economic forces that have been operating in the society concerned. Without pushing this view to its extreme form, and holding that no other factors are powerful, or even decisive, from time to time, it is assumed that the desire for a logically perfect or an ethically ideal solution to the problems of political and social organization cannot be satisfied in practice, since existing institutions and economic forces have a vitality and strength that must always be recognized and often yielded to.

Trade Unions are organizations that spring out of specific economic relationships (vocational rather than class), and, on the other hand, all modern States increasingly tend to add to their own economic functions. It would be surprising, therefore, if the forms and interactions of both types of institution did not follow very closely the major changes in industrial power, organization, and technique. We should not, a priori, expect to find that the characteristics of, and the relations between, Trade Unionism and the State were the same in a nation at a very primitive stage of economic development as in another nation that had reached an advanced stage. We should expect them to differ, again, in two countries which were respectively progressing and declining in economic power and importance.

But, it may be argued, the intrinsic nature of these institutions remains the same throughout all changes in their environment, and therefore varying economic systems and forces can only mean superficial alterations of their form and functions. The truth is, however, that no very intelligible meaning can be assigned to the term "intrinsic nature." The nature of an institution is only to be inferred from the sum total of its activities at any time. Both of the State and of Trade Unions is it true that they *are* what they *do*. At first sight, Trade Unionism to-day is essentially what it was a hundred years ago. Actually, as we have seen, the continuity of name misleads us; it is not the same as formerly. A century of economic change has produced something radically different.

There is, however, a continuity in forces and institutions which should enable us, not to forecast accurately, but at least to form an intelligent anticipation of the probable lines of development in the near future. It may seem to require courage to make such an assertion in the midst of a world economic collapse, but in fact it only requires a sense of historical continuity. Given this, we shall not merely say with Taine that it is better to build on the past than to start all over again;[1] we shall realize that we *must* build on the past, that we never can start again—as even the heroic experiment of Russia has shown. Consequently, despite world collapses, we shall not suddenly abandon our evolutionary hypothesis and revert to a belief in catastrophic change. To get a picture of the economic world of to-morrow we shall reason from the forces and institutions of the past and present, and not from the wishes or fears of an emotional public.

The dynamic aspect of economic forces and institutions is one upon which attention has been especially focused in recent discussion. It is a commonplace to say that everything is in a state of transition; it always is. The obvious has become even more obvious, to the man in the street, because change has been more rapid during the past quarter of a century than it used to be. As might be expected, however, the spectacular symptoms of change have been singled out and made the basis of superficial judgments and inferences, while the underlying and more important accompaniments have often been overlooked.

Thus, in the case of Britain's recent economic history, we are told in familiar terms how priority was gained in the development of machine production in the nineteenth century; how in consequence Britain led the way in supplying the markets of the world; how, later in the century, other nations went through the normal and inevitable evolution from agriculture to manufacture, helped by the very skill and machinery

[1] "En fait d'histoire il vaut mieux continuer que recommencer."

X

that had been sent from Britain; and how, finally, Britain found her former customers not merely supplying their own needs in manufactures, but even competing in other markets. From this the inference has been drawn by many that Britain must inevitably look forward to a future of steadily declining trade and (unless her population diminishes with equal rapidity) to a steadily declining standard of living for her people. Such an analysis is quite superficial, and there is no inevitability about the process thus described, but it has been used by Communists, for instance, as a corroboration of the theories of Marx and as evidence that intensified struggle between Capitalism and Socialism on Marxian lines is unavoidable. Yet it seems to have escaped the notice of Communists, and of many other people too, that the very changes to which so much importance is rightly attached have been accompanied by no less important though less spectacular changes in Capitalism itself (and consequently, one would imagine, in Socialist theory). The theories of Marx, like those of every other economist, were conditioned by the forces and institutions of his time, and can no more stand eternal, immune against change, defying time, than any other human creation.

Naturally, the Communist will argue that only the trappings of Capitalism, its superficial forms and trimmings, have changed, and that its real nature remains as it was a century ago. Again, one can only point out that this mystical inner nature does not exist, and that the Capitalism of to-day is radically different from that of a century ago despite the use of the same name. Of course, there is continuity and there are common features; that, as has been pointed out, is one of the striking facts about social and economic change. Nor need the change necessarily mean that there is any less conflict between Labour and Capitalism; that is irrelevant to the point at issue, which is that the system of fifty or sixty years ago and the theories based upon it must be quite different from those of to-day. It may still be thought by some people that there is an important core of principle or fact that has remained unaltered. The essential feature of Capitalism in the nineteenth century, they may say, was the power exercised over wage-earners by employers in virtue of the fact that the latter owned the industrial capital concerned. But in this respect we now see a change proceeding under our eyes. The private owners of capital, in fact, are not always those who exercise control; those who control are not always owners of the capital. In this highly important aspect, Capitalism is visibly changing its character. This is not to say that modern Capitalism is "better" or "worse" than the old variety; we are only concerned to point out that it is different.

This apparent side-tracking of the main argument is not irrelevant, for we must try to form some idea of the way in which industrial society in Britain is evolving, and of the way in which it is likely to change, in future, in the light of altered world conditions. For, if the Communists are right, it is improbable that the State and Trade Unionism will be quite like what they would be under conditions of expanding trade and rising standards of living.

In the past the predominant feature of economic life has been the scarcity of goods necessary to the well-being or even the existence of mankind. To economists the notion of scarcity has been fundamental in the definitions at the basis of economic science, but to manual workers scarcity has meant not merely that a choice had to be made between desired objects of expenditure; it has meant insufficient income to purchase in the aggregate the means of physical existence at a level of efficiency. Perlman has argued very acutely and convincingly that "manual groups . . . have had their economic attitudes basically determined by a consciousness of scarcity of opportunity."[1] "The manual worker is convinced by experience that he is living in a world of limited opportunity,"[2] the scarcity

---

[1] Perlman, S., *A Theory of the Labor Movement*, 6.
[2] *Ibid.*, 239.

being the result of natural conditions, of institutional differentiation in favour of privileged groups, or of individual preference for security. In fact, the whole economic mechanism has been dominated by the fact of scarcity of economic goods, and only individuals or groups specially favoured by their institutional privileges or by a particular type of ability could transcend this evil. Manual workers, argues Perlman, knew from experience that they themselves were at a disadvantage in these respects, and therefore they combined with the primary object of obtaining group control of the available opportunities of earning a livelihood. "Control of the job" thus became the immediate object of all Trade Union policy and tactics. This was quite different from "control of industry," a Socialistic concept which came much later. The worker did not want to undertake the functions and risks of the entrepreneur; he wanted a fair rationing of the available opportunities of obtaining a reasonable standard of life. This "scarcity consciousness" dominated not only working-class philosophy but the whole of economic thought in the nineteenth century. The wage-fund theory, once so popular, was a typical feature of this psychological phase of the struggle of a growing Capitalism to preserve institutional privileges against the pressure of an expanding proletariat. The State was not a "public service State," with positive functions. Its business was to "keep the ring" (a significant metaphor), and to allow the economic struggle to proceed unhampered, apart from maintaining the institutional advantages of the employing class and mitigating somewhat, by protective legislation, the worst rigours of life for the workers. It is instructive to notice that in preceding ages, from the time of the Guilds, "scarcity consciousness" was just as much a fact but, there being no entrepreneurs, and little or none of the economic optimism and competitive philosophy that dominated the early stages of Capitalism, the State or public authorities assumed the function of rationing opportunities and incomes. We have seen that it was for precisely this reason that Trade Unions were prohibited at that time.

It was because conservative business men and politicians perceived dimly that "control of the job" was the real aim of the Unions, and that this was preferable to more revolutionary aims born of repression, that Trade Unionism was finally allowed to develop, with the result that larger political objectives and movements did not appeal to the organized workers until very late in the nineteenth century when the whole position had changed. The converse process took place in Russia, and Perlman observes that "had Russian labor unions been let alone during the dozen years that elapsed between the two revolutions, it is not at all unlikely that they might have permanently remade the ideology handed down by the intellectuals, in the pragmatic mold of a trade unionism that seeks primarily to enlarge labor's opportunity and knows that it has 'more than its chains to lose.' Consequently, when the Government drove the trade unions back underground, it only succeeded in foisting upon labor for good the leadership of the revolutionary parties with their conception of industrial problems carried over uncritically from the political sphere. Thus, though the government spared capitalism the daily pains of an adjustment to the rising power of labor, it thereby sealed capitalism's fate."[1]

The modern change in British Trade Unionism is commonly supposed to be equivalent to a move to the Left, an endorsement of more revolutionary policies. This idea is based chiefly on the acceptance of Socialism by the Trade Union movement since about 1890, a departure often said to be due to the changing economic position of Britain.

We are told that while there was growing prosperity and security in the first three-quarters of the century, the nation's economic strength and prospects began to decline from that time, the result being to make the workers more revolutionary.

[1] Perlman, *op. cit.*, 47.

Analysis of the facts shows a quite different situation. It is probably true, and here one must differ from Perlman, that the acceptance of Socialism by organized Labour has implied a real change in Trade Union philosophy. Admitting that such a change affects leaders more than rank and file workers, it must nevertheless be asserted that the outlook of the mass of Trade Unionists is radically different to-day from what it was a century ago. But this is not due to a worsening economic situation. Quite the contrary is true. "Control of the job" remains important, but if it is not so exclusively important as it was, this is due to a steadily improving economic position. The "scarcity consciousness," in short, is becoming weaker because scarcity itself, if it has not disappeared, is at all events now seen to be unnecessary. A real revolution has quietly been happening, though its fruits remain to be gathered. The second half of last century saw a marked advance in material comfort, even for the mass of the workers, and the sense of economic expansion was strong enough to produce that complacency which is commonly referred to as "Victorian" and which must gradually have tended to blur the "scarcity consciousness" that had until then been predominant. During those fifty years the level of real wages doubled, and it is not surprising that larger aims and less immediate policies began to interest the Trade Union movement. This tendency should not be exaggerated, but its existence is distinctly traceable. Not until the war and post-war period, however, did the scarcity philosophy become really obsolete in economic thought. The advances in technology, in industrial organization, and in productive efficiency generally, in the space of ten years, were equivalent to a century's normal progress, and the effects on working-class thought and policy have been considerable. All the world now knows that science has carried us to the stage where we *could* produce for everybody, not merely enough for efficient physical existence, but sufficient for a reasonable level of material comfort. Economists tell us that in a hundred years' time we can be enjoying a standard of living eight times that of the present day.[1] Physicists, chemists, and biologists tell us of the astonishing savings in labour and material as a result of research in the last few years even,[2] and scientific industrialists[3] point out the great significance of the discovery of new alloys to the metallurgical industries, of the fixation of atmospheric nitrogen to the production of foodstuffs, and of coal as the source from which we can now get our fuel oils, and a hundred and one other important products. Working people are conscious, as never before, that the problem is no longer the technical difficulty of producing enough, but is rather the problem of planning production, together with distribution and consumption, so that the fruits of scientific progress become available to all. This is a matter of political and economic organization, and the thoughts of Labour turn more and more to this wider sphere. Institutions, Trade Unions among them, change their objectives and methods very slowly, and we should not expect the philosophy that evolved out of the hard conditions of scarcity to lose its power until long after the conditions themselves had changed. Scarcity, though no longer necessary, is still with us, and Trade Unions are likely to follow the policies of the past for some time to come, but signs of a wider outlook are not wanting. In the United States, for instance, where the psychology of abundance obtained a remarkable hold, as production jumped up and living standards were continuously raised, some Trade Unions advanced a considerable way beyond the traditional policy of job control, and deliberately pursued wider aims, including the expansion of production itself and the improvement of industrial organization and technical methods. True, the methods evolved when a scarcity consciousness was universal survived and are still

[1] Keynes, J. M., *Essays in Persuasion* (1931), 365.
[2] See, for example, the instances cited in Smith, Sir F. E., *Industrial Research and the Nation's Balance Sheet* (British Science Guild, 1932).
[3] E.g. Lord Melchett, *Modern Money* (1932), ch. 8 and 9.

practised, as is the way with institutions of all kinds, but the newer policy has come more and more to the front each year. It is also true that in the United States the change has not generally been accompanied by the conversion of the Trade Unions to Socialism. But there is no reason, *a priori*, why Trade Unions *as such* should be Socialistic under these conditions, if they believe that Trade Union aims can be satisfied by a continuously rising standard of life and by the specific needs of vocational associations being met, within a Capitalistic system. Socialists believe that there are reasons, inherent in Capitalist organization, why these conditions cannot permanently be fulfilled. American Trade Unions took the opposite view, and, whether they were right or wrong, believed the industrial mechanism could be modified in such a way as to preserve private enterprise while giving organized Labour the status, power, and standard of living that constituted their objective as vocational bodies.

In Great Britain, as in Germany, whether because of less rapid progress in living standards, or because of traditions less favourable to an individualist philosophy, the Trade Unions became convinced that the enlarged opportunities made possible by science could not be realized except by the supersession of Capitalist industry. In Great Britain they created the Labour Party for the express purpose of accomplishing this task, deeming it better to maintain themselves intact, as vocational associations, than to attempt to combine political propaganda with vocational functions. In Germany the Trade Unions, created by the Social-Democratic Party, became at once typical vocational bodies, with a philosophy of a Socialist character, as befitted their origin. In both Britain and Germany one of the most important and keenly contested issues in recent years, among the Trade Unions, has been their attitude towards the rationalization of industry and generally towards participation by the Unions in measures for increasing production and improving efficiency. The traditional policy was to concentrate on control of the job and on the fair rationing of scarce opportunities, rejecting the wider aims as outside the proper scope of Trade Unionism. Adherence to this policy has been urged mainly by Communists and semi-Communists, who are still under the influence of nineteenth-century economics and philosophy. The more modern attitude, accepted by the majority of Trade Unionists in both countries, has been to recognize the change in conditions and the need for a corresponding change in the methods of organized Labour, and to give at any rate a qualified support to all measures for utilizing in industry the advances in technology and in business organization. The extreme Right, like the extreme Left, is still dominated by the "scarcity" philosophy. The nineteenth-century mentality is observable, for instance, in the economists[1] who still think the concern of Trade Unionism is solely with the division of the product of industry and not at all with an enlargement of the product, with business organization and efficiency, or with the structure of industry as a whole.

Looking back on a century of development of Trade Unionism, it is possible to see that with the new economic possibilities a stage has now been reached at which the Unions can begin to supplement and even supersede their earlier limited, and on the whole negative, policies by positive, constructive policies based on a wider conception of vocational aims and functions. To carry this out completely means, in effect, a transformation of Trade Union institutions, but there will be nothing remarkable in the use of the same names and of as much of the same institutional pattern as can be used.

Will this transformation continue, and what will be the final form? These are important questions that will be examined in succeeding chapters. The answers depend mainly on what is going to happen in the economic sphere, both British and international. Will mankind fail to utilize, for the benefit of

[1] E.g. see Hutt, W. H., *Theory of Collective Bargaining* (1930), and Hicks, J. R., *Theory of Wages* (1932).

all, the enormous benefits made possible by science, and will the scarcity psychology accordingly prevail once more? If an optimistic answer is given, can—and if so, will—such a satisfactory solution be achieved under a system that is recognizably Capitalistic? In either case, can any suggestions be made as to the possible functions and place of Trade Unionism in the new society and as to its relations with the State?

CHAPTER XXVII

CONDITIONS OF ORDERLY DEVELOPMENT

IT has already been observed that from the purely technical point of view the problem of producing sufficient wealth for all has been, or is in process of being, solved. There remains the question whether the present economic and political mechanism can utilize the solution to the benefit of all, and can provide a satisfactory standard of living and a sense of security that have hitherto been absent, and that have been unobtainable whatever mechanism might be devised. To talk of "the present economic and political mechanism" is, however, in some respects misleading. As we have seen, the institutions of 1933 are not really fixed and unalterable, but are in a state of continuous evolution, so that even while we discuss the problem its terms undergo an unmistakable change. In recent times this change has taken us further and further from the *laissez-faire* system that was the classical form assumed by Capitalist economy, and has brought us nearer to a controlled, though we cannot as yet say a planned, system. Whatever explanations may be given of the failure of the distributive mechanism, in the widest sense of that term, the fact of its failure in recent times is undeniable. The increase in wealth and the technical possibilities of even more rapid increase have not resulted in the disappearance of poverty and want in any country in the world; increased output of goods and services has not risen to the level technically within our reach. It is no answer to point to the continuous rise in both production and average standards of life since the early part of last century. The outstanding fact of recent years in particular is the existence side by side of largely increased production, with the possibility of even vaster increases, and of world-wide unemployment and want. It is not necessary to see in this the collapse of a world system, or anything so dramatic. When familiar evils are magnified in extent people are apt to see in them something quite new and earth-shaking, but in fact the post-war depressions should serve to remind us that their smaller pre-war prototypes were themselves symptomatic of the failure to produce even then the amount of economic well-being that was technically attainable. That the economic and political institutions of the past performed a necessary historical function is perhaps true; that they performed it more efficiently than any alternative forms of institution could have done *in the circumstances* is arguable. But the present generation will decline to believe that those institutions are adequate, without great change, to the circumstances of to-day, and their belief is based as much on the present state of the economic world as on any theoretical considerations.

It has to be recognized also that the changed conditions of the modern world—the emergence of new nations and the consequent realignment of economic stresses, the development of new forms of motive power and new materials of commerce, and the resultant redistribution of economic forces—have created special problems for Great Britain over and above the problems arising from the obsolescence of institutions.

It is conceivable, and it is urged by many people, that this country is now situated so disadvantageously in relation to the rest of the world that no changes in the mechanism of production and distribution can avail to restore the former level of business activity. It is held that our foreign trade must dwindle rather than expand, that we do not possess sufficient resources to maintain the present population at anything like the present standard of living, and that while the United States, France, and other countries may, by reorganizing their social and economic systems, move to higher levels of prosperity, Britain must inevitably (failing a drastic fall in population) sink to lower levels. This argument assumes the absence of world planning, that is to say, of conscious international action designed to utilize the world's resources as a whole in the interests of all nations. Even with this assumption of continued competition, continuous decline in the case of Great Britain is not at all necessary, though this is not to say it will not happen. The argument implies a contraction of world markets for manufactured goods, or at least a contraction of international trade in manufactured goods. It is impossible to believe that such a contraction is necessary despite the advances in productive efficiency, for all history is witness to the fact that the desire for goods in ever-increasing diversity expands as quickly as the needs are supplied at lower levels of satisfaction. If continuous decline does take place, it will be due to a quite unnecessary failure of human institutions to grapple with the problem. We can, however, consider briefly what is likely to happen if material standards in this country do in fact fall steadily, a contingency that is at any rate possible and even probable if the situation is not faced with intelligence and courage. Let us suppose, then, that instead of drastic changes being made in the productive, distributive, and financial mechanism, so that modern scientific advances may be utilized to eliminate poverty and to give the entire population an adequate standard of life and leisure, the present absence of planning continues, traditional political and industrial methods remain, and there is a substantial decline in material well-being, with a continuance of heavy unemployment and great social and economic inequality. The outcome of such conditions must be, in the strict sense of the term, revolution. The historical attitude of Trade Unionism and its preoccupation with "job control" have been based not merely on scarcity but on the consciousness, the psychology, of scarcity. That has now gone. If the fact of scarcity remains, the knowledge that it is technically unnecessary must have profound reactions on the thought and policy of organized Labour. No situation quite analogous has hitherto arisen, but it cannot be doubted that the determination to realize an objective known to be within reach would effect a rapid overturn of existing economic institutions. This would not necessarily mean a revolution in the popular sense of the word, with military action, dictatorship by force, and so on. Indeed, action of this kind would almost certainly be an abject failure in Great Britain. Here, more than in most countries, continuity of forms and the influence of tradition will be important factors in any change that takes place. The English people have always been capable of the most drastic overnight revolution in outlook and policy while preserving appearances intact. Still, eggs have to be broken even for a constitutional omelette, and it might well be that many social and economic institutions that have most obviously outlived their usefulness would disappear. All this is a question of political action, however, and the Trade Unions would not be directly concerned apart from the moral support they would certainly give to the political forces making for change. Scarcely anyone nowadays believes in the "social general strike" as a means of overturning the social and economic structure. It is by political means, through the use of the ballot, that Labour in Great Britain must achieve its objective. Even if the attainment of political power led to resistance by hostile interests to constitutional measures of change, and there had to be forcible repression of what would then be unconstitutional opposition,[1] the Trade Unions as such would not be active parties; they would still have to carry on their work of safeguarding the interests of their members, unless they temporarily suspended their proper functions and completely changed their character in order to consolidate the political position, in which case Trade Unionism as we understand it would for the time being cease to exist. If events took this course, it would be impossible to foresee either the future structure of economic society or the future of Trade Unionism itself. A Socialist commonwealth might ultimately be estab-

---

[1] For a brilliant treatment of the entire situation on this assumption see Laski, H. J., *Democracy in Crisis* (1933).

lished, or on the other hand a reactionary regime; in either case a dictatorship of some kind, the duration and results of which could not be predicted, would probably be thought necessary at the outset. That Trade Unions would again assert themselves at some stage cannot be doubted, but the environment in which they would work and the forms of organization assumed by the State and other institutions must remain problematical.

While no serious student of affairs would say that this sequence of events is impossible, there are reasons for believing that matters will take a different course. In the first place, it seems unlikely that the factors already referred to as necessary for the production of a "revolutionary" frame of mind will exist in this country. When progress in political education, which may take place very quickly, puts a Socialist Government in power, it is unlikely that fundamental changes in the system can proceed so rapidly as to arouse the kind of resistance that has to be forcibly suppressed. In the mind of the general public, including the majority of Capitalists, there is not the stark, clear-cut opposition between something called Capitalism and something called Socialism that some people imagine. As has been said earlier, Capitalistic institutions themselves have changed considerably in the last few decades, and developments that would have shocked business men to the core fifty years ago have been accepted in our day without resort to drastic action. It is a mistake to take a too "dramatic" view of such changes. Those who tend to do so would doubtless have prophesied, before 1900, that the attempt to pass such measures as the Electricity Supply Act of 1926 would meet with open revolt on the part of Capitalist interests; in fact the Act was passed by a Conservative Government. Such a changed attitude should not be attributed to a "change of heart": it is a necessary consequence of changed technical conditions which compel the adoption of a "collectivist" policy.

Nor do such peaceful revolutions mean that "the more

things change the more they remain the same." That is an over-simplification, the truth being that most people, Capitalists included, have an unbounded capacity for imbibing whatever is "in the air" around them while remaining unconscious of its real meaning and ultimate effects. The idea, if not the fact, of divorce between Capitalist ownership and industrial control has even now become accepted so widely that the further transition to public control can hardly provide a controversy hedged round with contingent violence. The crux of ownership itself is now the legal right to "unearned" income, but even here the edge of controversy becomes dulled by substituting for confiscation such devices as terminable annuities, extinction of inheritance on Rignano lines, and so on; the disappearance of unearned income and of all forms of economic parasitism is not less certain merely because the process is sufficiently robbed of individual hardship to avoid giving a pretext for violent resistance. It is always the immediate that counts. The notion that Capitalists any more than other people calculate coldly in terms of long-term policies and results is mythical. The storm over the introduction of Death Duties in Gladstone's day was typical of what happens in this country when economic innovations of a fundamental kind are made by constitutional methods. With the British people the method is supremely important. Choking with cream is not the only way of killing a cat, but no civilized person would wish to deprive the animal of such a pleasant prelude, and there is much less fuss.

Most Marxians seem curiously incredulous about the efficacy of their own formula, and it is left to others to see with clarity the transformation of a *laissez-faire* economy into a Socialist economy as a result of factors generated by Capitalism itself.

In the early days of Capitalism the typical business undertaking was a small firm owned by one man, the wage-earners employed by the firm being entirely dependent upon this individual owner. As the need for a greater amount of capital became felt with the development of modern machinery the partnership became common. In this the ownership of the plant was vested in two or more owners. In both these cases the owners were almost always the actual managers of their businesses, and control was an essential part of ownership. As even greater amounts of capital became necessary the joint stock company evolved. At first sight, this appeared to be merely a device for raising the required capital from a very large number of people; actually it was a revolutionary development, for it marked the beginning of the divorce between ownership and control. For a considerable time the shareholders exercised some kind of control through the annual meeting, and the directors, who were much more real controllers, were themselves the chief shareholders. In time both these features changed. As the number of shareholders in large companies became very great the amount of the control they exercised through the annual meeting became more and more shadowy, until at the present day it can be said without exaggeration that in large undertakings the shareholders exercise no control whatever.[1] At the same time, the actual management of the concerns has tended to fall into the hands of either directors who are not themselves large shareholders, or of salaried officials. At the present day both these tendencies have proceeded even further. On the one hand there is the tendency to finance undertakings more and more by the issue of debenture stock which carries with it no voting rights, and on the other hand there is the invention of non-voting ordinary stock (i.e. stock carrying no voting rights, but not secured as debenture stock is). Parallel with this there has been the emergence of a definite class of salaried managers who are trained professional persons like lawyers, engineers, or architects. Even the private ownership of industrial capital has changed

[1] On this see Miller, M., and Campbell, D., *Financial Democracy* (1933), 11 ff.

Y

considerably since the advent of the joint stock company, for
there is an ever-increasing diffusion of ownership among the
population at large. There has grown up an investing public
consisting of people who know and care nothing about the
control of the industries in which they have invested their
money, and whose only concern is to receive regular dividends.[1]
This class is rapidly increasing, especially in the United States,
Great Britain, France, and Germany. In the United States
stocks and shares are commonly sold on the instalment system.
While it cannot be contended, as some people have suggested,
that industrial capital is very rapidly becoming the possession
of the people at large, it is true that the diffusion of ownership
is proceeding steadily. The greater part of industrial capital
still remains in the hands of comparatively few persons, but
the tendency above-mentioned is making itself more and more
felt. These new ideas as to industrial ownership and control
are seen most clearly in the cases of industries having as the
lawyers say "a public interest," e.g. electrical power supply,
tramways, railways, dock undertakings, gas supply, telephones,
telegraphs, and so on. The notion is even being extended
nowadays to steel, engineering, chemicals, and other manufacturing industries. In some cases the aim of public service
is becoming more prominent, and while much of the talk on
this theme is no doubt rhetorical and is indulged in for publicity
purposes, it cannot be denied that the ideal of public service
is receiving more and more recognition. The very fact that
such talk is an asset in advertising shows which way the public
mind is moving. The idea of a conventional rate of dividend
is also gaining increased acceptance, and it is now the practice
in many large public utility undertakings to pay a moderate
rate of dividend and to place the whole of the remaining profits
to reserve accounts to be used either during bad times when

[1] The opportunities afforded, by the ignorance of investors, for
large-scale gambling and swindling is another and a dangerous aspect
of this development. It is clear that further drastic revision of company
law is needed.

the conventional rate of dividend might not be maintained or for further development of the enterprise. Lord Milner's idea of Capital being hired by Labour at a fixed rate[1] is by no means utopian when we consider present-day practice in some of these large undertakings. In connection with price regulation in the public interest, also, significant advances have been made. In the United States the strict regulation exercised over many classes of undertaking by the Government Inter-State Commerce Commission, and less directly by the Federal Trade Commission, is astonishing to those who think of American business as the supreme example of private enterprise.[2] In addition, the separate States have their public utility commissions for regulating in detail the prices of electricity, gas, etc.[3] The criticism that these developments are only fragmentary and hesitating, that they do not as yet touch more than a fraction of the economic sphere, is easily made, but what does it amount to? No one claims that a transformation of nineteenth-century Capitalism has been completed. If it has begun, even if the tendencies are there, plainly and inevitably, the argument of this chapter is satisfied. To repeat, progress in Capitalist production and finance created the joint stock company which made necessary the divorce between industrial ownership and control, and so began the destruction of the main feature of the system; competition led to concentration

[1] Cf. opinion expressed by Mr. Owen D. Young (Chairman, General Electric Co., U.S.A.) at the opening of the new buildings of Harvard School of Business Administration, *Manchester Guardian*, June 30, 1927. "Perhaps some day we may be able to organize the human beings engaged in a particular undertaking so that they will truly be the employees buying capital as a commodity in the market at the lowest price. I hope the day may come when these great business organizations will truly belong to the men who are giving their lives and their efforts to them; I care not in what capacity. Then they will use capital truly as a tool and they will all be interested in working it to the highest economic advantage."

[2] It has to be recognized, however, that the degree of enforcement depends very much upon what Government is in power!

[3] For an admirable discussion of public regulation in the United States see Keezer, D. M., and May, S., *Public Control of Business* (1930).

in large units, and so created the professional manager whose power depends upon his *expertise* and not upon his shareholding; the drive for profits produced monopolies which tend to pass under public control and often into public ownership; the same urge led to the construction of expensive new plant and intricate new organizations the operation of which becomes an absorbing interest, in time a primary interest, of those responsible for them. These tendencies, it cannot be said too often, are not accidental or transient; they are inherent in the evolution of industry. The rate of change may be accelerated or retarded, to be sure, by propaganda and education from without as well as by the activities, enlightened or otherwise, of those intimately concerned with the operation of economic mechanisms. On these factors depend the kind and degree of resistance to change, but it seems unlikely that the steps proposed to be taken by the most eager "accelerationist" who has assumed the responsibilities of political office will provoke a resistance going beyond constitutional bounds. Such questions as "Will Capitalists acquiesce peacefully in the surrender of their privileges?" appear politically unreal. Not so do actual issues present themselves.

A criticism of a different kind suggests that the transformation of nineteenth-century Capitalism may be in the direction of a more dangerous twentieth-century Capitalism; it may not be a Socialist transformation at all. The ideas of Mr. Owen Young and Lord Ashfield, of Mr. Dannie Heinemann, Sir Harry MacGowan and the rest may, it is said, be directed towards "a big business" dictatorship, a scientific Capitalism more powerful and more ruthless than that of the past. With all respect, one can hardly think so. It may serve in a novel, but in the real world Mr. Huxley's Mustapha Mond, World Controller,[1] does not exist, and even Mr. Wells's Romer and Steinhart[2] are very ordinary people with very human limita-

---

[1] Huxley, Aldous, *Brave New World.*
[2] Wells, H. G., *The World of William Clissold.*

tions,[1] fortunately. What these critics really mean, perhaps, is that the new forces and tendencies mentioned above may lead us to an economic structure which, though planned (for it cannot be otherwise if the above analysis is correct), is not democratically controlled. English Socialism, at any rate, is rooted in democracy, and it is certainly possible that an undemocratic planned economy may be the outcome of the changes now taking place in industrial society. That depends upon the strength and intelligence of the democratic and Socialist movement, as well as on other factors. *Laissez-faire* democracy and *laissez-faire* Capitalism have had their day. A democratically controlled, planned economic system is what in England is meant by Socialism. What is a planned but undemocratic structure? Can it be called Capitalism? If so, it is an entirely novel type and one not likely to materialize at this date in our history. But is not all this perhaps unreal, this neat opposition of blacks and whites? Is there possibly some justice in the comment of one observer,[2] who says, "I am inclined, however, to agree with Sombart when he says that we must accustom ourselves to the thought that there is no great difference between a stabilized and regulated capitalism and a technified and rationalized socialism. They tend to come slowly together"? This does not mean that between the two systems there is common ground, but that events are driving us towards something that is neither Capitalism nor Socialism as these terms were understood in the past. Whether the old labels are used does not matter very greatly. From the point of view of organized Labour what does matter is that the economic mechanism shall be democratically and not auto-cratically controlled, on a national or if possible international plan, and that the functionless income receiver shall be eliminated. How the workers' organizations can find an adequate place in a society so based must now be considered.

[1] As was shown, for example, by the collapse of Stinnes in 1925.
[2] Shadwell, A., *Typhoeus, or the Future of Socialism* (1929), 115.

CHAPTER XXVIII

THE STATE AND ECONOMIC ORGANIZATION

THE transformation of Capitalist society is proceeding more rapidly now than at any previous time, but so far economic institutions have not outwardly kept pace with this change. We are still trying to use the mechanisms of the nineteenth century, both in industry and in the wider sphere of economic government as a whole. The most striking fact in post-war economic discussion is the almost unanimous acceptance of the view that *laissez-faire*, as a principle for the guidance of the State in such matters, is dead and indeed damned. Almost unanimous but not quite, for there are still a few of the old guard of theorists who have not yet realized what the modern world is like. Entangled in their fine-spun web of "equilibrium analysis," they seem unable to understand the revolution that has taken place in what might be called "economic dynamics."

Nor is the changed outlook confined to a small part of the world. On the contrary, economists and statesmen of nearly every country have testified to their rejection of the theory that "Man's Self-love is God's Providence."[1] Talk of planning has become fashionable everywhere; perhaps too fashionable, for the glib repetition of the word tends to gloss over the formidable difficulties that face the makers of a planned economy. Already there has been an international conference of people interested in national and international "plans,"[2] and even in the United States, the latter-day home of *laissez-faire*, President Roosevelt's National Recovery Administration has made large strides in the direction of the control and regulation of economic life. In industry, in finance, in agriculture, the old individualism has gone. Private enterprise remains, but its

[1] Toynbee, A., *The Industrial Revolution* (1908), 11.
[2] See *Social Economic Planning* (Report of I.R.I. Conference) (1931)

powers have been drastically curtailed in the public interest. Whether or not a permanent change has been made in the economic life of the United States, in this respect, the present domination of the psychology of "planning" and regulation can hardly be doubted.[1] Even before the Roosevelt regime President Hoover's Research Committee on Social Trends took the view that conscious control was necessary, that "nothing short of the combined intelligence of the Nation can cope with the predicaments here mentioned," in short that we must "lay plans for making plans,"[2] as a preliminary to more ambitious reconstruction. Mr. J. M. Keynes has written eloquently and decisively of the passing of the old order,[3] and another eminent economist, Sir Arthur Salter, has vividly described the chaos resulting from the failure to introduce deliberate control of the system after the abandonment of *laissez-faire*.[4] Industrialists like Lord Melchett[5] and Sir Basil Blackett[6] have vigorously repudiated the catch-as-catch-can policy of the nineteenth century.

The Labour Party has long been committed to a belief in a planned economy on Socialist lines, but nowadays the Liberal Party (historically the bulwark of Manchesterism) is also committed to a policy involving a high degree of conscious control in the economic sphere,[7] and even some sections of the Conservative Party have taken a few steps in the same direction.[8]

Looking back over the history of the post-war period we can

[1] See International Labour Office, *National Recovery Measures in the United States* (1933).

[2] Report of President Hoover's Committee, January 1933 (Summary in *U.S.A. Monthly Labour Review*, February 1933, 297).

[3] Keynes, J. M., *The End of Laissez-faire* (1926).

[4] Salter, J. A., *Recovery* (1932).

[5] Melchett, Lord, *Modern Money* (1932).

[6] Blackett, B., *Planned Money* (1932).

[7] E.g. Report of Liberal Industrial Inquiry (*Britain's Industrial Future*).

[8] E.g. MacMillan, H., *The State and Industry*, etc.

see that, despite Sir A. Salter's very sound emphasis on the dangerous situation that has resulted from having neither a *laissez-faire* system nor a planned economy, there has been a steady extension, both in industry and in legislation, of collective and conscious control where individual authority and the semi-automatic operation of competitive Capitalism used to prevail.[1] Few if any of the measures that have so far been taken have formed part of any wider scheme, even in the mind of their authors. They have been devised to meet an immediate situation, to supply a specific need at the time. Thus, one of the earliest post-war measures of national reconstruction was the Railways Act of 1921,[2] which reduced the chaotic system of several hundred railways to the comparative simplicity of four groups. Yet it was not visualized as part of any comprehensive plan for the whole of transport. That did not come until later, with the Report of the Royal Commission on Transport, 1931,[3] the Salter Report, 1932,[4] and the Government's measure covering the entire field in 1933.[5] The Road Traffic Act of 1930[6] and the London Passenger Transport Act of 1933[7] were, however, conceived as parts of a national transport scheme, though themselves dealing only with parts of the problem. Conscious control by the State in electrical power production has been more obvious, as it has been more simple. The Electricity (Supply) Act of 1919[8] laid the foundations by creating the Electricity Commission as an organ of government, and the further Act of 1926[9] establishing the Central Electricity Board to construct the national power grid, and to reorganize power generation throughout Great

[1] For an admirable account of the governmental agencies see Dimock, M. E., *British Public Utilities and National Development* (1933).

[2] 11 & 12 Geo. V. c. 55.   [3] Cmd. 3751.

[4] Report of the Conference on Road and Rail Transport.

[5] Road and Rail Traffic Act, 1933. 23 & 24 Geo. V. c. 53.

[6] 20 & 21 Geo. V. c. 34.   [7] 23 Geo. V. c. 14.

[8] 9 & 10 Geo. V. c. 100.   [9] 16 & 17 Geo. V. c. 51.

Britain, on the basis of ten regions, set the seal upon this major piece of economic reorganization. By 1933 a really national scheme of electrical power generation and main line transmission was actually in operation without the majority of the population being aware that a new and significant economic development had taken place.[1]

The third important example is agriculture. After much tinkering with the difficult problems of British farming, measures were at last taken to organize the marketing end. The Agricultural Marketing Act of 1931[2] was passed, for the purpose of co-ordinating and controlling the sale of agricultural products, through the formation of co-operative selling agencies, and this was followed in 1933 by another Act[3] carrying the principle farther and establishing a greater measure of regulation, coupled with control of imports where necessary. Already Marketing Boards have been set up for hops, milk, pigs, and bacon, and if this progress is continued the notoriously haphazard character of British agriculture will soon be profoundly modified and the beginnings of a controlled system for the entire industry will be established.

In coal, too, a start has been made with the Coal Mines Act of 1930,[4] which not merely introduced a wide measure of regulation of coal production, through central and district boards, but set up a Reorganization Commission with, in the last resort, power to compel the fusion of colliery undertakings in order to form efficient units. These compulsory powers are being applied already, slowly it is true, to districts where the coal owners refuse to submit schemes voluntarily. Thus, some of the vital steps in the evolution of a nationally regulated coal industry have now been taken despite the unpromising outlook only a few years ago. There are some signs that even the new system of tariffs may be used to promote the same objective

[1] See *Annual Reports* of the Central Electricity Board from 1928 onwards.
[2] 21 & 22 Geo. V. c. 42.
[3] 23 & 24 Geo. V. c. 31.
[4] 20 & 21 Geo. V. c. 34.

in other industries. The steel industry, at all events, having had plain warning that continued protection by import duties would be dependent upon drastic reorganization by the industry itself, is being compelled to formulate a scheme of unification on a nationally planned basis.[1] The Coal Mines Act, the first Agricultural Marketing Act, the Road Traffic Act, and the London Passenger Transport Scheme were among the fruits of the second Labour Government (1929–31), which thus, despite its critics, made a major contribution to the reorganization of the national economic life. The other measures and the final stages of the London Passenger Transport Bill were carried through by Conservative or Coalition Governments.

In the meantime, industry itself has, independently of Governmental action and legislation, made some small advances in the substitution of collective control for haphazard competition. In some branches of textiles, in iron and steel, electrical engineering, building, shipbuilding, heavy chemicals, and road transport, for example, this process has been at work not only nationally but in some cases internationally. In these instances the gradual concentration into large units, the weakening of internal competition, and the establishment of centralized control have not meant the introduction of public ownership or socialization in any form. Nevertheless, most Socialists and many upholders of private enterprise believe that such changes must eventually lead to a State regulated and controlled economy as the logical outcome.[2] On the international side especially the importance of the growth of cartels, production and sales agreements, and similar devices has been recognized by the States members of the League of

[1] See Statement issued by the Import Duties Advisory Committee, April 6, 1933.

[2] In a recent conversation with the writer a French industrialist bitterly deplored these present-day tendencies for this reason. Holding that the Bank of England is the moving force, he asserted that the leading British Socialist to-day is Mr. Montague Norman!

Nations, the Economic Consultative Committee of which has for some years been observing their effects on national and world economic life.[1] As an example of a modern concern of a purely Capitalist kind which endeavours to plan its activities, both nationally and internationally, the organization of Imperial Chemical Industries may be cited. The Chairman states:[2] "Our principal subsidiary companies in the United Kingdom are organized in eight groups. . . . Every group contains a number of separate companies, the products of which are cognate to each other. For all purposes of control and administration we treat the companies that form one group as a unit. The statutory Board of each of these companies is the parent company, viz.: Imperial Chemical Industries, so that there is a uniform legal controlling authority vested in your own Board. This method of control ensures harmonious working and co-ordinated direction over the whole wide field of our activities. Group or company inter-competition is avoided and there is no conflict of authority, and wasteful duplication is eliminated. Each group has a subordinate Board, which is in reality the Group Executive, consisting entirely of members of our staff, some attached to the companies within the group and the remainder to head office; none of your Directors acts in this capacity. All technical, commercial, financial, and administrative problems concerning one group are therefore studied in the first place as affecting one entity. . . . The necessary co-ordinating link between myself and my full-time colleagues on our General Purposes Committee and the various Group Executives is provided by an intermediate body which we call the Central Administration Committee." On the international side "My colleagues and I have been convinced believers in the long-range

[1] See, for example, the League's monographs on the economic and legal aspects of International Industrial Agreements, and the Report of the Preparatory Commission of the World Monetary and Economic Conference (1933).

[2] Imperial Chemical Industries Ltd., Proc. at Fifth Annual General Meeting, April 14, 1932.

wisdom of international agreements as instruments of world rationalization of industry. Co-operation, we have always found, is better in the long run than competitive warfare." He goes on to describe agreements with the continental countries on dyestuffs, with Germany on synthetic nitrogen, and with German, American, and Anglo-Dutch interests on coal oil, and refers to subsidiary organizations of I.C.I. in Canada, Australia, and South Africa. This concern is exceptional in its comprehensive range and in the organization of central control while permitting a high degree of devolution to its constituent groups, but there can hardly be any doubt that it broadly foreshadows the future development of industry whether, as in this case, uncontrolled, or subject to the regulation of the State, or owned by the State.

Looking at the British economic structure as a whole, we are scarcely aware that tendencies towards planned organization exist, and the chief reason for this, perhaps, is to be found in the fact that there is no national co-ordinating authority. There are piecemeal schemes in operation, but there is no central body pulling the separate elements together and directing or even influencing economic development as a whole. This is the most serious defect in the present structure. It is quite impossible for Parliament to exercise such a function, nor is the Cabinet itself a more suitable instrument. The modern tendency is for the Cabinet to act less and less in a collective sense. It is merely an assembly of heads of State departments and of *ad hoc* committees, each member having barely time to look after the affairs of his own office, much less those of other departments or of the nation as a whole. In any case, few people will feel confident that politicians are suitable for this kind of work. In considering this problem, however, we must distinguish between the different conceptions that are current concerning a central economic authority. In some quarters it is apparently thought that the entire industrial structure is to be organized on a logical plan, with properly unified, rationalized industries at the base controlled by a central Board at the apex; that this Board will plan out the whole economic life and development of the nation; and that it will, either on its own account or in conjunction with similar central Boards for finance, etc., allocate new capital to this industry, labour to that, supplies of raw materials here and there, and generally act as a kind of economic directorate for the nation. All things, even such a logical and tidy plan as this, are possible after a thoroughgoing revolution, but if we assume, as will be wise, that no such complete overturn is going to take place, this omnipotent economic authority must take its place as a piece of imaginative propaganda. It is extremely unlikely that the workers in this country will think it either practicable or desirable that a Board should be created with powers of detailed control similar to those possessed by, say, the Supreme Economic Council in the U.S.S.R.

A central body (or bodies) will be necessary, however, for several distinct purposes; to supply initiative and driving force for the unification and reorganization of individual industries; to maintain a continuous survey of economic events and problems; to effect co-ordination and balance between social, industrial, and financial activities. Perhaps these various functions cannot efficiently be carried out by one Board, but more will be said on this point, and on the organization of the necessary bodies, in later paragraphs. Here it is sufficient to note that at present no organs either of government or of industry exist for any of these purposes. The stimulation and, if need be, compulsion to unify and reorganize might be undertaken by a department of State (say, the Board of Trade), or by a statutory authority outside the normal machinery of government (like the German *Reichskuratorium für Wirtschaftlichkeit* with greater powers), but in fact the Board of Trade is neither empowered to exercise such functions nor organized on lines that would make it a suitable body for the purpose. Nor is there any statutory or semi-statutory mechanism outside.

The entire machinery of government is out of date from this point of view, as was emphasized more than a dozen years ago by the Haldane Committee.[1] We have a miscellaneous collection of Government departments and statutory bodies, each with its own part of the field to cover but lacking, either individually or collectively, any power to think or act comprehensively. Interest in economic development is divided between the Board of Trade, the Ministry of Transport, the Ministry of Agriculture, the Ministry of Labour, the Department of Overseas Trade, and the Treasury among the departments, and in addition there are the Coal Mines Reorganization Commission and the Committees of Investigation under the Coal Mines Act, 1930, the Central Electricity Board, the Railway Rates Tribunal, the Railways and Canals Commission, the Road Traffic Commissioners, the Industrial Transference Board, the Department of Scientific and Industrial Research, the Development Commission, the Forestry Commission, and the Import Duties Advisory Committee among the permanent statutory bodies, as well as the Bankers Industrial Development Company, which may be regarded as semi-official. Now, the multiplicity of organizations is not necessarily bad in itself; quite the contrary, indeed, for this so-called "English" lack of a logical structure has the merit of having grown naturally out of the needs of the time, and the solid advantages of flexibility and internal strength. It would not be true, either, to suggest that there is no contact whatever between any two of these bodies. But there is an absence of balance and proportion, there is overlapping and waste of effort, and there are gaps where important interests are not covered at all, simply because there is no organization and no department whose function it is to keep contact with and effect some co-ordination between the various boards, commissions, and departments, and to survey and influence economic developments as a whole. The Prime

[1] See Report of Committee on Machinery of Government. Cd. 9230 (1918).

Minister's Economic Advisory Council might have been such a body, but in the event it quickly degenerated into futility, so restricted were its scope and powers. Among the reasons for its failure were that it was given no power of initiative, but could only consider matters referred to it; that it was created as a personal appendage of the Prime Minister, who seldom paid any attention to its advice; and that it was composed of members appointed as individuals and not as representatives of important economic interests. In all probability there should be a Council or Board drawn from the economic world itself (production, commerce, and finance), with functions that include the continuous survey of economic tendencies and problems, the establishment of commissions for individual industries for the purpose of promoting and if need be compelling unification and reorganization, and perhaps the formulation of legislative measures within a defined field. It is necessary, however, that there should be a central authority to co-ordinate and maintain the proper balance between economic and social activities, home and foreign policies, material and other objectives—in short, to promote simultaneously, as far as may be possible, the harmonious activity of the community as a whole and the welfare and liberties of the individual citizen. In a democratic country this must be the task of the popularly elected Government, but the present mechanism needs considerable modification to meet the needs of our complex civilization to-day. Not only must the Ministers concerned be free from routine departmental duties, but they must be assisted by advisory bodies to keep them in constant touch with changing events and opinions. Such consultation must be systematic and not, as at present, spasmodic. Further, the private Member of Parliament must play a positive part in making legislation, and not merely act as a "rubber stamp" for the Government's decisions (or for decisions of Opposition leaders).

At first sight, the movement towards a more controlled

economic structure seems to mean a high degree of centralization. This is more evident in the schemes of those who visualize a quite new and logical mechanism being created after a drastic overturn of existing institutions. Even if, as has been suggested is the more probable course of events, the reconstruction of our economic institutions takes place piecemeal, the necessity for greater centralization seems obvious. Yet there are important tendencies the other way. In the steps that have so far been taken to give various industries and services a more orderly structure and a more thought-out control, care has been taken to work as far as possible through either existing institutions, modified and expanded perhaps, or new *ad hoc* bodies possessing a good deal of autonomy. There has been no enthusiasm for the complete centralization of the activities and functions of these industries and services in the State mechanism itself. Mr. Keynes has admirably expressed the idea behind these developments: "Progress lies in the growth and the recognition of semi-autonomous bodies within the State—bodies whose criterion of action within their own field is solely the public good as they understand it, and from whose deliberations motives of private advantage are excluded."[1]

Even bodies with semi-governmental functions, like the Import Duties Advisory Committee, the Industrial Transference Board, and the Coal Mines Reorganization Commission, have been constituted on a basis of detachment from existing State institutions and from direct political interference. In setting up central and district committees to allocate production quotas, the Coal Mines Act worked through the industry itself. The Central Electricity Board, appointed by the Government, is a semi-autonomous body, as is the British Broadcasting Corporation after an earlier career in which it was constituted by the radio manufacturers themselves. The London Passenger Transport Board is three parts autonomous, while Imperial and International Communications (the cable and wireless

[1] Keynes, J. M., *The End of Laissez-faire*, 41.

combine) is really an instance of private ownership planned and controlled by the State. In the case of the Agricultural Marketing Acts, again, the controlled system foreshadowed is being developed by the agricultural interests themselves. The emergence of "semi-autonomous" bodies, or public corporations, as they have come to be called, is one of the outstanding facts of modern economic life, and this form of mechanism has been accepted as a model (not necessarily the exclusive model) for present-day socialization.[1] Socialists naturally believe that this form will be—and indeed must inevitably be—increasingly adopted in the future, private ownership and private profitmaking being in due course extinguished, in all important industries at any rate. Advocates of private profitmaking (other than those who vigorously oppose all methods of control and all methods of concentration and consolidation in industry) think that the right line of evolution is to exclude from the operation of industry both the State department and the public corporation, and to organize industry on an orderly basis from within, preserving Capitalistic forms, with some measure of State control or regulation as a safeguard for the consumer against monopoly power. This system, the "new Capitalism" popularly associated with names like Owen D. Young, Lord Melchett, Sir Josiah Stamp, and Sir B. Blackett, is, whatever name may be used, something quite different from the Capitalism of the nineteenth century. Whether Capitalism can save itself on such lines as these or whether the Socialist conception of planned economy is accepted, it is evident that the future lies with the consolidation or association of smaller units in "industry" organizations each having a large measure of autonomy or self-government in its own sphere of work. The only other possible forms of economic structure—old-fashioned, individualistic, and highly competitive small units on the one hand, or the rigid centralization of all economic

[1] See Annual Reports of the Labour Party and of the Trades Union Congress, 1932 and 1933.

z

activity in the State mechanism on the other hand—are alike unthinkable. The former would be a clear reversal of all modern tendencies, and the latter would be quite foreign to the mentality and institutions of our people. Internationally, too, there are obvious limits to centralization of economic functions in an international body. No one would care to prophesy that in any reasonable period to which the nations can look forward a "world State," a super-national authority, will be created. Rather is the emphasis, in these days, on nationalist policies. But if we assume that nationalism in its cruder forms will give way to a wise internationalism—a probability in any case, one hopes, and a certainty if Socialist doctrines continue to spread—the creation of a super-State is outside practical politics. A greater measure of international regulation is inevitable. Organs of supervision, information, and statistical agencies, better methods of conference and of closer association between nations will doubtless be evolved, either through the League of Nations or otherwise, but the national group for some purposes, and for other purposes the economic group cutting across national boundaries, will always be important and will function actively as autonomous organs. As the State to-day has its "vertical" (geographical) units like County Councils and Municipalities, upon whom greater powers have to be devolved in their own sphere, and "horizontal" (functional) associations like Trade Unions, whose inherent vitality and autonomy have to be recognized, so it is easy to see that the planned world of the future may well have its vertical groups—the national States—and its horizontal groups—economic associations evolving from international Trade Unionism, etc.

A division of powers, with the recognition of autonomous groups, is seen not merely to accompany, but to be a necessary part of, any efficient national or international planned system. However industry may evolve from the point of view of ownership, this central fact of functional decentralization must be accepted.

CHAPTER XXIX

THE TRADE UNIONS AND DEMOCRACY

THROUGHOUT the long history of political and economic institutions there has been the dilemma that every major gain in efficiency appeared to involve a loss of freedom, and every advance in liberty seemed to mean greater opportunity for waste and inefficiency. Democracy, being a philosophy that attaches a high positive value to freedom, has either attempted to reconcile efficiency with liberty, or has frankly preferred to sacrifice the former, as in Sir H. Campbell-Bannerman's famous phrase, "Self government is better than good government." The modern movement towards centralization and conscious control in industry and trade emphasizes the efficiency aspect of the problem, while the growth of autonomous groups stresses the reaction against centralized power and the struggle to preserve and extend freedom, on functional lines. Since individual freedom to exercise a vocation under tolerable conditions and to escape from industrial autocracy has only been found possible by means of combination, Trade Unions have developed as voluntary groups. As organizations they have been faced with the same dilemma; they have had to perform efficiently their specific function of advancing the standards of their members and protecting their freedom from industrial tyranny, while imposing as little restriction as possible upon their members individually in their daily work. Like the State itself, the Unions have tried to reconcile these conflicting aims by a process of trial and error which has led to the creation of various checks and safeguards and to a network of sub-groups giving the individual member the opportunity of real participation in the group government.[1]

[1] See Chapter x *supra*; and for the history of these developments see Webb, S. and B., *Industrial Democracy* (1920 ed.).

It will not be suggested that restrictions on individual freedom are not involved in Trade Union as in all other forms of group organization, including the State and (so far as it exists) the society of nations. The Unions and analogous bodies exist, however, to further the vocational objectives of their individual members, as conceived by the members themselves, and every interposition of such a voluntary group between the individual and the State must, unless the idealist position is adopted with all its implications, result on balance in an enlargement of freedom. Unconsciously, the Trade Union movement has always acted upon this principle. In practice, the result at first was conflict with the existing industrial autocracy, which, not professing to be democratic, complained of the Unions' interference with efficiency, and later with the State, which has complained of interference with democratic methods of government. Employers have criticized Trade Unionism because of its belief in industrial democracy, while Governments have attacked it because of its refusal to accept all the implications of nineteenth-century political democracy, with its unitary basis. As the meaning of democracy and the structure of democratic society are central issues, it will be advisable to survey briefly the present tendencies and the probable future developments in this connection, before going on to discuss concretely the place and functions of Trade Unions in the planned industry of the future and in the State itself.

It is a commonplace of contemporary political writing that the events of the post-war period have all over the world raised once again, but in a new form, the choice between democracy and dictatorship. Never before have the claims of dictatorship been presented with such weight of philosophical argument, and never before have the position and achievements of Capitalist democracy been so much criticized.[1] There are many reasons for this. The war itself contributed a great deal both because it seemed to many people that the spread

[1] See Laski, H. J., *Democracy in Crisis*.

of democratic institutions had done nothing to prevent the calamity and because the aftermath of political disintegration and economic misery in some countries created a fertile soil for the growth of nationalism and therefore.of regimes of force. Again, democracy in its classical forms has been evolved to deal mainly with issues of a political kind—the franchise, religious freedom, guarantees of personal safety, and the like. The rapid industrialization of the western world has created a highly complex economic structure, and has provoked a series of economic, semi-technical problems which Parliamentary democracy and its mechanisms were not designed and were incompetent to handle. Many socialists have jumped to the conclusion that the existing institutions cannot be adapted to the new needs, and have impatiently rushed to the other extreme of a belief in autocracy. Behind all these factors there is the mechanization not merely of industry but of life, which in the past century has transformed the activities and thought of the Western world. As a result, apparently, there has been a widespread conversion to types of philosophy that exalt the mass and depreciate the individual human being,[1] that find virtue in uniformity and in some kind of mystical absorption of individual wills, desires, and standards into a wide, impersonal current of aspiration and activity directed by a central superior authority.[2] This type of philosophy is diametrically opposed

---

[1] Cf. "It is only by such external functions as the millions have in common, their uniform and simultaneous movements, that the many can be united into a higher unity: marching, keeping in step, shouting 'hurrah' in unison, festal singing in chorus, united attacks on the enemy, these are the manifestations of life which are to give birth to the new and superior type of humanity. Everything that divides the many from the one, that fosters the illusion of the individual importance of man, especially the 'soul,' hinders this higher evolution, and must consequently be destroyed." Fulop-Miller, R., *The Mind and Face of Bolshevism.*

[2] See, for instance, Hecker, J., *Moscow Dialogues* (1933); Schneider, H. W., *Making the Fascist State* (1928). See also Rowse, A. L., *Politics and the Younger Generation* (1931).

to democracy, which is based on the notion that individual welfare and happiness is in itself a final end. At first sight this fashionable philosophy of dictatorship (common, incidentally, to both Communism and Fascism) seems to have a Socialistic flavour, but English Socialism, at all events, has never had such a basis, and has always been founded on a democratic belief in the individual citizen's freedom, his values, even his prejudices. English Socialism assumed this character largely because of its ethical origins. Rooted in a more purely intellectual grasp of the democratic philosophy, French Socialism exhibits the same feature; that outlook is indeed more deeply imbedded in the French character than in that of any other people.[1] In both countries Socialism has been essentially personal and individual in the sense that the "community," the collectivity of human beings, has been regarded as a convenient fiction and not as a mystical divinity. Social action has been exalted as a necessary means to individual freedom and fulfilment and not as an end in itself. Those people in the British Labour movement who have recently been flirting with notions of dictatorship have scarcely appreciated the underlying philosophy of Socialism, as understood in this country. The victims of this infantile disorder of the Left have discovered for the nth time in history that working men and women sadly need the leadership of a few supermen. As the entire history of Trade Unionism shows, the workers have an inveterate preference for working out their own salvation in their own way. This is not to say they have succeeded in evolving a perfect theory or fashioning a perfect mechanism of democracy. The mechanism is very imperfect as yet and the theory is still more so, but there has been no disposition on that account to fly to the latest political novelty that has appealed

[1] "Because there can be no agreement about the nature of Paradise so long as France insists that it depends on the sum of individual well-being and other people tell us we must please be guided by the notion of the general welfare." Sieburg, F., *Is God a Frenchman?* (1931).

to quite different people situated in quite different circumstances. There is a keen desire to think more deeply about the implications of democracy and to modernize the old mechanism in the light of new requirements. In particular, the close bond between material progress and technological advances has focused attention upon the functions of the expert in the democratic State and the inadequacy of primary democracy to cope with the complexities of modern economics. On analysis, it may be as dubious a proceeding to put to a popular ballot the policy of cheaper food as that of departing from the gold standard, but it certainly does not seem so to the electorate. Present-day controversies have made it obvious to the most untrained layman that many of the issues that have to be faced involve highly technical matters which are no more within the knowledge of all than is the special knowledge of the bricklayer, the cotton-spinner, or the miner. Hence it becomes realized that the main function of the democratic vote is to determine ends, general objectives, directions of policy, and not detailed means of attaining those ends. Means are not always separable from ends, but this is only to say that on occasion means become ends and have to be determined accordingly. It is the distinction, often a fine one, between the two that often gives rise to controversy and that makes the need for continuous political education the more pressing. In the early days of the modern movement for "self-government in industry," the crudest notions of democracy were current. There was to be a popular vote in the workshops on all matters of policy and on the appointment of foremen and managers. The mass of the workers were to be asked to vote not only on the arrangement of their working hours and the settlement of their conditions of labour, but on the right man for a position of technical responsibility, the right kind of sales policy for a particular market, the best means of financing a new extension, and innumerable other questions requiring technical or commercial knowledge. This is a travesty of democracy and would be as sensible as taking a popular vote on the kind of disease affecting a sick person or the legal liabilities of a property owner in respect of drains. The Guild Socialist movement did something to put these claims in their proper perspective, but there was still a good deal of muddled thinking on the subject. The process of education has gone on until, latterly, a much clearer distinction has been drawn between the functions of the expert and those of the democratic representatives. It is now recognized[1] that the day-to-day management of an industrial concern, even when this is publicly owned, is an expert matter calling for the appointment of persons qualified by their training and experience for the work. On matters of broad policy, affecting directly or indirectly the security and livelihood of the Labour employed, it is recognized that this Labour, through its own organizations, should have an effective voice. The particular body of workers that is most nearly affected should, in other words, participate in the formation of policy determining the general direction and aims that are being pursued. The community as a whole should also participate because it is also affected and because it is responsible for the wider plan of which the industry in question forms only part. There are many practical difficulties, and opinions differ as to the best means of giving effect to the principle, but the principle itself is truly democratic and has been recognized in some recent extensions of public ownership. It is the only course that can be followed between the primitive and inefficient "democracy" of Syndicalism and the autocratic rule of an industrial dictatorship, whether of Capitalist interests or of the State. The Trade Unions thus become an essential vehicle of industrial democracy, a necessary means for giving the workers an effective voice in the determination of the broad aims industrial concerns are designed to serve. They have had no such voice in the Capitalistic concerns of the traditional kind; Capitalistic

[1] See *Annual Report* of the T.U.C., 1933, and *Annual Report* of the Labour Party, 1933.

aims were fixed and pre-determined, the immediate objective being to produce profits and the less immediate to satisfy consumers in proportion to their effective demand. They have no such voice under a dictatorship, where they become mere propagandist agencies on behalf of the dictator whose policy and aims dominate the community.[1] The democratic view of industry postulates that productive enterprises should exist neither to provide profits for private owners nor solely to furnish cheap commodities for consumers. The satisfaction of consumers must be an important aim, but public service in the widest sense implies more than this. It must take account also of the lives and vocational interests of the producers themselves, and it must satisfy their claim to honourable standards of labour and livelihood and to a properly recognized status. It must also mean that each enterprise is part of a general scheme planned for the benefit of all citizens and not an anarchic growth serving the interests of the few. The vocational point of view and the vocational association are thus vital in the organization of economic democracy, and institutions framed to meet the needs of political democracy are not suitable for the representation of the workers as workers. As long as the State was almost purely "political" in functions the vocational associations could safely be treated as voluntary independent bodies. Their relations with the State could be of a shadowy kind, providing merely for certain forms of business recognition and financial security. As the State becomes more and more involved in the ownership of and responsibility for economic enterprise this negative relationship is no longer

---

[1] See Chapter xxv, *supra*, and cf. the following comment on Trade Unions in Soviet Russia: "Their duties at the moment form an amalgam of Taylorism and Communist Evangelism. They have to improve production: they must also spread the true faith. In fact they rather resemble certain Christian missionaries, who preach at and put to work the simple-minded savage until texts and textiles are indissolubly confused in his mind." Crottet, A. A., and Childs, S. L., *Economic History*, January 1933, 625.

possible. There must be a positive relationship, and if the economic system is to be brought into harmony with democratic principles vocational bodies, being part of the necessary means of giving effect to those principles, must clearly have organizational relations with the State. They must not become part of the State (using the term in its political sense) for this would involve the surrender of the vocational outlook which is their *raison d'être*. They must become part of the recognized institutional mechanism of the community, performing definite functions in the operation and organization of economic democracy, and having clearly defined relations with the political State. It is a half-conscious recognition of this development that has led on several occasions in recent years to the assertion of the views of the Trade Union movement on great economic issues. On the other side, political elements have charged the workers' organizations with attempting to "coerce the Government." Instances of alleged dictation by the Trades Union Congress that have been given[1] include the Coal Dispute of 1921, the withdrawal of the prosecution of J. R. Campbell in 1924, the National Strike of 1926, the withdrawal of the Labour Government's Trade Disputes and Trade Unions Bill in 1930, the constitution of the Holman Gregory Commission on Unemployment Insurance in 1930, and the Financial Crisis in 1931. The supposed attitude of Trade Unionism on these cases is called "a serious challenge to democratic government." Such charges are fantastic and display not merely ignorance of the facts in these affairs but ignorance of the real nature of democratic government. The withdrawal of the prosecution of J. R. Campbell in 1924 was not in the least due to Trade Union pressure; the Unions were not even interested in J. R. Campbell. As to the withdrawal of the second Labour Government's Trade Disputes and Trade Unions Bill, the fact is that a Liberal amendment was carried, in Committee, which made the measure not worth having from the point of view of

[1] *Politics or Power?* (Liberal Party Publications Dept., 1932).

organized Labour. The Trades Union Congress intimated as much—and every organization affected has the right to express its opinion on the merits and value of a measure, both as introduced and as amended—and the Government decided not to proceed further, believing, doubtless, that a Bill designed to remove a grievance would hardly be a success if the grievance was restored in another form. The setting-up of the Holman Gregory Commission was another instance in which no exception whatever could be taken to the Trade Union attitude. Asked to participate in an Inquiry, the Trades Union Congress declined on the ground that the terms of reference were so drawn as to make a genuinely comprehensive and unbiased investigation impossible. An effort was made to persuade the Government to widen the scope of the Commission. How could this be criticized as undemocratic? The position of Trade Unionism in serious industrial disputes in which the Government becomes involved raises issues of a different kind, but before discussing these, something should be said about an outstanding case in which accusations of attempting to coerce the Government have been freely made. On the fall of the second Labour ministry as a result of the financial crisis in 1931, the General Council of the Trades Union Congress was repeatedly charged with undemocratic attempts to bring pressure to bear on the retiring Cabinet. "The assumption by the General Council of the right to dictate to Governments, or at least to meet Governments on equal terms . . . the General Council asserts this claim to control the policies of Governments; . . ." these are phrases used by a responsible organ of opinion[1] and many other journals as well as politicians have used language of a similar kind. Certainly the uninstructed citizen often believes that the T.U.C. has dictated, or tried to dictate, to Governments on large issues of policy. He would be astonished to find what really took place in 1931. The phrases quoted above grossly misrepresent the position.

[1] *The Times*, November 13, 1931.

What happened was simple enough. On the Prime Minister's initiative the T.U.C. was invited to express an opinion on certain proposals that would vitally affect the standards of members of Trade Unions. Few people would assert that it was improper to seek this opinion. The T.U.C. considered the proposals and quite temperately expressed its views to the Prime Minister, again a perfectly correct proceeding. There were no threats, no blusterings, simply a statement of views, and the T.U.C. was cordially thanked by the Prime Minister.[1] The Government thereafter decided upon its course of action without any further communication with the T.U.C. Doubtless it took the opinion of organized Labour into account, and the opinion of many other interests and persons affected. Was this undemocratic? Was it not rather a perfectly correct democratic procedure, to ascertain first the views of the various parties chiefly affected? Eminent Civil Servants told the Donoughmore Committee that in their opinion this practice was vital to the successful working of democratic government.[2] Yet this was the alleged "dictation" exercised by the T.U.C.! Would the procedure adopted have been called undemocratic if the organized workers had happened to agree with the proposals? Would it not rather have been hailed as a triumph of democratic methods?

Although large-scale industrial disputes have most often provoked newspaper denunciation of Trade Union "dictation," this, as we have seen, only happens because such occasions are more spectacular. In fact, opportunities for conflict between Trade Unions, as well as other groups, and the State occur more frequently as the State assumes all kinds of economic functions. However, strikes and lockouts in which the Government has at some stage become involved have provided the most conspicuous instances. The legal aspects of these clashes

[1] Trades Union Congress *Annual Report* (1931), 515.
[2] See Committee on Ministers' Powers (1932), Cmd. 4060, *Minutes of Evidence*; e.g. evidence of Sir A. Robinson, pp. 120, 129; Sir C. Hurcomb, pp. 270, 274.

and the theoretical considerations that arise have been discussed in earlier chapters. What are the present and probable future tendencies, and how do they fit into a planned economic system of the type that we are discussing? If the so-called general strike of 1926 be taken as typical of large-scale conflicts between organized Labour and the Government, we may see in the controversy that followed ample evidence of the muddled thinking indulged in by politicians and journalists whenever a strike dislocates the normal routine of life. Every time an issue arises in our social life of a kind that moves large numbers of people to deep feeling, those affected—on both sides—use their influence to secure the triumph of their own point of view. Provided no illegal means are used, and conduct should only be made illegal if it tends to destroy the very basis of the democratic society that exists, no exception can be taken. The widespread use of all the agents of publicity that are at the command of those who have the wealth to employ them; the use of meetings and processions, of a deluge of postcards falling upon M.P.s, of personal intrigue and wirepulling; the boycott of goods; the refusal to buy or to sell; all these expedients, regrettable as they may be from some points of view, are recognized and are in fact employed frequently. There is little likelihood that they will ever disappear so long as human beings continue to feel strongly on issues that arise. There is a certain unfairness in the use of these methods, since, as has been said, many of them are only available to the wealthy. It is one of the obvious evils of economic inequality that the power of influencing public opinion is possessed dispropor-tionately by moneyed people and institutions. But the unfairness and inequality are only accentuated if certain of these expedients are forbidden, those available to the workers, for instance, while others are allowed which can only be utilized by those opposing the workers' claims. Publicity of all kinds is a way of drawing people's attention to a question, of inducing interest and concern, of making it impossible for people to forget the problem is there. So is a large-scale sympathetic strike of the kind that took place in 1926. It may be that such action is far more effective than ordinary publicity, but mere effectiveness cannot be held to convert a rightful method into a wrongful one. The view that all action to influence public opinion, and therefore the Government, is undemocratic is really based on the unitary concept of the democratic State that has been shown to be untenable. The idea that once a Government has been elected every decision it makes must be unquestioningly obeyed, until another general election or a succession of by-elections destroys its majority in the House of Commons, is one that, as has been said repeatedly, cannot and will not be accepted by vocational and other groups. It is not accepted at present by any important group, whether of employers or workers, whether a religious body or an educational society. Nor, if the foregoing argument is sound, should it be. One of the conditions of successful majority rule is that minority views must not be outraged. Only through the constant vigilance of group organizations and their vigorous activity in pursuit of their own objectives can democracy be really alive and responsive to changing opinion and circumstances. This is quite different from the use of force to overthrow a democratically elected Government. What is the difference between the use of physical force to overturn existing institutions, and the use of publicity or the cessation of work to influence a Government? The difference is precisely that in the latter case the Government is not in danger of being forcibly overthrown, and therefore the democratic principle is not threatened. No one suggests that the object of the Trade Union movement in 1926 was to overturn the Government and put in a rival Government which had not been returned as the result of a general election. The democratic basis of our political system was not menaced. The Government might have altered its policy as a result of the influence exerted, but it would not have been the first time a Government changed its mind owing to an agitation in the country. In the event, it stood by its policy and obtained sufficient popular support to bring the stoppage to an end. And, throughout the affair, the constitution, law and order, and democratic institutions were not for a second endangered. The surest way of provoking a *revolutionary* strike is to attempt to prohibit a *constitutional* strike of the 1926 kind.[1] During the discussions in Parliament on the Labour Government's Trade Disputes and Trade Unions Bill, in 1930, the demand was made in some quarters for all strikes to be completely banned in what were termed "essential" industries and services. The proposal is just as illogical as the idea of prohibiting action which tends to "coerce the Government." It means that a strike which is really effective because it impinges on the normal routine of life (transport, coal, etc.) is to be forbidden, while one not felt immediately by the ordinary citizen (cotton, boots, tinplate, etc.) may be permitted! The line that should increasingly be taken is rather to provide more adequate machinery for bringing Trade Unions into the councils of industry and the State, for it is only by fully recognizing and making provision for group activities and points of view that violent clashes will be avoided. People will acquiesce, or at any rate will be far more likely to acquiesce, in decisions they dislike if they have shared in the entire process which has led up to those decisions, and have had adequate scope for using their influence throughout. The mere establishment of machinery for "settling" disputes is not enough, though of course it has its place, as must any expedient that facilitates investigation, cool judgment, and a comprehensive view of the issues at stake. The machinery must be provided in the earlier stages. Conferences, consultation, participation, must be continuous, covering all the stages of policy-making that are antecedent to the final decisions and

[1] As to the constitutional nature of the 1926 strike, see Goodhart, A. L., "The Legality of the General Strike," *Yale Law Journal* (1927), XXXVI, 464.

therefore avoiding at the source many of the causes of ultimate conflict. If it is impossible and unnecessary to leave technical problems of "means" to a popular vote, it is equally impossible and foolish to leave the determination of "ends" to experts; experts, by their nature, are not concerned with ends. Since it is unlikely that there will ever be complete agreement about means and ends, it seems unlikely at first sight that the most careful provision of machinery for consultation and participation will entirely prevent the occurrence of grave conflicts between groups and the State. There will surely be cases, it may be said, in which differences are so profound that minorities will feel nonconformity is imperative. Such occasional clashes may be a necessary consequence of the freedom of thought, of the spiritual integrity, that human beings will prize as long as they are human beings and not robots. But this very consideration holds out hope that social anarchy may not always be just round the corner, for it presupposes the dominance of those factors that are the surest guarantee of democracy. When the problem is analysed it is seen that emphasis on group autonomy and group rights, and the provision of machinery for allowing them the fullest opportunity for expression on democratic lines, are, in this country, far less likely to lead to violent conflict than are the methods of dictatorship and State absolutism. A dictatorship may have a practical programme with which the Trade Union movement, for instance, agrees in every detail, but the workers will not regard the abrogation of democratic methods as a desirable means of achieving this objective; they will consider the maintenance of the democratic system that gives them and their members a definite status in industry and a share in formulating economic policy to be supremely important in itself and not merely as a means to something else. Within the democratic system the State will be right from its own point of view in pursuing the aims of the majority, while allowing freedom of expression and persuasion to minorities. The group may be equally right from its own standpoint in challenging the State, provided its challenge does not imply the overthrow of democracy. But finally education in political thought and action, together with the modernization of democratic institutions, may lead to the universal acceptance of the view that the maintenance of democratic methods is a principle transcending in importance any group purpose whatsoever, so that in case of conflict a group will voluntarily accept what is to it a wrong decision rather than destroy the democratic principle itself. This will be to accept democracy in the widest sense as the ultimate and most compelling objective of all; under no other conditions can any real approach to social harmony be achieved.

CHAPTER XXX

THE NEW FUNCTIONS OF TRADE UNION INSTITUTIONS

IT is clear that in no State and in no social system can Trade Unionism permanently cease to be a real living force. Its vitality and its power do not depend upon local economic circumstances, upon the precise form of political organization adopted in any community, nor even upon the existence of Capitalist industry. They are the result of the profound need for organization and self-expression felt by vocational groups. The grave conflicts that occur between Trade Union organizations and Governments are due to the failure to accord these vocational institutions a status comparable with their actual position in the economic system, and an effective voice in the formulation of policy affecting their interests. The democratic principle is not rejected by Trade Unionism: on the contrary, it is an essential factor in this movement, but it has to be transplanted into modern terms to accord with the realities and complexities of the economic life of to-day. The immediate task of economic organization is to make the potential triumph over scarcity a reality, and to distribute wealth and leisure democratically up to the limits made possible by modern science. Conscious control of economic institutions and the planning of economic activities in the public interest are necessary to this end. Neither human freedom nor economic efficiency can be achieved unless this planned system is also democratic, not merely in form but in reality. Real democracy is now seen to involve a high degree of functional decentralization, of freedom for autonomous groups, and of participation by these groups in the control and direction of our economic life. Trade Unions are among the more important groups of this kind, but there has been very little attempt made to bring them into full recognition and participation. Science is doing its part in vastly increasing the mastery of mankind over nature. The tendency towards a planned and controlled economic system has made rapid strides. The establishment of autonomous groups and the decentralization of responsibility are becoming more and more the accepted policy in financial, commercial, and technical fields. But in the sphere of Labour, the most vital sphere of all, progress is hampered by the persistence of obsolete ideas and prejudices. Trade Unionism, the group expression of Labour, is still fantastically encumbered with legal disabilities that belong to the dark ages, and is constantly forced to take the defensive against attacks based on ignorance and political hostility. Small wonder need be felt that serious clashes occur from time to time. The attitude of the State, as expressed both through the mechanism of government and through the law, must be changed if the menace of more serious conflict is to be removed. In other words, the reconstruction of economic life and government that is just beginning must be on democratic lines and must provide for the participation of organized Labour as one of the most important functional groups. It would be useless to add one more to the multitude of elaborate "paper" plans for the future government of industry and of economic life generally. The reality will be different from them all. It will be enough to make a few suggestions as to possibilities and probabilities.

Although most people are agreed that our democratic institutions need modernizing, to enable them to cope with the new and complex problems of to-day, there is (barring a violent revolution) little likelihood that the whole machinery of government will be reconstructed on a new model. As is customary with us, the old institutions will be adapted and the old names retained, though there will doubtless be unobtrusive but important additions. Such radically new mechanisms as the Webbs' dual Parliament to supplant the existing legislature, or as Mussolini's Chamber based on Corporations, are not at all likely. Dissimilar as these projects are, they have in common, however, an emphasis on economic organization and its place in the making of national policy. This is the direction in which the current of public opinion is still flowing strongly, and it will probably receive expression in this country before long, though in a very restrained form. In industry itself, neither the centrally controlled State Trusts of Soviet Russia nor the Fascist Corporations of Italy are likely to be copied here, yet our major industries will be unified under the control of corporations having responsibilities solely to the public. To consider industrial organization first, it may be said that further progress towards planned development will almost certainly take the lines indicated by the measures already passed in connection with London Passenger Transport, electricity generation, and radio broadcasting. The semi-autonomous public corporation, operating under statute within a defined field and with carefully defined powers, and managed by persons having no financial stake in the concern but working in the public interest, would seem in most cases to be the type of organization favoured by all parties. The application of the principle to ordinary industries serving a highly competitive market is not so simple, of course, but in view of the policy that is being pursued by the iron and steel industry, where the formation of a series of sectional bodies under the ultimate supervision of a national corporation is in progress, it seems likely that this highly competitive and complex productive industry is on the way to complete reorganization and unification. The final step of placing it under *public* ownership and control can only be a matter of time. There is no reason to suppose that the practical difficulties cannot be overcome or that organizations broadly similar could not administer our other large industries efficiently and well. The workers of all grades who at present carry on these industries will for the most part co-operate under the new management, but they will not give the most effective co-operation if their work and conditions of service are either too little or too much controlled from without. They will expect that in what is essentially a public service they shall be assured of honourable terms of service, security, and so on, but at the same time, they will not be able to work efficiently if they are under a rigid day-to-day control on matters of detail. The policy of the Trade Union movement in this country distinguishes between three aspects of the government of a Public Corporation. There is, first, the determination of "labour conditions"—wages, hours, overtime, shift working, holidays, works amenities, and so on. It is contemplated that these factors will remain matters for negotiation between the Board of the Corporation and the appropriate Trade Unions (subject to any minimum standards that may be laid down by the statute establishing the Corporation, or by the general law). This leaves the workers with the fullest right to strike and the Corporation with a similar right to lock-out, but the likelihood of these rights being exercised will undoubtedly be minimized as a result of the new provisions for consultation and participation. The point has already been discussed and need not be elaborated further.

There is no reason why Trade Unions, after the necessary rationalization of their own organization,[1] should not make themselves increasingly responsible for the entire function of labour supply and regulation. The result might ultimately be that "collective contracts" for specified jobs became the normal method, the Union allocating labour and settling conditions, including the division of the contract price. Would this be outside strictly vocational functions? At any rate, the need for closer association of the Unions with the determination of labour conditions will probably be admitted generally. Machinery in the form of joint industrial councils, works councils, etc., working in the closest contact with, and having the workers' representatives appointed by, the Unions, can give the opportunity for intelligent‑discussion and healthy

[1] See p. 381 *infra*.

criticism on all phases of work and welfare in individual establishments. Such devices need not and would not interfere at all with the executive management of a concern. The day-to-day work of the technical and commercial management is a job for the expert trained in the craft. Management is generally recognized nowadays as a profession which is developing its own standards, its own code, and its own vocational bodies. It is a specialized form of labour. It has nothing in common with the profit-making element and it is not, as some writers have tried to show, a "third factor" in industry. True, its functions include the co-ordination and direction of other workers' effort, but this factor enters at every stage of the labour hierarchy and the higher management itself is subordinate to the supreme controlling Board. Management is thus a specialized function, and neither considerations of shareholding nor of popular ballot should be deemed relevant in the appointment and work of this grade.

The functions of the supreme controlling board of a Public Corporation are another matter altogether. This body will have to be responsible, subject to the limitations laid down in the statute establishing the Corporation and subject also to the needs of economic planning in general, for the broad policy to be pursued and for the major decisions on finance, production, markets, and so on. Since every such decision may ultimately affect the position and well-being of the workers employed the Unions must have some share in determining policy at this stage. The method may not be the same in all cases. The simplest form of participation is to give organized Labour in the industry representation on the Board that controls policy. Where the Unions demand such representation it will be difficult to deny them, though a Board composed of persons appointed solely on grounds of ability and having no interest to serve but that of the public will be preferred by many.[1] The issue is perhaps

[1] For a full discussion of this question see Morrison, H., *Socialisation and Transport* (1933).

not as important as it sounds, for it is certain that no more than a minority representation will either be claimed by the Unions or conceded by public opinion. Also, the Board will in any case be appointed by the Government, and the representation of organized Labour will probably be secured by selection from a panel nominated by the Unions concerned. If direct representation of Trade Unionism is not sought in some cases, the device of an Advisory Committee may be adopted. It will often be very desirable for the Board of a Public Corporation to have associated with it such an Advisory Committee consisting of persons appointed by various interests closely concerned with the industry or service in question, and by consumers in general. Though unable to interfere with the actual control of the Corporation this Committee may have valuable powers of access to data on costs, profits, etc., the right to question the Board at regular meetings, and the duty of publishing an annual report. Its functions may become of great importance, and its influence may be far wider than would appear on the surface. If the organization of Public Corporations is interpenetrated with some such mechanisms for Trade Union participation or consultation at both the highest and the lowest stages, the possibilities of serious industrial conflict will be perhaps eliminated, and certainly minimized.

The modernization of the system of democratic government as a whole and its better organization for economic functions present a problem of equal or perhaps greater complexity. It is essential to avoid changes which, under the guise of making democracy more efficient, merely succeed in relegating the wishes of the mass of the people to a back place and substituting the wishes of a small governing clique. It is very easy for high-minded enthusiasts for some specific policy to persuade themselves that they are the heaven-sent rulers, that they intuitively have so much knowledge of the desires of ordinary men and women that they need not trouble to consult the nation by means of a general election. From this attitude to a revival of "general will" theories, and thence to dictatorship, is a very short step. Criticism of the slowness of Parliamentary procedure is very often criticism of the need to consult the wishes of the people who elect members to the House of Commons. It is very easy to say, and perhaps to think, that people who have views of their own are indulging in "obstruction." The plain fact is that if industrial and political freedom mean anything, no decisions on major objectives and issues of policy can rightly ignore the desires, the views, and even the prejudices of all sections concerned. Absolute truth is a mirage. Political truth is what can get itself accepted as such, and the suppression or curtailment of ample and free discussion is perhaps the surest way of making acceptance unlikely. It is not by the ruthless forcing through of legislation and the machine-gun fire of "Orders in Council" that democratic institutions can be truly reformed, but rather by the devolution and splitting-up of authority.

From the point of view of organized Labour a more satis-factory as well as more rapid output of legislation can be secured by devolution on functional lines than by expedients involving undemocratic suppression of freedom of discussion and criticism. The device of a Second Chamber based on occu-pational representation, such as was suggested by Bismarck many years ago,[1] would be of no value; in fact, there is no justi-fication for a Second Chamber at all, in the opinion of the workers' movement. Nor would the substitution of an occu-pational for a geographical basis for the House of Commons be a progressive step. Necessary as it is that functional bodies should be given not only freedom but, in their own sphere considerable authority, the final responsibility for government

[1] It is interesting to notice that the Malta Constitution Letters Patent in 1921 established two Houses, the Senate consisting of representatives of interests, including the Trade Union Council of Malta.

as a whole must reside in a Parliament elected by *citizens* and not by economic or other special interests. The greater importance of specialization of function makes it all the more imperative that final ends and broad policies should be determined by the common people. The primary need in general issues of government is that Parliament should be aided by a network of consultative bodies which can give expert advice from their own special knowledge and experience. In the field in which organized labour is chiefly interested, a National Economic Council could perform this function. The Webbs' scheme[1] for a Social Parliament, co-ordinate with the Political Parliament and possessing full powers of legislation, would involve an artificial division of power that would be quite unworkable in practice, as would all other plans for a duality or plurality of authorities. The creation of a National Economic Council representing in the main the chief industrial and commercial interests, including the Trade Union movement, would give rise to no such difficulties, but could be the means of ensuring that Parliament was made continuously aware of the views and criticisms of the chief economic institutions. Either at the request of the Government or on its own initiative the Council could advise on problems as they arose, propose legislation for the consideration of Parliament, criticize measures under discussion, and carry on continuous investigation into economic questions generally. The Trade Unions, being adequately represented on this body, would feel that they were participating in the work of government in a valuable, creative way, and not merely in a negative fashion, at the points where their special experience was of most use. The Council could also exercise certain functions of administration and regulation, in its own sphere, so relieving the ordinary machinery of government of a good deal of work. Many "internal" problems of industry could be handled in this way without interfering with the legitimate autonomy of Public Corporations in their

[1] See p. 292 *supra*.

own specific field, and without robbing the democratically elected Parliament of any of its powers of government.

A general picture of the structure that is here contemplated may be attempted, to draw together the threads of the discussion. It would be foolish to suggest any detailed scheme, for the circumstances and forces that mould the future must determine the precise way in which these broad tendencies work themselves out. It is contemplated that in future there will be a great deal more emphasis than in the past upon the development of semi-autonomous functional groups within the State. It is thought that these groups, in the form of statutory associations or corporations (statutory only in the sense that they are recognized and given specific powers by Government, and not necessarily that they are created by statute) will be responsible for the performance of certain functions within the field delimited for them. It is not contemplated that Parliament and the machinery of government as a whole will be "functionalized" or will cease to be representative of and responsible to the people voting as citizens. It is thought, however, that Parliament, modernized in certain ways to drop obsolete and troublesome procedure without losing any of its democratic features, will be surrounded with a network of consultative and advisory bodies, able to speak with an expert knowledge of specific interests and functions. In the economic field, which will be a very important but not the sole field in which this principle will operate, the National Economic Council, on which Trade Unionism will be strongly represented, will act in such a capacity. In matters especially affecting Trade Union interests the General Council of the T.U.C. itself will be recognized as the authoritative body to advise on behalf of organized Labour, as individual Unions will be on questions of particular concern to Labour in specific industries. As the area of interest and expert knowledge narrows, the more specialized institutions will be the appropriate advisory bodies. The Trade Union organizations, then, will be neither agents of the State nor entirely outside bodies playing a critical and hostile role. They will remain autonomous institutions, within the general framework that has been described, but with functions that link them to the State in a consultative and constructive way.

As the planning of the economic life proceeds (and, if the foregoing analysis is sound, it must proceed along the lines of transforming the major industries and services into public services) the Trade Union movement will also assume new functions *within* industry. Each Public Corporation will secure the participation of organized Labour either by direct representation of the Unions on the supreme controlling board or by some other mechanism of a similar kind, as desired by the Unions concerned. In addition there will be a network of consultative bodies, Works Councils and the like, to which the Unions will appoint members. Industries not for the time being transformed into public services will nevertheless be placed under some measure of control, with the objects of bringing about unification, eliminating redundant units, safeguarding wages and hours standards, securing publicity for financial details, etc. This control will perhaps be most conveniently exercised by the National Economic Council, through subordinate organs, under powers conferred by statute, and the Trade Union movement will thus participate in this important task. It will no doubt be found desirable in most cases that the supervising body for a specific industry should be selected in the main from the personnel of the industry, and the Unions concerned will find a place here, too.

It will be seen that the main principle underlying these suggestions is that where the interests of Labour are most directly and concretely affected, the Unions will actively participate, and that where general policies and the wider economic issues of government are concerned, the Trade Union movement will have a recognized consultative and advisory role. This would seem to be quite consistent with the tendencies that are becoming more and more evident in the evolution of government and industry. These tendencies may work out in a different form, but unless the fullest regard is paid to the participation and consultation of organized Labour it is folly to suppose that large-scale industrial conflict will be avoided. No measures that are taken can guarantee immunity from struggles of this kind, but at least their occurrence can be made far less likely by associating Labour with control at all stages, somewhat on the lines suggested in the preceding discussion.

Internationally the recognition of vocational associations is likely to be of slower growth and to take a different form. The two tendencies already noticed in this field, the spread of international industrial and professional groups, and the slow development of the League of Nations, will almost certainly continue. There is a steady multiplication of international, scientific, educational, artistic, and administrative associations year by year, some of which become linked up with the League and hence play a part in government, while some have more direct administrative powers. Industry has its international trusts, cartels, and agreements[1] which at some stage will certainly have to come under the control or supervision of the League. Trade Unionism has its horizontal "trade internationals" and its vertical structure of the International Federation of Trade Unions. On the other hand the League itself will (failing a world catastrophe) develop its scope and powers towards the point at which it becomes a genuine world authority in certain fields not merely of political but of economic activity. It seems inevitable that the League, based on national States, must at some stage establish an organic relationship with the important international associations which for specific functions exercise considerable authority in their own spheres. Their connection may be very close or, more probably, they may act as advisory or consultative bodies. For international Labour problems there will doubtless con-

[1] See *Planning*, May 23, 1933, for up-to-date list.

tinue to be the dual mechanism that already exists. The International Labour Organization of the League will include direct representatives of national Trade Union Centres, while the International Federation of Trade Unions will both act as a co-ordinating body for these national representatives and will itself have a recognized place as an international organ. On wider economic issues the mechanism for international policy-making has still to be fully developed. Trade Unionism has been recognized at the two World Economic Conferences so far held. The 1927 Conference consisted of Governments, organized employers, and organized Labour, and the full status of delegates was therefore secured by Trade Union Centres. The 1933 Conference was a meeting of Governments only, the Trade Union representatives having the status of industrial advisers. This latter model will probably be followed in future when operative decisions and not merely resolutions are sought. As administrative and supervisory mechanisms are developed by the League in the economic sphere, there will have to be provision for Trade Union participation either through national Centres or through the I.F.T.U.

International organization is so new that, as is shown by the structure of the International Labour Organization of the League of Nations, there will be less difficulty than is experienced in national economic structures in finding an adequate place for organized Labour, especially as "legislative" functions will not, for a long time to come, be conferred upon League organs.

At this final stage of our consideration of the future place of Trade Unionism, two questions that are often asked may be discussed. In the first place, are Trade Union institutions at present organized in a manner that fits them to go forward on this basis of fuller participation? Or will they need some measure of reorganization themselves? The answer has been given by the Trades Union Congress which, in the Report on

Trade Unionism and the Control of Industry[1] adopted in 1933, stated that "If this development takes place Trade Unions must realize that some readaptation of their forms of organization will be necessary." In many cases that readaptation has been proceeding, in others it has still to be undertaken. It ought to be pointed out that where organization and methods have not been modernized this is largely due to the fact that the industries concerned have themselves been unprogressive and the Unions have not been given an opportunity to enlarge their scope, nor encouraged to exercise wider functions. Traditions are powerful in Trade Unonism as elsewhere, but when Governments show a full appreciation of the status of organized Labour in the planned economy of the future it seems likely that the response will be rapid and far-reaching. At the present time it is hardly logical to reproach Unions for not having fitted themselves perfectly for functions that have always been denied them.

The second question is whether the larger powers that tend to be assumed by autonomous groups may mean the substitution of one tyranny (or perhaps many tyrannies) for another. It is a very important question and it has been referred to many times in the foregoing discussion. So far as Trade Unions are concerned it is hardly possible to maintain seriously any charge of tyranny. The working of every social organization involves some limitation upon complete freedom of individuals. In a democracy the consent of the majority is obtained and the minority is safeguarded as far as may be possible. Trade Unions are in reality as well as in form democratic bodies. It was no idle figure of speech that Mr. and Mrs. Webb used in applying to the Trade Union movement in this country the title "Industrial Democracy." The rank and file members do in fact, on the broad issues and general objectives, determine the Unions' policies. The excitement and publicity attaching to occasional "revolts" and "unofficial" movements within Trade Unionism

[1] *Annual Report* of the Trades Union Congress, 1933.

only serve to emphasize the infrequency of these occurrences. Doubtless, undesirable practices and indefensible violations of freedom can be found in this as in all other institutions: no democracy yet was perfect. But a first-hand study of Trade Union methods leaves no room for serious criticism of the movement as a whole, in this respect.

If the interpretation that has been given of Trade Unionism in the foregoing chapters is correct, freedom, democracy, the refusal to accept either industrial autocracy or State absolutism have been the keynote of the history of organized Labour ever since men and women first banded themselves together to defend their vocational interests. To-day, the sway of dictatorships and the denial of the peoples' liberties threaten to extend over the greater part of the civilized world. State absolutism menaces democracy in the name of philosophies that are utterly alien to the history and spirit of Trade Unionism. At such a time lovers of freedom will seek to enlarge the sphere of all institutions that, democratic in their own working, impose a check upon the tyranny of would-be dictatorships and compel a decentralization of powers. This, indeed, is the ultimate meaning that emerges from our long survey of Trade Unionism in its relation to the State. The workers' organizations, seeking both betterment and industrial freedom for their members, have passed through a period of the State's open hostility into a period of puzzled and fearful toleration. The innate strength of the movement has defied suppression and won an unwilling recognition, but it has not established a positive status and constructive functions. Industrial conflict has become a menace to the State, but no effective steps have been taken to resolve the clash by finding an agreed basis on which Trade Unionism can fit into the economic life and institutions of the community without sacrificing its independence and freedom. This is the great task which now has to be faced if both economic political and freedom are to be made a permanent part of our national and international life.

"Political and social institutions," says Mr. Russell,[1] "are to be judged by the good or harm that they do to individuals. Do they encourage creativeness rather than possessiveness? Do they embody or promote a spirit of reverence between human beings? Do they preserve self-respect? . . . Institutions, and especially economic systems, have a profound influence in moulding the characters of men and women. They may encourage adventure and hope, or timidity and the pursuit of safety. They may open men's minds to great possibilities, or close them against everything but the risk of obscure misfortune. They may make a man's happiness depend upon what he adds to the general possessions of the world, or upon what he can secure for himself of the private goods which others cannot share. Modern Capitalism forces the wrong decision of these alternatives upon all who are not heroic or exceptionally fortunate." Modern Capitalism has moulded the character of both individual human beings and the institutions they create, Trade Unionism included. It has forced a concentration on the maintenance of material standards and has left little or no encouragement for the creative aspect of vocational organization. As economic scarcity becomes a thing of the past and public planning replaces private Capitalism the Trade Unions will be freed for the constructive functions they alone can undertake in making industrial government truly democratic. In so doing they will not merely demonstrate the value of the vocational outlook and its contribution to economic welfare, but will provide a channel for the creative activities of the workers through which every man and woman in industry will find an enlargement of freedom and an enhancement of personality that are impossible to-day.

[1] Russell, Bertrand, *Political Ideals*.

SHORT BIBLIOGRAPHY

IT is not possible to give anything like a full bibliography for such an extensive field as that touched by this book. Only a short list is given, therefore, of works in English which the reader may consult who wishes to go further into the topics discussed. Books in other languages and articles in periodicals have been omitted in order to keep the list as short and simple as possible, but the footnotes to the text indicate many other sources, and full bibliographies are given in many of the books listed below. Reference should also be made to the bibliography and sectional lists of sources in Milne-Bailey, W., *Trade Union Documents* (1929).

ADAMS, M. (ed.)   The Modern State. (1933).
BARKER, E.   Political Thought from Spencer to To-day. (1915).
BATT, F. R.   Law of Master and Servant. (1929).
BEARD, C.   An Economic Interpretation of the Constitution of the United States. (1925).
BEER, M.   History of British Socialism (2 v.). (1929).
BOOTHBY AND OTHERS.   Industry and the State. (1927).
BOSANQUET, B.   Philosophical Theory of the State. (1899).
BRISSENDEN, P. F.   The I.W.W. (1919).
BUKHARIN, N.   Historical Materialism. (1926).
BUKHARIN, N., and PREOBRASCHENSKY, E.   ABC of Communism. (1924).
BURNS, E. M.   Wages and the State. (1926).
CARPENTER, N.   Guild Socialism. (1922).
CATLIN, G. E. G.   The Science and Method of Politics. (1927).
CATLIN, G. E. G.   The Principles of Politics. (1930).
CHANG, S. H. M.   The Marxian Theory of the State. (1931).
"CINEF."   Survey of Fascism. (1928).
CITRINE, W. M.   The Trade Union Movement of Great Britain. (1926).
CLARK, J. M.   The Social Control of Business. (1926).
COLE, G. D. H.   Social Theory. (1920).
COLE, G. D. H.   Guild Socialism Restated. (1920).
COLE, G. D. H.   The World of Labour. (1928 ed.).

COLE, G. D. H. Trade Unions and Munitions. (1923).

COLE, G. D. H. Labour in the Coal Mining Industry. (1923).

COMMONS, J. R. Legal Foundations of Capitalism. (1924).

COMMONS, J. R., and ASSOCIATES. History of Labor in the United States (2 v.). (1921).

CROOK, W. H. The General Strike. (1931).

DAVIDSON, W. L. Political Thought from Bentham to Mill. (1915).

DEWEY, J. Human Nature and Conduct. (1922).

DICEY, A. V. Law of the Constitution. 8th ed. (1926).

DICEY, A. V. Law and Public Opinion in England. (1926).

DIMOCK, M. E. British Public Utilities and National Development. (1933).

DONALDSON, J. International Economic Relations. (1928).

DUGUIT, L. Law in the Modern State. (Tr. F. and H. Laski). (1921).

DUNNING, W. A. A History of Political Theories (3 v.). (1902–1921).

ELLINGWOOD, A. R., and COOMBS, W. The Government and Labor. (1926).

ELLIOTT, W. Y. The Pragmatic Revolt in Politics. (1928).

FIGGIS, J. N. Churches in the Modern State. (1913).

FINER, H. Representative Government and a Parliament of Industry. (1923).

FLORENCE, P. S. The Statistical Method in Economics. (1929).

FRANKFURTER, F., and LANDIS, J. M. The Business of the Supreme Court. (1927).

FRANKFURTER, F., and GREENE, N. The Labour Injunction. (1930).

GELDART, W. M. Elements of English Law. (1914).

GITSHAM, E., and TREMBATH, J. F. Labour Organization in South Africa. (1926).

GOOCH, G. P. Political Thought from Bacon to Halifax. (1914).

GOODHART, A. L. Essays in Jurisprudence and the Common Law. (1931).

HANSSON, S. The Trade Union Movement in Sweden. (1927).

HARDMAN, J. B. S., and ASSOCIATES. American Labor Dynamics. (1928).

HASLAM, A. L., and STALLYBRASS, W. T. S. Law Relating to Trade Combinations. (1931).

HAWTREY, R. G. Economic Aspects of Sovereignty. (1930).

HECKER, J. Moscow Dialogues. (1933).

HEDGES, R. Y. The Law Relating to Restraint of Trade. (1932).

HEDGES, R. Y., and WINTERBOTTOM, A. Legal History of Trade Unionism. (1930).

HENDERSON, A. Trade Unions and the Law. (1927).
HILLER, E. T. The Strike. (1928).
HOBHOUSE, L. T. Metaphysical Theory of the State. (1921).
HOBSON, J. A. Free Thought in the Social Sciences. (1926).
HOLMES, O. W. Collected Legal Papers. (1921).
HOLMES, O. W. Dissenting Opinions of Mr. Justice Holmes (arr. A. Lief). (1929).
HSAIO, K. C. Political Pluralism. (1927).
INTERNATIONAL LABOUR OFFICE. Trade Unions in Soviet Russia. (1927).
INTERNATIONAL LABOUR OFFICE. Freedom of Association (5 v.). (1927).
INTERNATIONAL LABOUR OFFICE. Studies in Industrial Relations (2 v.). (1930–32).
INTERNATIONAL LABOUR OFFICE. International Survey of Legal Decisions on Labour Law (Annually from 1925).
INTERNATIONAL INDUSTRIAL RELATIONS ASSOCIATION. Social Economic Planning (2 v.). (1932).
JENKS, E. Short History of English Law. (1924).
KEEZER, D. M., and MAY, S. Public Control of Business. (1930).
KEYNES, J. M. The End of Laissez-faire. (1927).
KO, T. T. Governmental Methods of Adjusting Labor Disputes. (1928).
KOPALD, S. Rebellion in Labor Unions. (1924).
LABRIOLA, A. Essays on the Materialistic Conception of History. (1908).
LAIDLER, H. History of Socialist Thought. (1926).
LASKI, H. J. Authority in the Modern State. (1919).
LASKI, H. J. Political Thought from Locke to Bentham. (1915).
LASKI, H. J. Foundations of Sovereignty. (1921).
LASKI, H. J. Grammar of Politics. (1925).
LASKI, H. J. Communism. (1927).
LASKI, H. J. Liberty in the Modern State. (1930).
LASKI, H. J. Studies in Law and Politics. (1932).
LASKI, H. J. Democracy in Crisis. (1933).
LENIN, N. The State and Revolution. (1917).
LIPPMAN, W. Public Opinion. (1922).
LIPPMAN, W. The Phantom Public. (1925).
LONDON SCHOOL OF ECONOMICS. Annual Survey of English Law (Annually from 1928).
LORWIN, L. L. Labor and Internationalism. (1929).

LOSOVSKY, A.   The World's Trade Union Movement. (1925).

MACIVER, R. M.   The Modern State. (1926).

MAITLAND, F. W.   Collected Papers (3 v.). (1911).

MAITLAND, F. W.   Intro. to Gierke's "Political Theories of the Middle Age." (1900).

MERTENS, C.   Trade Union Movement in Belgium. (1925).

MILNE-BAILEY, W.   Trade Union Documents. (1922).

MOGI, S.   The Problem of Federalism. (2 v.). (1931).

MOGI, S.   Otto Von Gierke. (1932).

MONTGOMERY, B. G.   British and Continental Labour Policy. (1922).

MORRISON, H.   Socialisation and Transport. (1933).

OAKES, E. S.   Organised Labor and Industrial Conflicts. (1927).

PERLMAN, S.   A Theory of the Labor Movement. (1928).

PIPKIN, C. W.   The Idea of Social Justice (1927).

PITIGLIANI, F.   The Italian Corporative State. (1933).

POLLOCK, F., and MAITLAND, F. W.   History of English Law (2 v.). (1903).

POTTER, P. B.   Introduction to the Study of International Organisation. (1929).

POUND, R.   Spirit of the Common Law. (1921).

POUND, R.   Introduction to the Philosophy of Law. (1924).

RATHENAU, W.   The New Society. (1921).

RATHENAU, W.   In Days to Come. (1921).

ROBSON, W. A.   Justice and Administrative Law. (1928).

ROWSE, A. L.   Politics and the Younger Generation. (1931).

SALTER, SIR J. A.   Recovery. (1932).

SAPOSS, D. J., and B. T.   Readings in Trade Unionism. (1926).

SASSENBACH, J.   Twenty-five Years of International Trade Unionism. (1926).

SCHNEIDER, H. W.   Making the Fascist State. (1928).

SCOTT, J. W.   Syndicalism and Philosophical Realism. (1919).

SEIDEL, R.   The Trade Union Movement of Germany. (1928).

SLESSER, SIR H. H.. and BAKER, C.   Trade Union Law. (1927).

SMITH, H. A.   Law of Associations. (1914).

SOPHIAN, T. J.   Trade Union Law and Practice. (1927).

SOREL, G.   Reflections on Violence. (1914).

STALIN, J.   Leninism. (1925).

SUTCLIFFE, J. T.   History of Trade Unionism in Australia. (1921).

TAWNEY, R. H.   The Acquisitive Society. (1921).

TILLYARD, F.   Industrial Law. (1928).

WALLAS, G.   Human Nature in Politics. (1908).

WALLAS, G. The Great Society. (1914).
WALLAS, G. Our Social Heritage. (1921).
WARD, P. Sovereignty. (1928).
WEBB, S. and B. History of Trade Unionism (1920 ed.).
WEBB, S. and B. Industrial Democracy (1920 ed.).
WEBB, S. and B. Constitution for a Socialist Commonwealth. (1920).
WEBER, M. The Protestant Ethic and the Spirit of Capitalism. (1930).
WHEELER-BENNETT, J. W., and others. The World Court. (1929).
WILLOUGHBY, W. W. Fundamental Concepts of Public Law. (1925).
WITTE, E. The Government in Labor Disputes. (1932).

INDEX

For Product Safety Concerns and Information please contact our EU
representative GPSR@taylorandfrancis.com
Taylor & Francis Verlag GmbH, Kaufingerstraße 24, 80331 München, Germany